Public Order: The Criminal Law

John Marston, LL.B, Solicitor,
de Montfort University
and
Paul Tain, BA, M.Jur, Solicitor,
District Judge (Magistrates' Courts), Recorder

London
Callow Publishing
2001

John Marston and Paul Tain have asserted their rights under the Copyright, Designs and Patents Act 1988 to be identified as the authors of this work.

ISBN 1 898899 54 1

First published 2001

Every care is taken in the preparation of this publication, but the authors and publishers cannot accept responsibility for the consequences of any error, however caused.

Published by Callow Publishing Limited,
4 Shillingford Street, London N1 2DP
www.callowpublishing.com
Printed and bound in Great Britain by MPG Books Ltd, Bodmin, Cornwall

Preface

In this book we provide an examination of the law relating to public order offences and powers. Our intention is to achieve a practical account of use to those involved in the criminal justice system. Although there will always be disagreement as to the boundaries of public order law, the contents of this book reflect our view of those areas that are of interest and use to practitioners, albeit that the treatment of some points may be brief where we judge them to be peripheral to the mainstream. We do not claim to be encyclopaedic and apologise if some topics may have been omitted and others preferred. For the main part, the text is descriptive of the legal principles as we understand them, but from time to time we do address the issues which reside below the surface of those principles. These issues often arise in the context of the burgeoning case law under the Human Rights Act 1988 and will ultimately become the coinage of many arguments at all levels.

As ever, there are those to whom gratitude is owed, especially our families, for their understanding, and our publisher for her forbearance and her excellent editing. Errors and omissions are our responsibility.

We have attempted to state the law as we understand it at 1 July 2001, although we have managed to include references to a few more recent cases.

John Marston, Paul Tain

September 2001

Contents

Table of Cases

Table of Legislation

Chapter 1

Introduction

This book deals with the criminal law relating to public disorder; it does not focus on civil law, although there are references to civil law matters where they directly affect particular aspects of the criminal law. It does not review the psychology or sociology of group action in public disorder, or examine the methods used by public authorities to police protest, although these matters are discussed where they are directly relevant in the criminal law context. Since 1 October 2000 cases on public order law have been considered in the context set by the Human Rights Act 1998. This new and developing jurisprudence is referred to in this book where relevant.

1   The Human Rights Act and the European Convention
The starting point for some people with legitimate grievances against the state, organisations or even individuals may be that they have an inherent and unhampered "human right" to make their points of view known. If they are unaware that in most cases their rights are circumscribed, they face disappointment when their chosen method of protest is restricted by a hierarchy of provisions starting with the European Convention on Human Rights and working down via UK legislation through to, for example, decisions of police authorities. It is as critical to issues relating to trespass and raves as to any other aspect of public order law that civic education be used to disseminate knowledge of the parameters that constrain each "right".

Protestors may be anxious to take advantage of the Human Rights Act 1998 ("HRA") to extend and redefine their rights. Some will seek to invoke art 8 (protection of the right to respect for private and family life). Some will look to art 14 (enjoyment of Convention rights "shall be secured without discrimination on grounds such as sex, race, colour, language, religion, political or other opinion, national or social origin, association with a national minority, property birth or status"). Others will look to arts 10 and 11. They may find that even though the legislative framework in question is not itself incompatible with the Convention, they can ask the appeal courts to analyse whether, in a particular case, the powers exercised were proportionate.

During the build-up to the implementation of the HRA, there was much speculation that the Act would have a wide impact on many aspects of English criminal law in general, and public order law in particular. The reality at this stage is that the Act has had its impact. Issues have been tested. In general, the appeal courts have interpreted the HRA, the Convention and the jurisprudence relating thereto in ways which have tended to support pre-existing approaches in the legal areas concerned (see for example the Privy Council decision in *Brown v Stott* [2001] 2 All ER 97, and *DPP v Jones* [1999] 2 AC 240, [1999] 2 All ER 257, [1999] 2 Cr App R 348 (HL)). This may not continue to be the case in respect of every issue raised before the appeal courts, and some issues will be taken to the European Court of Human Rights notwithstanding appeal decisions in this jurisdiction.

Four articles of the Convention are likely to provide the basis for applications suggesting that the law, or a particular application of the law, is non-compliant with the requirements of the Convention.

Article 6 deals with the right to a fair trial. It is a right with no provisos attached to it and constitutes the absolute minimum rights of a person facing trial. Article 6(1) provides that ". . . everyone is entitled to a fair and public hearing within a reasonable time by an independent and impartial tribunal . . .". The House of Lords has already looked at the question of bias (in *R v Gough* [1993] AC 646, [1993] 2 WLR 883, [1993] 2 All ER 724 and *R v Bow Street Metropolitan Stipendiary Magistrate ex p Pinochet Ugarte (No 2)* [2000] AC 119, [1999] 2 WLR 272), as has the Court of Appeal in *Locabail Ltd v Bayfield Properties and Another* [2000] QB 451, [2000] 1 All ER 65, *The Times* 19 November 1999 and *Director General of Fair Trading v Proprietary Association of Great Britain, The Times*, 2 February 2001, where a minor adjustment to the "real danger" test in *R v Gough* was thought to be necessary in the light of the HRA. Bias could be an ongoing issue in relation to specific benches in particular localities dealing with certain categories of public disorder. Magistrates' courts should keep in mind the need to guard against the risk of bias, particularly in areas where, for example, trials relating to incidents in connection with fox-hunting regularly take place.

Article 6(2) provides ". . . everyone charged . . . shall be presumed innocent until proved guilty according to law". On its face this paragraph places the burden of proof on the prosecution. The House of Lords has now reviewed the concept of the "transferred burden of proof" and modified it significantly in a drugs case (see page 91 and *R v Lambert and Others* [2001] All ER (D) 69 Jul). Thus far, there has been no appeal on the various transferred burden provisions in the field of public order law, but it is likely that the same logic will be applied and the law on transferred burdens modified.

Article 9 sets out the right to freedom of thought, conscience and religion. It incorporates the right "either alone or in community with others and in public or private, to manifest his religion or belief, in worship, teaching, practice and observance". This right is subject only to ". . . limitations as are prescribed by law and are necessary in a democratic society in the interests of public safety, for the protection of public order, health, morals, or for the protection of the rights and freedoms of others".

A public authority must, if challenged under this article, show that its action is based on law which is accessible to the public, can be shown to be required for one of the specified reasons, and is proportionate to the circumstances of the case. If it can do so, its action is compatible with the Convention. The potential for public disorder issues to raise questions of proportionality under this article is apparent, and "prescribed by law and necessary in a democratic society" has been considered in the context of breach of the peace (see page 21).

Article 10 provides for freedom of expression and includes the right to "impart information . . . without interference by public authority . . .". It is subject to a proviso in that:

". . . it carries with it duties and responsibilities, may be subject to such formalities, conditions, restrictions . . . as are prescribed by law and are necessary in a democratic society, in the interests of . . . the prevention of disorder or crime . . . for the protection of the reputation or rights of others . . .". (art 10)

The potential for this article to be raised during some categories of public order case is apparent. If it is raised, and if the public authority has sought to restrict freedom of expression, then the authority must show that it complied with the proviso above. The authority must show that what it did was prescribed by law and necessary in a democratic society for one of the reasons set out. The response must be proportionate, ie the least intervention consistent with compliance with the terms of the proviso.

Article 11 provides for freedom of assembly and association: "Everyone has the right to freedom of assembly . . .". Again this right is subject to a proviso that it can be restricted, but only if the restrictions are "such as are prescribed by law and necessary in a democratic society . . . for the prevention of disorder or crime . . .". The article reflects arts 9 and 10. Any interference with the right must be in accordance with law that is accessible to the people. It must be necessary in a democratic society in one of the prescribed ways. It must be proportionate.

The reality in relation to public disorder is that the law is contained (generally) in statute, and most tests relate to the necessity for particular interventions in a democratic society. The question will be whether the action was proportionate, or inappropriately heavy-handed. Courts will have to decide whether the approach taken was the least necessary to achieve a legitimate objective. Did the end justify the particular means? In relation to the absolute right to fair trial, it may be that, notwithstanding the appeal decisions thus far made, the cases will, in due course, come before the European Court of Human Rights. Some might see the present decisions as placing a restriction on an absolute right.

2   History

The report of Lord Scarman into the Red Lion Square disorders (a violent assault on a police cordon leading to a riot on 15 June 1974) (Cmnd 5919) began in the following terms:

"There is a case – some would think a strong case – for codifying our law as to public order so as to ensure that the fundamental human rights set out in the United Nations Declaration of 1948 and the European Convention of 1951 are protected by statute . . . the real issue is . . . whether our law confers upon those whose duty it is to maintain public order sufficient powers without endangering the right of peaceful protest."

Twenty years later substantial changes were made to public order law in the Criminal Justice and Public Order Act 1994 ("CJPOA"), leaving the same central questions unresolved.

Even with the HRA and its implementation, the difficulties of managing the interface between protest and protecting public order continue, albeit in a context where the rights are express and will be subject to careful analysis as criminal cases are brought under the new regime.

Lord Scarman went on to define the historic requirements of the common law in relation to public order:

"There must be disorder or the threat of disorder before police powers may be used: but when they are needed the powers exist, and are strong. Moreover it is a policeman's duty to use them . . . The law requires of the citizen as the necessary condition for the exercise of his rights that he respects the rights of others, even though he may fundamentally disagree with them and totally disapprove of their policies."

He then set out the public order dilemma arising from the question of protest in a passage cited in the Green Paper issued prior to the Public Order Act 1986 (Cmnd 7891):

"Civilised living collapses – it is obvious – if public protest becomes violent protest or public order degenerates into the quietism imposed by a successful oppression. The fact that those who at any one time are concerned to secure the tranquillity of the streets are likely to be the majority must not lead us to deny the protestors their opportunity to march: the fact that the protestors are desperately sincere and are exercising a fundamental human right must not lead us to overlook the rights of the majority."

The focus of Lord Scarman was protest and demonstration. Yet the law upon which he and the legislature concentrates has wider implications, incorporating individual acts of small-scale criminality as well as complex issues relating to the right or freedom to protest and the right of peaceful passage.

Until 1986 the serious offences affecting public order were the common law offences of riot, rout, affray and unlawful assembly. They were complex and archaic, out of touch with developing society. Covering the lower end of the scale of public order matters, s 5 of the Public Order Act 1936 had been based on breach of the peace, rendering the Act less effective than was required in relation to processions. The main aim of the 1936 Act had been to counteract the growth of political violence associated with qua-si-military groups. The Public Order Act ("POA") 1986 placed in statutory form the serious public order offences and removed reliance on breach of the peace for the less serious offences. It left in force the preventive powers of the police and the powers of the lower courts in relation to binding over to be of good behaviour or to keep the peace. Both of these are reviewed in Chapter 2. The 1986 Act regulated processions, certain assemblies, aspects of racial hatred and violence at sporting events.

The CJPOA 1994 dealt with a range of public order issues which had developed since the 1986 Act. The principal themes were that lawful activity should be protected and interference with it penalised. Quiet enjoyment of property should be protected and interference with it penalised. Legal provision for assemblies and processions should be developed to reflect current circumstances. The Act modified the position between the majority and the minority of sincere protestors to whom Lord Scarman had referred. It increased the extent to which regulation impinged on ill-defined rights to protest, both in connection with processions and assemblies, and in relation to protestors such as hunt saboteurs who had taken their protest to the hunting fields.

More recent developments reflect the focus on particular problems. The law on football-related problems has been extensively revisited (see Chapter 9) and there have been developments in respect of the removal of masks (see page 39); on-the-spot penalties (see page 52); and harassment – generally (see page 125), at home (see page 127) and collectively (see page 130). There have also been preventive schemes such as child curfew provisions which fall outside the scope of this book.

3   Dilemmas of Public Order Law

While it may be necessary to have a body of law dealing with public order, there are inherent difficulties in the UK in resolving precisely where public order law fits into the system. If public order is isolated, it is difficult to relate the preventive powers which enable interventions by individual members of the community to the statutory offences of riot and violent disorder which have precise requirements and definitions. These ancient preventive powers lie alongside serious offences recently defined by statute. There is no all-embracing statutory code placing each aspect of public order law in context with the rest of the subject.

The statutory offences embrace such a wide range of conduct that the Acts deal with different classes of behaviour. At the higher end of the scale are offences involving serious community disruption. At their worst, these offences strike at the root of the proper organisation of the community. At the lower end is conduct by an individual which is essentially nothing more than disorderly.

If a man threatens another with unlawful violence it is an offence. Such an incident features conduct by one person, aimed at another, which is clearly wrong to most observers. It does not matter that the offence is governed by a statute on public order as opposed to a statute dealing with offences against the person. It is something that most people understand as unlawful. The more serious group public order offences, where an individual may appear to do nothing, yet by his presence and defined participation he may be committing an offence, may be more difficult to comprehend. The public, who may not appreciate that the person is acting unlawfully, may be offended. Indeed the public may believe that inappropriate legal assumptions of complicity are being made to the detriment of an individual accidentally in the wrong place at the wrong time. Or, conversely, the public may regard presence as tantamount to participation and sufficient to condemn even an accidental presence at the scene of disorder. Moreover, perceptions of public disorder are likely to depend on an individual's view of the particular group involved in the protest or demonstration.

In some public order cases it is clear that defendants have no perception of the restrictions that are legitimately placed on the right of protest. Even when a police officer tells persons at an assembly that a s 14 notice (see page 160) authorises him to require them to move in a certain direction, they may never have heard of s 14; they may perceive the officer as trying to exercise arbitrary authority, and regard their "right" of protest as absolute. The significance of the HRA and the Convention and its provisos needs to be disseminated if there is to be any prospect of distinguishing protestors who would comply with the law if they knew it, and those who will continue in their conduct in the knowledge that it is criminal.

This diversity of legal provision affects both those charged with policing the community and the community itself. The responsible authorities have to determine the approach to take in varying circumstances and where to draw the line between permitted and proscribed conduct. Deciding when to impose conditions on processions or assemblies, and when to impose an order prohibiting processions or trespassory assemblies, are not necessarily perceived as objective assessments of public safety and other appropriate considerations. The use of the statutory powers is inevitably regarded by some of those affected as abuse. If the authorities pitch their interventions at a level that the community dislikes, they risk falling into disrepute with sections of the public, and the statutory scheme becomes less effective. The use of discretions to set boundaries for protest, movement and assembly poses the greatest risk to public faith in the system of laws. At a time when television and video cameras are everywhere and news is often broadcast live, the importance of ensuring that the policing of public order is appropriate to the context cannot be overstated.

4   Perception of Rights

Many people believe that they have readily ascertainable rights in relation to protest, assembly, movement and speech. In reality the position in the UK is that the individual is generally permitted to do that which is not proscribed by statute or common law. What a person is permitted to do is not set out, and he may test the interpretation of the legal provisions to see if he is straying into something which is contrary to law. If it is not, he may do whatever it is, but if he is wrong then he commits an offence. Establishing what can and cannot be done is a matter of trial and error. Taking, for example, the public right to pass along a public right of way, if the person uses the right of way for any purpose other than passage, he may become a trespasser (*Harrison v Rutland* [1893] 1 QB 142). If he stands and protests, he may become a trespasser in civil law. The public at large is unlikely to be conscious of these legal refinements, and indeed the House of Lords has only just addressed some of the difficulties of equating this historic position with the rights of the public to enjoy a highway for any reasonable purpose (see *DPP v Jones* [1999] 2 AC 240, [1999] 2 All ER 257, [1999] 2 Cr App R 348 and page 166).

Restrictions which prevent a person being assaulted or goods being taken are easily understood. The restrictions which keep peace between neighbours and prevent large gatherings are much less easily understood, particularly by the innocent neighbour or the member of the large gathering with an honourable motive. Even the HRA seems not to have helped people to understand what they can and cannot do.

Lord Scarman intimated that a right to protest existed in English law, and Lord Denning has spoken of:

"a right to demonstrate and the right to protest on matters of public concern. These are rights which it is in the public interest that individuals should possess; and indeed they should exercise without impediment so long as no wrongful act is done" (*Hubbard v Pitt* [1976] QB 142, [1975] 3 WLR 201, [1975] All ER 1).

This was repeated in *R v Coventry City Council ex p Phoenix Aviation* [1995] 3 All ER 37, [1995] COD 300, (1995) NLJ 559 (QBD):

"Some protest is lawful; some alas is not. The precise point at which the right of public demonstration ends and the criminal offence of public nuisance begins may be difficult to detect" (Simon Browne LJ).

These expressions of principle fit uneasily, however, with the judgment in *Duncan v Jones* [1936] 1 KB 218, [1935] All ER 710; (1935) 52 TLR 26, in which it was held that "the right of assembly . . . is nothing more than a view taken by the court of the individual liberty of the subject".

Because the HRA does not recite anything other than a right to assemble and a proviso to that right, it is difficult to see it simplifying things for the person who might turn out for a protest meeting.

In 1949 Sir Alfred (later Lord) Denning sought to define freedom in his Hamlyn Trust lectures:

"By personal freedom I mean the freedom of every law abiding citizen to

think what he will, to say what he will, and to go where he will on his
lawful occasions without let or hindrance from any other persons."

Even in 1949 freedoms or rights were subject to community disciplines for
the protection of individuals, and the potential for the improper exercise of
discretions was also reviewed by Lord Denning in a formula which some
might view differently now. He stated that:

"the police are not regarded here as the strong arm of the executive, but
as the friends of the people . . . and no one is inclined to resist the authority of the police, because it can be safely assumed to be lawfully used".

Today, when police officers are called upon to police public order in all its
myriad forms, these words might be accepted less universally. They express
what was to become a crucial problem for police forces, that of appearing to
be the strong arm of the executive.

The willingness of the courts to preserve rights or balance freedoms is
a vital ingredient in public order law. The fact that those rights are now part
of our statute law simply means that the courts' obligation is now clear and
enforceable by appeal. As the *Phoenix Aviation* case demonstrates, the
touchstone for the courts tends to be the rule of law; see also *Bennett v
Horseferry Road Magistrates' Court* [1994] 1 AC 42, [1993] 3 WLR 90,
[1993] 3 All ER 138, albeit in a different context. The judicial control over
discretions exercised by the police or the executive must be real in order to
preserve the confidence of the community. Although significant cases are
generally dealt with by the higher courts, it is the lower courts, in particular
magistrates' courts, which face the difficult task of questioning the discretions of individual police officers (see *Piddington v Bates* [1961] 1 WLR
162, [1960] 3 All ER 660).

5 Aspects of Group Disorder

There has been considerable analysis of the freedoms of individual citizens
and the responses of groups as they exercise these freedoms:

"There might be relevance to the present day in studies of the response
of the authorities to potential trouble. Where these were inept, short-
sighted or limited by the absence of appropriate means of enforcing order the result could be disastrous. For many incidents it is possible to
trace how protest turned into violence or an attack on property became a
bloody battle as a consequence of the readily available policing force . . .
It was the local yeomanry who turned the Manchester reform meeting in
the St Peter's fields at which all the leaders had called for a respectable
and peaceful occasion into the bloody incident of "Peterloo'." (Norman
Tutt, *Violence*, DHSS Social Work Development Group, 1976, p 43).

The policing of protests has a historic dimension. Crowd problems are
hardly new either:

"Although collective behaviour in crowds is usually sensible and incon-
spicuous, the potential stupidity, irrationality and childlike behaviour of

the crowd have been noted by many observers . . . In such situations a mob is itself dehumanised but at the same time dehumanises others so that remorseless violence can occur without shame or guilt feelings." (Tutt, p 187)

Public order may be prejudiced by the individual, but it is group activity that is the primary concern and has the greatest potential for short term damage and long term disruption to community security. The way in which groups respond has been analysed:

"The explanation rests on the premise that, where social strains are present and conditions are structurally conducive, a 'generalised hostile belief' among the disaffected and thence a 'hostile outburst' occurs. Structural conduciveness is characterised by (1) the presence of an agency to which the blame for an unsatisfactory state of affairs may be attached; (2) the absence or failure of grievance channels; and (3) the possibility of effective communication among the aggrieved." (D Waddington, *Contemporary Issues in Public Disorder*, Routledge, 1992, p 12)

Significant group disorders have immediate as well as longer term causes. The violence on the Broadwater Farm estate in London in 1985, for example, was triggered in the short term by the death of the illegal immigrant Mrs Jarrett, whatever the longer term background (Waddington, p 91).

A more recent trend has been to internationalise protest and direct it at the concept of globalisation and at multi-national companies controlling events to the detriment of poorer communities in the world. Thus, international protesters take advantage of modern transport facilities to protest at international government gatherings in the UK and around the world. These protesters use the internet and e-mail to keep in touch, to organise and to avoid the police becoming aware of their specific plans. Among them are some who are prepared to ignore the law entirely, seeking to make their protest at any cost. No doubt in due course provisions on the surrender of passports, akin to those applying in cases of football hooliganism, will be implemented to restrict the movement of some of this category of protester (see page 237).

6   Policing

Police powers and the criminal law tend to reflect particular problems. For example, the provisions of the 1986 Public Order Act relating to disorderly behaviour, tampering with goods and illegal encampments followed a spate of incidents which gave rise to difficulties. Statutory powers for the police in relation to demonstrations, processions, assemblies and other gatherings have widened over recent years. The very existence of powers has been sufficient to cause objection. A variety of groups opposed the CJPOA, on the grounds that it interfered with the freedom of movement of new age travellers, or that it revoked the right of silence, or that it prevented the activities of hunt protestors. All these groups voiced anxiety about the encroachment of state powers on the individual's freedom. When those powers are essentially discretionary, much depends on the way they are used in practice and controlled by the courts, as well as on the developing culture of the community. The widespread use of video surveillance at football matches has created little visible anxiety that the cameras are reducing individual freedom. Instead they are seen as protective. This is very much a matter of how they are described and perceived:

> "London demonstrations are routinely monitored by sixty cameras placed at symbolic locations, enabling an area of 200 square miles to be covered by the Scotland Yard operation room . . . The resolution of these cameras is good enough to pick out number plates or the faces of individual demonstrators." (Waddington, p 184)

The right to express dissent at Hyde Park, which has existed since 1872 and is perceived as inalienable, has evolved to a point at which police now see a need to use video cameras to monitor the expression of dissent. This follows complaints about the extremist and threatening nature of some of the speeches and comments of various groups using the Hyde Park forum.

Lord Scarman expressed the view that "the sombre lesson of recent British history is that the balance between public order and individual liberty . . . is in its operation the business of the police" (Papers of 7th Commonwealth Law Conference, 1983). Community policing was one method recommended by Lord Scarman. As the maintenance of public order depends on the relationship between the community and those who police it, the use of "beat officers" and significant community liaison were seen as ways of improving community and police relationships to the advantage of public order. The extent to which they have worked is a matter for conjecture, as there has subsequently been a variety of substantial public order difficulties.

A single violent demonstration without public support has the power to rally public support behind what might otherwise be seen as over-restrictive legislation:

> "the few unpopular and highly inconvenient demonstrations have already produced, in recent months, demands for tighter legal control and these in turn threaten to force the hand of the law to the detriment of the freedom of expression." (V T Bevan, *Protest and Public Order* [1979] PL 163)

7   Developing Police Roles

Whether or not police officers prefer a wide discretion, or clear and specific rules, their discretions appear to be widening progressively from their common law preventive powers, through the POA 1986 and the CJPOA 1994. The only obvious challenge to those powers is the implementation of the HRA with its guarantee of the fundamental rights of the individual. Police discretion has developed since 1986 when the police were given powers to condition marches and assemblies in order to avoid serious disruption, through to the 1994 Act which gave them powers to direct people away from specified open air parties, the revised powers of search and the power to place a *cordon sanitaire* around ancient monuments to prevent gatherings. All these developments require the police to make judgements about events before they happen. Since these judgements may reflect a particular view of society and impinge on groups or individuals who take particular views, the police risk being seen in a political role supportive of one point of view as opposed to another. They now have the additional and difficult task of pitching their decisions so as to reflect and protect the individual rights of the particular people whom they must of necessity seek to control.

Fox hunting imposes on the police an unenviable task. On the one hand, the law acknowledges a "right" of protest; on the other, protecting the exercise of lawful rights is the foundation of the aggravated trespass provisions in the 1994 Act. Caught between the two extremes are the police, attempting to find a balance. Their position has always been difficult in that they may be seen as an arm of the executive when part of their function is to help preserve the individual's rights by the proper exercise of discretion in relation to matters of civil liberty. The problem has become even greater while Parliament discusses, but fails to resolve, whether or not fox hunting should remain lawful. The dilemma has not changed; it was described in the Canadian case *R v Zwicker* [1938] 1 DLR 461:

"The well known saying from Gilbert and Sullivan that 'A policeman's lot is not a happy one' is true – at times, but is also true with regard to public officials. They must expect more or less so called abuse . . . In this country a policeman is a peace officer, and his duty is not only to the public generally but to every individual citizen, and to protect that citizen, and to protect him as far as possible, even against his own weakness and not to hail him before the magistrate for every foolish thing he does."

The danger of police officers misapplying their discretion is reviewed in Home Office Research Study 135, *Policing Low Level Disorder: Police Use of s 5 Public Order Act 1986*. The purpose of the study was to review fears that the section was:

"used where the police rather than vulnerable members of the public were the victims; and its use in a wide variety of situations prompted concern that the provision might fall into disrepute in the way that the former 'sus' laws had done by their disproportionate use against ethnic minorities".

There are potential problems in the use of police discretions in this area, and the summary of the study identifies the police as commonly using s 5 as a mechanism for enforcing respect for the police rather than to protect the vulnerable in the community:

"In conclusion, the report raises the questions about the extent of police intervention in incidents of low level disorder and whether it is always appropriate to use section 5 to make arrests. First, although the behaviour leading to section 5 arrests is often genuinely offensive, judged by any standard, it is for consideration whether in some cases the conduct described is serious enough to cause real offence to those members of the public present or the police themselves . . . There is a danger that undiscriminating use of section 5 will bring it into disrepute. The section 5 provision will be most efficacious if it is reserved for precisely those cases for which it is intended: in which vulnerable members of the public are genuinely likely to, or do, suffer from offensive behaviour."

In parallel with the developing and expanding legal framework there are developments in policing tactics. Her Majesty's Inspectorate of Constabulary's Report for 1999, entitled *Keeping the Peace*, deals with the policing of disorder across the country and cites evidence of good practice. Its recommendations make clear that there are important issues about the adequacy of legislation to deal with new and old forms of disorder, and about the need for co-operation with partners in dealing with crime and disorder generally, intelligence, leadership and training. The report recognises that:

"The policing of new and emerging forms of disorder present a number of problems to forces. The balance between the rights of the individual and those of society as a whole is delicate and complex, and is inevitably open to challenge."

The development of laws and tactics to tackle disorder adversely affects many groups, who feel marked out or otherwise disadvantaged. It is in the application of the law that much cause for genuine concern is felt; see, for example, Home Office, Police Research Series, paper 127, *The Impact of Stops and Searches on Crime and the Community*.

Finally, the Government's Consultation Document on what it terms *Animal Rights Extremists* (Home Office, March 2001) has already produced the changes to the Protection from Harassment Act 1997 noted in Chapter 4, and no doubt more changes will follow soon.

8   The Future

Public order law is not codified and indeed is probably incapable of codification. Nor is it comprehensible to the community at large. The HRA seems merely to have reinforced a perception among protestors that their rights are absolute and unfettered. At the moment, the capacity of the public authorities is stretched as they try to distinguish between genuine and lawful protestors and those who are prepared to commit serious criminal offences in pursuit of their aims. The increasing experience of protestors means that confrontations between them and the public authorities (often the police) are much more subtle than the outward displays of violence might suggest. Targeted use of the internet and e-mails leading to "out of the blue" occupations, demonstrations or acts of group violence suggest a level of sophistication that is very much of our time. The State has an obligation to build into the education system awareness of the law relating to public order to ensure that individuals develop an accurate perception of the extent of individual rights. In the absence of that knowledge it is hardly surprising that there is widespread misapprehension as to how far individuals can go if they choose to make a protest.

Our law is constantly changing as society changes. What was perfectly tolerable 50 or 100 years ago may be perceived differently now, in the field of public order law as in any other area of law, but it will mean little if the community at large is not aware of what that law provides and that it is consistent with international requirements on individual rights.

Chapter 2

Preventive Powers and Duties

1 Introduction

The Public Order Act 1986 ("POA"), the Criminal Justice and Public Order Act 1994 ("CJPOA") and other legislation do not purport to constitute a comprehensive codification of the law relating to public order. While certain common law offences have been abolished, and certain statutory provisions have been repealed or amended, much of the pre-existing common law framework remains intact. Importantly, the common law powers to deal with or prevent breaches of the peace are unaffected by statute, and are specifically preserved by the 1986 Act (see s 40(4)). This approach is consistent with that adopted in s 17 of the Police and Criminal Evidence Act 1984 which expressly preserves powers to enter premises to deal with breaches of the peace. Despite the development of wider powers of arrest or statutory preventive powers, the arrest and preventive powers in connection with actual or apprehended breaches of the peace continue to play important roles in the policing of public disorder. Professor Glanville Williams described breach of the peace as:

"A notion . . . of immense historical significance and . . . the foundation of modern rules of law. Nevertheless, the courts have failed to resolve precisely what they mean by it, largely because they are constantly under the temptation to make it do far too much work." (146 JPN 199)

Frequently, the principal motivation behind police intervention is the preservation of the peace and good order rather than an arrest for a specific offence. It is in that context that the common law preventive powers fall for consideration, either as justification for interfering with a citizen's freedom, or as the basis for applying for a bind-over.

In this chapter, the common law powers to prevent or deal with breaches of the peace are reviewed. Given their central importance, it is unsurprising that their scope and application have fallen for consideration in the European Court of Human Rights (see page 21). There will be continuing scrutiny under the Human Rights Act 1998.

This chapter also deals briefly with measures introduced by the Crime and Disorder Act 1998 and the Criminal Justice and Police Act 2001: anti-social behaviour orders, local child curfew orders, on-the-spot fines, and certain provisions concerning alcohol.

2   Breach of the Peace

2.1   *General Nature of Breach of the Peace*

In England and Wales breach of the peace is not a substantive criminal offence, although in Scotland the law recognises it as a crime. The extensive range of powers available both to the police and the courts, in connection with breaches of the peace, persuaded the European Court of Human Rights, in *Steel & Others v UK* (1998) 28 EHRR 603, 5 BHRC 339, [1998] HRCD 872, [1998] Crim LR 893, that a breach of the peace is a criminal offence within the meaning of art 5(1)(c) of the European Convention on Human Rights and Fundamental Freedoms. This view accords with the recognition in English law that, although the procedures before magistrates' courts are "primarily civil . . . they have some of the hallmarks of criminal proceedings" (*DPP v Speede* [1998] 2 Cr App R 108), and involve a criminal standard (*Everett v Ribbands* [1952] 2 QB 198, [1952] 1 All ER 823, [1952] 1 TLR 933; *R v Bolton Justices ex p Graeme* (1986) 150 JP 129, (1986) 150 JPN 271 (CA), and *Percy v DPP* [1955] 1 WLR 1382, [1995] 3 All ER 124, [1995] Crim LR 714 (DC)). Accordingly, in *Steel v UK*, it was found that each of the applicants had been arrested and detained with a view to being brought before a competent legal authority on suspicion of having committed an offence.

The European Court of Human Rights in *Steel* concluded that, as an alternative, the arrest had been because "it was considered necessary to prevent the commission of an "offence". If, as must commonly be the case, detention is effected not with a view to bringing an arrested person before a court, but with a view to stopping or preventing a breach of the peace, then it is clear that, following the decision in *Steel*, detention is justifiable under art 5(1)(c) as detention effected for the purpose of preventing an offence.

It is also arguable that detention in such circumstances may be justifiable under art 5(1)(b) as detention effected to secure the fulfilment of an obligation prescribed by law. This was the view of the UK Government in the case of *Steel*, but was not further analysed by the Court. The contention may not be sustainable in the light of the decision in *Engel v Netherlands* [1976] 1 EHRR 647, that to satisfy this requirement the obligation must be "specific and concrete", rather than a general duty imposed upon citizens; see also *McVeigh and Others v The United Kingdom* [1983] 5 EHRR 71.

2.2   *Breach of the Peace and Execution of Duty*

Often, the common law preventive powers arise in the context of an offence under s 89 of the Police Act 1996 (assault or wilful obstruction of a constable acting in the execution of his duty), or a civil action such as a claim in damages for trespass to the person. Whether a police officer is acting in the execution of his duty is often answered by asking whether or not he is acting to control a breach of the peace; that this elementary point is often overlooked was illustrated in the House of Lords' decision in *Albert v Lavin* [1982] AC 546, [1981] 3 WLR 955, [1981] 3 All ER 878. A police officer may also justify interventions in a citizen's liberty by reference to common law powers.

It is also trite law that these preventive powers are available both to ordinary citizens and to the police, and that reasonable force may be used in support of those powers. A constable who is acting within this preventive capacity is within the execution of his duty for the purposes of s 89(1) and (3) of the Police Act 1996 (assaulting and wilfully obstructing a constable in the execution of his duty). Assault or wilful obstruction of a citizen assisting a police officer is also an offence contrary to s 89.

There may occasionally be circumstances where a constable is doing something which at law he is not strictly compelled to do, eg assisting in or supervising the exclusion of trespassers. The question that may arise is whether the constable is acting merely in a private capacity rather than as a constable. If the former, then the constable is in no better (or worse) position than, say, a security guard employed by the owner of the land. A constable is, of course, acting lawfully when assisting a citizen to achieve what the citizen is lawfully entitled to do, provided that excessive force is not applied. Suppose a constable is assaulted or obstructed while so engaged? At the very least, any assault on the constable would constitute a common assault (or similar, depending on the degree of injury), regardless of his precise status. But it has been said that in such an instance the constable is not only acting lawfully, but is also acting in the execution of his duty for the purposes of the Police Act 1996. This proposition also applies if he anticipates an imminent breach of the peace; see *Coffin v Smith* (1980) 71 Cr App R 221. There, police officers attended a youth club whose leader was ejecting youths. The youths returned to the area and assaulted the police officers. The Divisional Court held that the police officers were acting in the execution of their duty.

Coffin v Smith casts doubt on *R v Prebble* (1858) 1 F & F 325, where it had been held that a police officer clearing licensed premises was not acting in execution of his duty where there had been no actual or threatened breach of the peace. These two authorities conflict. There is also some doubt about the true *ratio* in *Coffin v Smith*. On the facts, the result is certainly correct, but the statement of principle may have been *obiter* given that the conduct of the youths was such as to cause the officers to believe that a breach of the peace was imminent. The point was briefly considered by the Court of Appeal in *Porter v Commissioner of Police for the Metropolis*, 20 October 1999, unreported, where, on the facts, the Court of Appeal was not called upon to decide the correctness of the statement in *Coffin v Smith*, but May LJ thought it was probably part of the *ratio* of the case; Sedley LJ recognised that the reasoning could not be accepted as wholly correct; and Judge LJ declined to comment.

Although the matter is not free from doubt, it is submitted that the better view is that *Coffin v Smith* stated the principle correctly. The case is entirely consistent with the broad approach to police duty developed in cases such as *Rice v Connolly* [1966] 2 QB 414, [1966] 3 WLR 17, [1966] 2 All ER 649 (DC) and *Lavin v Albert* (above). The point is also largely academic given that in an appropriate case the difficulty of the phrase "execution of duty" can be avoided by charging the defendant with simple assault rather than the more technically demanding s 89 offence – a result which was achieved in *R v Prebble* (above), where the defendant was convicted of common assault.

Ordinarily, the legality of police intervention is justified by direct evidence. But where a serious disturbance involving breaches of the peace is taking place, the court may draw the inference that an attempted arrest by an unidentified police officer is lawful, and accordingly interference with that arrest by another person amounts to an offence contrary to s 89 of the Police Act 1986 (*Plowden v DPP* [1991] Crim LR 850 (DC)). Such inferences may not be drawn where police officers involved are readily identifiable and direct evidence to support the legality of the original arrest is available (*Riley v DPP* (1990) 91 Cr App R 14, (1990) 154 JP 453, [1990] Crim LR 422 (DC); see also *Chapman v DPP* (1989) 89 Cr App R 190, [1988] Crim LR 843, (1989) 153 JP 27 (QBD)).

2.3 Powers and Duties in Connection with Breach of the Peace

Section 40(4) of the 1986 Act is clear that the full range of preventive powers based upon actual or apprehended breaches of the peace is preserved: "Nothing in this Act affects the common law powers in England and Wales to deal with or prevent a breach of the peace".

The Citizen's Duty

The common law imposes a duty on all citizens to suppress actual breaches of the peace. This duty is of ancient origin and is illustrated by clear and uncompromising statements in the *Bristol Riots* case (1832) 3 State Tr NS 1, *R v Pinney* (1832) 3 B & Ad 947 and *R v Kennett* (1781) 5 C & P 282. The authoritative modern statement of the duty in respect of both actual and apprehended breaches of the peace is found in Lord Diplock's speech in *Albert v Lavin* (above):

> ". . . every citizen in whose presence a breach of the peace is being, or reasonably appears to be about to be, committed has the right to take reasonable steps to make the person who is breaking or threatening to break the peace refrain from doing so; and those reasonable steps in appropriate cases will include detaining him against his will. At common law this is not only the right of every citizen, it is also his duty, although, except in the case of a citizen who is a constable, it is a duty of imperfect obligation."

In *R v Pinney* the court considered the obligations of a public officer, but the more general observation was made that: "The King's subjects are bound to be assistant to them [magistrates] in suppressing the riot, when reasonably warned".

And, in the *Bristol Riots* case, it was said that:

"by common law every person may lawfully endeavour of his own authority and without any warrant or sanction of the magistrate, to suppress a riot by every means in his power . . . it is his bounden duty of a good subject . . . to perform this to the utmost of his ability. If the riot be general and dangerous he may arm himself against evil doers to keep the peace."

In the light of modern police structure and methods, the wider comments in the older cases as to the duty of the citizens to suppress riots may now be otiose; but the importance of the duty to deal with breaches of the peace is that it is placed upon every citizen, and that in acting to suppress breaches of the peace police officers, and others, act lawfully.

Duty to Assist a Constable

It is an offence at common law for a citizen to fail to come to the assistance of a constable when that constable sees a breach of the peace and there is reasonable necessity to call on the citizen to assist. The offence is an extension of the duty to deal with or prevent breaches of the peace. In *R v Brown* (1841) Car & M 314, the court said that "It is no unimportant matter that the Queen's subject should assist the officers of the law, when duly required to do so, in preserving the public peace . . ."; and that "every man is bound to set a good example to others by doing his duty in preserving the public peace".

It seems likely that the offence will extend to occasions where the constable apprehends an imminent breach of the peace. The appropriate *mens rea* is unclear. There is a defence of physical impossibility or lawful excuse, although the scope of the defence is uncertain. See *R v Brown* (above), *R v Sherlock* (1886) LR 1 CCR 20, and *R v Waugh, The Times,* 1 October 1976. The Royal Commission on Criminal Procedure (Cmnd 8092) indicated that there have been prosecutions for this offence in modern times, and cited an example from Gwent where a police officer was attacked by a group while arresting another person for being drunk and disorderly. The constable called upon a passer-by to come to his assistance but he failed to do so. The passer-by was fined £50 in respect of the offence. Where a person is assisting a constable acting in the execution of his duty, the offences under s 89 of the Police Act 1996 are relevant.

2.4 Definition of Breach of the Peace

Until recently it was possible for a leading writer to comment that "Rather oddly it may seem, the creation of a breach of peace is probably not a substantive crime . . . Problems of definition exist." (Brownlie's *Laws of Public*

Order and National Security, 2nd edn, Butterworths, 1981). Professor Glanville Williams was also driven to observe the "surprising lack of authoritative definition of what one would suppose to be a fundamental concept in criminal law" ([1954] Crim LR 578).

In his report on the Red Lion Square disorders of 15 June 1974 (Cmnd 5919), Lord Scarman noted with apparent approval the view expressed in Moriarty's *Police Law* (1972, 21st edn) that: "The 'Queen's Peace' or shortly 'the peace' is the normal state of society, and any interruption of that peace and good order which ought to prevail in a civilised country is a breach of the peace". Although this view may reflect the state of public tranquillity which is generally desirable, its emphasis on mere breaches of tranquillity amounting to breaches of the peace is too broad to be sustained. Breach of the peace was referred to by the craftsman of the Draft Criminal Code as "a somewhat vague notion" and the suggested formulation, based on *R v Howell* (below), was:

"A breach of the peace occurs when, by unlawful violence, harm is done to a person, or in his presence his property, or a person fears on reasonable grounds that unlawful violence likely to cause such harm is imminent."

The 1986 Act departed from the 1936 Public Order Act and based its principal offences on the concept of "unlawful violence", rather than on breach of the peace. The common law, however, continues to depend upon this ill-defined but useful concept.

R v Howell

Although the courts have consistently refused to provide a definition of breach of the peace, the Court of Appeal in *R v Howell* [1982] QB 416, [1981] 3 All ER 383 considered that:

". . . there is a breach of the peace whenever harm is actually done or is likely to be done to a person or in his presence to his property or a person is in fear of being so harmed through an assault, an affray, a riot, unlawful assembly or other disturbance."

A disturbance not involving violence or the fear of violence does not amount to a breach of the peace, and mere noise and disturbance is insufficient (see *R v Howell*; *Wooding v Oxley* (1839) 9 C & P 1 NP 170; *Hardy v Murphy* (1795) 1 Esp 294; *Green v Bartram* (1830) 4 C & P 308; *Jordan v Gibbon* (1863) 8 LT 391). Noise and disturbance may provide a constable with evidence from which he may conclude that a breach of the peace is imminent. In the same way, mere trespass does not amount to a breach of the peace (*Green v Bartram*; *R v Chief Constable for Devon and Cornwall ex p Central Electricity Generating Board* [1982] QB 458, [1981] 3 WLR 867, [1981] 3 All ER 826; *Porter v Commissioner of Police for the Metropolis*, 20 October 1999, unreported (CA)), although there may be additional circumstances from which it might reasonably be apprehended that a breach of the peace is likely as a natural consequence of the trespass, eg continued incursions into property in the face of clearly expressed threats to use violence to resist the trespass (see *Percy v DPP* [1955] 1 WLR 1382, [1995] 3 All ER 124, [1995] Crim LR 714 (DC)).

The Court of Appeal in *Parkin v Norman* [1983] QB 92, [1982] 3 WLR 523, [1982] 2 All ER 583 (DC) approved the statement in *R v Howell*, and it has been approved and applied in *Percy v DPP* and *Nicol & Selvanayagam v DPP* [1966] JP 155. The approach in *R v Howell* now represents the authoritative statement of the law and is preferred to the more widely expressed *dictum* of Lord Denning MR in *R v Chief Constable for Devon and Cornwall ex p Central Electricity Generating Board* (above), which is too wide for general application:

> "There is a breach of the peace whenever a person who is lawfully carrying out his work is unlawfully and physically prevented by another from doing it . . . if anyone unlawfully and physically obstructs the workers, by lying down or chaining himself to a rig or the like, he is guilty of a breach of the peace."

Where the physical obstruction involves actual or threatened personal violence there is scope for accepting the first part of Lord Denning's *dictum*, but passive obstruction cannot of itself be a breach of the peace. Of course, such action may well give rise to a reasonable belief that a breach of the peace may be imminent, eg where there is an attempt to force a passage and a belief that the physical but passive obstruction may take a more violent course. The remaining members of the Court of Appeal in *R v Chief Constable of Devon and Exeter ex p CEGB* did not join in with Lord Denning's *dictum*, although there was disagreement about the exact point at which police might intervene to deal with the demonstrators in that case.

The analysis in *R v Howell* was doubted in *Lewis v Chief Constable of Greater Manchester, The Independent,* 23 October 1991, where the Court of Appeal, in a civil action, considered that an act which places a person in fear of harm is not of itself a breach of the peace but is merely the ground upon which the power of arrest is activated. The actual infliction of harm is necessary to constitute a breach of the peace. The court drew a distinction between the conditions justifying arrest and the definition of a breach of the peace. The court acknowledged that the distinction made little practical difference, and the decision may do no more than reflect the attempt in *R v Howell* to provide a distillation of relevant factors drawn from the earlier cases.

Accordingly, there is currently a close correlation between "violence" as defined in s 8 of the 1986 Act and breach of the peace, although the latter may be more flexible in its application. For example, the type of disturbance in the older cases – such as *Howell v Jackson* (1839) 9 C & P 437; *Ingle v Bell* (1836) 1 M & W 516, (1836) 5 LJMC 85, [1836] 150 ER 539; *Cohen v Huskisson* (1837) 2 M & W 4877, (1837) 6 LJMC 133; *Webster v Watts* (1847) 11 QB 311, (1847) 12 JP 279, [1847] 116 ER 492 (where the breach of the peace was seen to arise from the gathering of a crowd which, because of its size and general manner, threatened the peace) – would not readily fall within ss 1–4 of the 1986 Act in the absence of actual threats or use of violence. Certainly, since the earlier cases tend to turn on the pleadings, caution is needed, and in *R v Howell* Watkins LJ observed that "the older cases are of considerable interest but they are not a sure guide to what the term is understood to mean today".

The meaning of breach of the peace for the purposes of the law relating to binding over follows the same principles set out above (*Percy v DPP*). The equation, in *Everett v Ribbands* (above), of breach of the peace with any breach of law has been disapproved (*Percy v DPP*).

The European Convention on Human Rights
The principle in *R v Howell* has met with the approval of the European Court of Human Rights in *McLeod v UK* [1999] Crim LR 155 and *Steel v UK* (1998) 28 EHRR 603, 5 BHRC 339, [1998] HRCD 872, [1998] Crim LR 893, and the lack of absolute certainty regarding the definition of a breach of the peace has not prevented the European Court of Human Rights from identifying the core elements as satisfying the requirements of the Convention in two major regards.

To be lawful, arrest and detention has to be in accordance with the terms of art 5 of the Convention, which provides that:
"Everyone has the right to liberty and security of person. No one shall be deprived of his liberty save in the following cases and in accordance with a procedure prescribed by law:
(a) the lawful detention of a person after conviction by a competent court;
(b) the lawful arrest or detention of a person for non-compliance with the lawful order of a court or in order to secure the fulfilment of any obligation prescribed by law;
(c) the lawful arrest or detention of a person effected for the purpose of bringing him before the competent legal authority on reasonable suspicion of having committed an offence or when it is reasonably considered necessary to prevent his committing an offence or fleeing after having done so. . .".
The European Court of Human Rights, in *Steel v UK,* treated breach of the peace as a criminal offence within the meaning of art 5(1)(c) of the Convention.

The various rights to privacy, freedom of conscience, freedom of expression and freedom of assembly guaranteed by arts 8, 9, 10 and 11 respectively of the Convention may be curtailed by limitations which are "in accordance with the law" and "necessary in a democratic society" (art 8(2)), or "prescribed by law" and "necessary in a democratic society" (arts 9(2), 10(2) and 11(2) respectively) in pursuit of certain objectives specified in the relevant article of the Convention, such as prevention of disorder or crime.

The expression "in accordance with the law" has a specific meaning in the context of the Convention. In *McLeod* the European Court of Human Rights said that the expression:

> "requires firstly that the impugned measures should have a basis in domestic law. It also refers to the quality of the law in question, requiring that it be accessible to the person concerned and formulated with sufficient precision to enable them – if need be, with appropriate advice – to foresee, to a degree that is reasonable in the circumstances, the consequences which a given action may entail. However, those consequences need not be foreseeable with absolute certainty, since such certainty might give rise to excessive rigidity, and the law must keep pace with changing circumstances."

The degree of certainty which has now been achieved by the domestic courts was sufficient to permit the court to conclude that the power of the police to enter private premises was "in accordance with the law". There is no reason to suppose that the same result will not follow in respect of the other preventive powers of the police outlined below (see page 34).

According to the European Court of Human Rights, the expression "necessary in a democratic society", "implies that the interference corresponds to a pressing social need and . . . that it is proportionate to the legitimate aim pursued".

In *McLeod v UK* the question was whether there had been a fair balance between the interest of the applicant in her private life and the prevention of crime or disorder. On the particular facts, the Court held that the entry by police to private premises could not be justified despite having been upheld as lawful by the High Court in civil proceedings, and despite the Court of Appeal's refusal to upset that finding; see *McLeod v Commissioner of Police of the Metropolis* [1994] 4 All ER 553. The reasoning of the European Court of Human Rights was that, although the power to enter premises in connection with an actual or threatened imminent breach of the peace existed under English common law, the *particular* exercise of that power could not be justified because the police officers could not, *on the facts*, have had reasonable cause to believe that a breach of the peace was imminent. Accordingly, the intrusion breached art 8 of the Convention (right to respect for private life and home), because, as an unlawful act, it could not be said to be "necessary in a democratic society".

Within art 5 the expressions "lawful" and "in accordance with a procedure prescribed by law" require that arrests and detention should fully comply with national law. Although English law fulfilled the criteria of providing sufficient guidance to the individual and sufficient precision, in *Steel and Others v UK*, the European Court of Human Rights itself reviewed the legality of the arrests, even though this was primarily a matter for the national courts, "since failure to comply with domestic law entails a breach of Article

5(1), the Court can and should exercise a certain power of review in this matter . . .". This approach is entirely consistent with the decision in *Winterwerp v Netherlands* (1979) series A 33.

The Court concluded that the behaviour of some of the applicants might have provoked others to violence, and accordingly their arrests had been lawful. Other applicants were in a different position in that their behaviour was entirely peaceful and non-provocative. According to the Court:

"it would not appear that there was anything in their behaviour which could have justified the police in fearing that a breach of the peace was likely to be caused. The arrest and subsequent detention of the applicants did not comply with English law and could not be described as 'lawful' for the purposes of Article 5(1)".

It was also held in *Steel* that there had been no breach of art 6 because the charge sheets contained sufficient information and were given to the applicants in sufficient time to satisfy the requirements in art 6(3)(a) – that everyone charged with a criminal offence should be informed promptly, in a language the person understands and in detail, the nature and cause of any accusation.

The various applicants in *Steel* also claimed that their arrests and subsequent detention had been in breach of art 10 as interferences with rights of expression. The Court held that the applicants' behaviour fell within art 10 as amounting to expressions of opinion, even though in some instances the behaviour factually amounted to obstruction of others. But where the applicants had been unlawfully arrested, the illegality meant that the measures taken against them could not be described as "prescribed by law". Thus, even though the measures were in pursuance of a legitimate object under art 10 (the prevention of disorder), there had been breaches of art 10 in respect of those applicants.

2.5 Breach of the Peace in a Private Place

A breach of the peace may occur on private premises even though no member of the general public is likely to come into the vicinity of the disturbance amounting to a breach of the peace. The point was not taken in *Wilson v Skeock* (1949) 65 TLR 418, (1949) 113 JP 293, *Robson v Hallett* [1967] 2 QB 939, [1967] 3 WLR 28, [1967] 2 All ER 407 (DC), or in *R v Chief Constable of Devon and Exeter ex p CEGB* (above), where the conduct amounting to breach of the peace occurred on private property; the point was decided in *McConnell v Chief Constable of Greater Manchester* [1990] 1 WLR 364, [1990] 1 All ER 423, (1990) 91 Cr App R 88 (CA) and applied in *McQuade v Chief Constable of Humberside Police, The Times* 3 September 2001. The nature of the property and the presence of the public are matters which go to whether or not a breach of the peace is likely to occur as a result of a particular course of conduct (*McConnell v Chief Constable of Greater Manchester*).

2.6 Lawful Action as Breach of the Peace

Whether lawful action may constitute a breach of the peace should not be confused with the separate issue of whether or not a constable may restrict or terminate a lawful activity when he reasonably apprehends an imminent breach of the peace; see pages 27, 34 and 40. Lord Denning, in *R v Chief Constable of Devon and Exeter ex p CEGB* (above) seemed to suggest that lawfulness is irrelevant to whether or not a breach of the peace exists:

> "But in deciding whether there is a breach of the peace . . . the law does not go into the rights and wrongs of the matter, or whether it is justified by self help or not".

Despite this *dictum*, which was unsupported by the other members of the Court of Appeal, it is suggested that in the absence of unlawful violence (or threat thereof) no breach of the peace can be said to occur. In normal circumstances any exchange of violence inevitably amounts to a breach of the peace, even if one of the parties is acting lawfully. In deciding whether or not there is a breach of the peace the courts are not concerned with allocating responsibility; there need only be some unlawful activity involving violence or threat thereof. Responsibility is an issue to be considered only at the stage of deciding whether action is reasonable and appropriate.

In *Marsh v Arscott* (1982) 75 Cr App R 211, [1982] Crim LR 827 (QBD), a struggle occurred when an individual attempted to eject police officers from his property. McCullough J remarked:

> ". . . the police officers, having been told to leave, were acting unlawfully in remaining. If the defendant was using no more force than was reasonably necessary to evict them he was acting lawfully, and in arresting him the police were acting unlawfully. This violent incident amounted to a breach of the peace but it was one for which the police officers were responsible and not the defendant himself . . . Suppose . . . that the defendant's threats and use of force towards the police had been unlawful, once again there would have been a breach of the peace. In this event the defendant would have been responsible for breaching the peace. Thus, regardless of who was acting lawfully and who was acting unlawfully there was at the time of the incident a breach of the peace."

This approach can also be seen in *Joyce v Hertfordshire Constabulary* (1985) 80 Cr App R 298 (DC). The court decided that one police officer could intervene in a struggle between the appellant and another police officer and need not be certain that there had been a lawful arrest. The court observed that "What was going on was in fact a struggle and a breach of the peace and the rights and wrongs do not matter". In *McBean v Parker* [1983] Crim LR 399 (DC) Dunn LJ said, of the requirement in *R v Howell* for "harm", that it seemed to him that ". . . the harm done or likely to be done must be unlawful harm".

The problem with Lord Denning's approach is that it is difficult to see why a lawful action should be classified as a breach of the peace and therefore susceptible to intervention. Is the ejection of a trespasser, under the common law power of self-help, a breach of the peace where the trespasser does not struggle and reasonable force is employed? To label this a breach of the peace, and thereby excuse the intervention of police officers, is to extend inappropriately the range of breach of the peace, a point similarly made in *Bibby v Chief Constable of Essex, The Times*, 24 April 2000 (CA).

Of course, the removal of demonstrators may, in appropriate circumstances, give rise to a reasonable anticipation that a breach of the peace will occur. Whether it does or not was discussed somewhat inconclusively by the Court of Appeal in the *CEGB* case (above).

2.7 Reasonably Apprehended Breach of the Peace

Action may be taken not only in relation to breaches of the peace which are actually occurring, but also in respect of reasonably apprehended imminent breaches of the peace. The difficulties of identifying the risk of breaches of the peace can be seen from the disparate views of the court in the *CEGB* case (above). Lord Denning accepted the possibility that the simplest obstruction of the Board's employees might give rise to a reasonable apprehension of a breach of the peace. But Lawton LJ did not see any risk of a breach of the peace in mere removal of the protectors:

"... police officers ... cannot act unless they see a breach of the peace or have reasonable cause for suspecting that there is a real imminent risk of one occurring ... If those obstructing do allow themselves to be removed without struggling or causing an uproar (which seems to me unlikely ...) the police will have no reason for taking action, nor should they."

On the other hand, Templeman LJ took the view that:

"An obstructer who will not leave the site unless he is forcibly removed presents a threat and danger of a breach of the peace even if he disclaims any intention of causing a breach of the peace."

In any event, he went on to say:

"... the police will be entitled to intervene if an obstructer resists being carried away from the site or runs to another part of the site or tries to return to the site, thus obliging the board's representatives to seize him so that he may be permanently excluded. Such conduct by an obstructer ... will create an imminent and serious danger of a breach of the peace for which the obstructer will be responsible and liable to arrest or removal by the police."

The Objective Standard

As will be seen, the correct approach is a two-stage approach. The first stage is the question of the objective standard to decide whether a breach of the peace was reasonably apprehended as imminent. The second stage is to decide where the threat to the peace is coming from, and what action is reasonable in the light of the facts; see page 34.

Whether a breach of the peace is reasonably apprehended as imminent is a question of fact, and a belief as to the imminence of a breach of the peace must not only be genuine, but founded on reasonable grounds. The courts have been reluctant to interfere with decisions of magistrates on this point, while stressing the need for objective scrutiny of police discretion: see *Piddington v Bates* [1961] 1 WLR 162, [1960] 3 All ER 660 (DC); *Kavanagh v Hiscock* [1974] QB 600, [1974] 2 WLR 421, [1974] 2 All ER 177 (DC); and *Tynan v Balmer* [1967] 1 QB 91, [1966] 2 WLR 1181, [1966] 2 All ER 133 (DC).

There must be grounds for the constable's reasonable belief. A mere statement by the constable that he anticipated a breach of the peace is insufficient (*Piddington v Bates*). There must be a real and not merely a remote possibility of a breach of the peace (see *Piddington v Bates*). In *R v Chief Constable of Devon and Exeter ex p CEGB* [1982] QB 458, [1981] 3 WLR 867, [1981] 3 All ER 826 (QBD), Lawton and Templeman LJJ both refer to the need for a "real and imminent risk" or "imminent and serious danger" of a breach of the peace. It has also been said that "[t]he possibility of a breach must be real to justify any preventive action. The imminence or immediacy of the threat to the peace determines what action is reasonable" (see *Moss v McLachlan* (1985) 149 JP 167, [1985] IRLR 76, (1985) 149 JPN 149 (DC)). And in *McLeod v Commissioner of Police for the Metropolis* [1994] 4 All ER 553 (CA) Neill LJ emphasised that:

> "It seems to me it is important that when exercising his power to prevent a breach of the peace a police officer should act with great care and discretion; this will be particularly important where the exercise of his power involves entering on private premises contrary to the wishes of the owners or occupiers. The officer must satisfy himself that there is a real and imminent risk of a breach of the peace, because, if the matter has to be tested in court thereafter there may be scrutiny not only of his belief at the time but also of the grounds for his belief."

Despite these judicial observations, the degree of judicial scrutiny of police discretion may not have been more than superficial. But two cases – *McLeod* and *Steel* – before the European Court of Human Rights have reinforced the requirement that the scrutiny, by both civil and criminal courts, should be strict and not merely formulaic. This has been applied by the Divisional Court in *Redmond-Bate v DPP* (1999) 163 JP 789, [1999] Crim LR 998, *The Times* 28 July 1998 (QBD), where the test was described as objective but without the benefit of hindsight:

> "It is for the court to decide not whether the view taken by the constable fell within the broad band of rational decisions but whether in the light of what he knew and perceived at the time the court is satisfied that it was reasonable to fear an imminent breach of the peace."

The same point was also effectively made by the Court of Appeal in *Foulkes v Chief Constable of the Merseyside Police* [1998] 3 All ER 705, [1998] 2 FLR 789, [1999] FCR 98 (CA); see page 32, a domestic law case decided contemporaneously with the cases in the European Court:

> "There must . . . be a sufficiently real and present threat to the peace to justify the extreme step of depriving of his liberty a citizen who is not at the time acting unlawfully. The factors identified by the Recorder in the present case do not in my judgment measure up to a sufficiently serious or imminent threat to the peace to justify arrest. Accordingly I would hold that [the police officer] though acting honestly and from the best of motives did not in fact have reasonable ground for the arrest."

The most recent decision is the case of *Bibby v Chief Constable of Essex*, see page 25.

The application of the law to particular cases must call for critical judicial scrutiny of the evidence and objective assessment of the factual basis for any exercise of police discretion. The willingness of the European Court of Human Rights, in *McLeod v UK*, to reopen and reverse the findings of fact (and the decision of the appellate court) demonstrates that there must be effective control of police officers' discretions at the time of trial or binding over, or on an action for damages should this be the context in which the matter falls to be tested. The warnings in such cases as *Piddington v Bates*, to apply strictly an objectively reasonable test of the officer's belief that a breach of the peace is imminent, must be borne in mind when weighing the evidence.

Finally, as the decision in *Redmond-Bate* demonstrates, the advent of the Human Rights Act 1998 makes absolutely certain that the values inherent in the Convention must be at the forefront of decision-making by courts. This is so whether the courts are acting within their binding-over jurisdiction or on the trial of offences where particular exercises of police power have been called into doubt.

2.8 The Person Against whom Preventive Action Should be Taken

The courts appear to expect that the police will take action against the party "responsible" when that person can clearly be identified. For example, in the *CEGB* case, Lord Denning MR and the other members of the Court of Appeal clearly had it in mind that the police would operate only against the obstructers as the party "responsible". Notions of causation and responsibility are notoriously difficult to pin down in law and the observations in this case are not necessarily either helpful or of current authority.

Police officers, and presumably others, may, in appropriate circumstances, take action against anyone who is acting otherwise lawfully (see *Humphries v Connor* (1864) 17 ICLR 1 21). Whether such preventive action is lawful depends on all the circumstances, and in this context there are important issues relating to peaceful protest.

The Hostile Audience and Human Rights

The dilemma facing police officers, and others, in controlling public behaviour is often summed up in debate as "the hostile audience problem". This problem is not restricted to the exercise of the common law preventive powers, but is also readily apparent in the exercise of the statutory preventive powers in the context of those public processions and public assemblies falling within the scope of the 1986 Act; see Chapter 5.

At the simplest of levels, where the lawful activity of a person or group is met by unlawful action or threats of violence by opponents, then the police officer is faced with the questions, should the lawful activity be curtailed, or should the unlawful activity be dealt with and the lawful activity protected? The risk of creating a "heckler's veto" is apparent, and interference with an individual's lawful action in response to threats by opponents was described in *Humphries v Connor* "as making, not the law of the land but the law of the mob supreme". The possibility of abuse of the preventive power was noted in *Humphries v Connor*. Fitzgerald J was reluctant to agree with his colleague because he thought that the police ought not to act against those who are carrying out lawful acts which others find displeasing and use as an excuse to break the peace. Rather, the police should act against those who threaten to, or who actually, break the peace. O'Brien J perceived that there was a risk and specifically excluded abuse of power from the scope of his decision:

> "Our decision would not be applicable to a state of facts where the power was abused; and . . . it would not protect any constable from any unnecessary, excessive, or improper exercise of such power in other cases."

As will be seen, these comments reflect modern cases, although this case might well be decided differently today, given the impact of the rights afforded by the Human Rights Act. The same issue arises in the context of the justices' power to bind over; for recent illustrations see *R v Inner London Crown Court ex p Benjamin* (1987) 85 Cr App R 267, [1987] Crim LR 417 (DC); *R v Morpeth Ward Justices ex p Ward* (1992) 95 Cr App R 215, [1992] Crim LR 497, (1992) 142 NLJ 312 (DC); *Nicol & Selvanayagam v DPP* [1966] JP 155. Unsurprisingly, the approach to this problem in the statutory preventive context is likely to lead to the same result (see Chapter 5).

In *Beatty v Gillbanks* (1882) 9 QBD 308, [1881–5] All ER Rep 559, (1882) 47 LT 194 (QBD), the lawful activity of Salvation Army marchers was violently opposed by the Skeleton Army, a group which had often engaged in violence to thwart the aims of the Salvationists. At the time, in order to bind over, an actual or apprehended crime – here the offence of unlawful assembly – had to be established. The binding over order imposed on the leader of the Salvationists' procession was quashed on the basis that there had been no intention on his part to cause the disturbance, and, by implication, that the disturbance was not the natural and necessary consequence of his action.

The principle in that case received support in *R v Londonderry Justices* (1891) 28 LR IR 440, but has found little support elsewhere; see *O'Kelly v Harvey* (1883) 15 Cox CC 435; *Duncan v Jones* [1936] 1 KB 218, [1935] All ER Rep 710, (1935) 52 TLR 26; *Humphries v Connor* (above); and particularly *Wise v Dunning* [1902] 1 KB 167, [1900–3] All ER Rep 727, (1902) 85 LT 721, where the court was prepared to sanction a more realistic view of the natural consequences of the use of insulting and abusive behaviour. In *R v Chief Constable of Sussex ex p International Traders' Ferry* [1999] 2 AC 418, [1999] 1 All ER 129, Lord Slynn observed, in a wide *dictum* which has not yet fallen for consideration, "I do not accept that *Beatty's* case lays down that the police can never restrain a lawful activity if that is the only way to prevent violence and a breach of the peace".

Although the matter is primarily one of the proper exercise of discretion by the police officer, the courts have ultimate authority over that discretion and seek to ensure that the formally guaranteed rights of assembly and expression are not subverted by the improper exercise of the discretion. *Dicta* in a range of cases (for example, *R v Coventry City Council ex p Phoenix Aviation* [1995] 3 All ER 37, [1995] COD 300, (1995) NLJ 559 (QBD)) indicate the view of the higher courts that the rule of law must prevail and that, save in exceptional circumstances, any exercise of discretion should favour the continuance of the lawful activity, including freedom of peaceful assembly, procession and speech. That broad approach has been vindicated by decisions of the European Court of Human Rights and the Divisional Court in the case of *Redmond-Bate v DPP* (1999) 163 JP 789, [1999] Crim LR 998, *The Times* 28 July 1998 (QBD) (see page 33).

The current approach of English law reflects the principles developed by the European Court of Human Rights in the case of *Steel and Others v UK* (1998) 28 EHRR 603, 5 BHRC 339, [1998] HRCD 872, [1998] Crim LR 893 (ECHR), a complex case involving several applicants and several distinct events.

Applicant no 1 had been arrested for a breach of the peace when she walked in front of a grouse-shooter. She was detained for a total of 44 hours both at the shoot and in the police station, "to prevent any further breach of the peace". The applicant was proceeded against by way of complaint for a binding-over order under s 115 of the Magistrates' Court Act 1980, and was also charged with an offence contrary to s 5 Public Order Act 1986. She was convicted, and the magistrates' court held that the complaint under s 115 was also made out. The applicant's appeal failed and the Crown Court upheld the fine and ordered the applicant to agree to be bound over for twelve months in the sum of £100. The applicant refused to be bound over and was committed to prison for 28 days.

Applicant no 2 had been obstructing work on a motorway and was arrested for conduct likely to provoke a disturbance of the peace. She was detained for seventeen hours on the basis that, if released earlier, she would cause a breach of the peace. A complaint under s 115 was upheld, and the applicant was ordered to agree to be bound over to keep the peace in the sum of £100. She refused and was committed to prison for seven days.

Applicants 3, 4 and 5 were protesting outside an arms conference; they were holding banners and handing out leaflets. They were arrested for conduct which was or was likely to provoke a disturbance of the peace. The applicants were detained at court for seven hours before the case was adjourned for lack of time. The prosecution ultimately called no evidence and the case was dismissed.

The European Court of Human Rights concluded that the behaviour of the first and second defendants might provoke others to violence and accordingly their arrests had been lawful. The behaviour of the third, fourth and fifth applicants was entirely peaceful and non-provocative. According to the Court:

"it would not appear that there was anything in their behaviour which could have justified the police in fearing that a breach of the peace was likely to be caused. The arrest and subsequent detention of these applicants did not comply with English law and could not be described as 'lawful' for the purposes of Article 5(1)."

The applicants also claimed that their arrests and subsequent detention had been in breach of art 10 as interferences with rights of expression. The Court held that the behaviour of the applicants fell within art 10 as expressions of opinion even though, in the cases of the first and second applicants, factually amounting to obstruction of others. In respect of the third, fourth and fifth applicants (but not the first and second) the illegality of the arrests meant that the measures taken against those applicants could not be said to be "prescribed by law" and, even though the measures were in pursuance of a legitimate object under art 10 (the prevention of disorder), there had been breaches of art 10. For the same reason the action taken breached art 10 since the illegality as against the first, second and third applicants meant that the measures could not be said to be "necessary in a democratic society".

Dealing with Fights

In *McBean v Parker* [1983] Crim LR 399 (DC), a police officer intervened to stop a struggle between the appellant and the officer's colleague who was attempting to carry out an unlawful search of the appellant. The police officer was present throughout the stop and attempted search and could not be said to have been acting in the execution of his duty to prevent a breach of the peace, since he knew that the initial detention had been unlawful. Dunn LJ said that:

". . . in a situation of this kind where two officers are involved and all that was needed was for the appellant to be told the reason for the search to make what was done lawful, it follows that if, thereafter, the person who is apprehended uses reasonable force to repel a search by one officer he is doing nothing unlawful. The other officer . . . cannot be said to be acting in the execution of his duty if he then attempts to restrain him . . . I will limit my decision to those facts."

But if a police officer comes across a struggle between an individual and another police officer, he can intervene, since there is a breach of the peace. In *Joyce v Hertfordshire Constabulary* (1984) 80 Cr App R 298 (DC), at a football match, the police officer responsible for the initial detention of the defendant, with whom he then had a struggle, could not be identified. Another constable saw the struggle as part of a general and violent disturbance involving a group of fans, and intervened to seize the defendant, who then resisted. The defendant was charged with conduct contrary to s 5 of the 1936 Act. The defence suggested that since the initial struggle was a result of an unlawful detention, the defendant had simply been using reasonable force to escape and the second officer should not have intervened.

The Divisional Court saw no merit in this view and made two points: first, the court had been entitled to assume that the first detention was lawful; and secondly, even if it had been unlawful, there was still a breach of the peace and the officer to whose attention it came was obliged to intervene: "What was going on was in fact a struggle and a breach of the peace and the rights and wrongs do not matter". In intervening, the officer was acting in the execution of his duty and further struggles by the individual amounted to threatening behaviour and to offences contrary to s 51 of the Police Act 1964.

An individual who is in fact freeing himself from an unlawful detention may well find himself in difficulties vis-à-vis all but that constable and any other who may be tainted with the illegality of his colleague. A constable who comes across a general mêlée, in which it is possible that some of the parties are acting in self-defence, need not assess who is responsible and may proceed against all concerned since there is a breach of the peace; see *Timothy v Simpson* (1835) 1 Cr M & R 757, (1835) 3 Nev & MMC 127, (1835) 5 Tyr 244:

"If no-one could be restrained of his liberty in cases of mutual conflict, except the party who did the first wrong, and the bystanders acted at their peril in this respect, there would be very little chance of the public peace being preserved by the interference of private individuals . . . [or] of peace officers. . ."

Other Situations

The cases of *Percy v DPP* [1955] 1 WLR 1382, [1995] 3 All ER 124, [1995] Crim LR 714 (DC), *R v Morpeth Ward Justices ex p Ward* (1992) 95 Cr App R 215, [1992] Crim LR 497, (1992) 142 NLJ 312 (DC), and *Nicol and Selvanayagam v DPP* [1966] JP 155, concern the application of the preventive powers in circumstances where the police reasonably fear a breach of the peace as a consequence of the lawful acts of a person who is then arrested. Taken together, these cases require that, to justify interference in a case of provocation to violence, there must have been unreasonable behaviour on the part of the defendant, including interference with another's rights, the natural consequence of which is that the other party was provoked to violence.

The same principles apply to a decision on a summons under s 115, Magistrates' Courts Act 1980.

In *Nicol and Selvanayagam v DPP* protestors disrupted a fishing match in a non-violent way and a summons was issued under s 115. The case makes it clear that it need not be shown that the disruption amounted to a criminal offence (see also *R v Morpeth Ward Justices ex p Ward*), but it must be shown that a breach of the peace was the natural consequence of the defendant's behaviour. In addition, the court held that a necessary prerequisite to such a finding is that it must be shown that the defendant was acting unreasonably and in breach of the rights of others. Putting it another and negative way, the court suggested that a complaint under s 115 could not be made out unless the violence provoked would be not only unlawful but also unreasonable.

Another example is *R v Inner London Crown Court ex p Benjamin* (1987) 85 Cr App R 267, [1987] Crim LR 417 (DC), where the decision to imprison the respondent for refusing to be bound over was upheld despite the absence of any threat of violence on his part. The risk to the peace came from those who objected to his persistent sounding of a conch shell in a crowded market. In *Percy v DPP* (above), there was no reasonable likelihood that trained military personnel would be provoked to unlawful violence by trespassers. By contrast, in *R v Morpeth Ward JJ, ex p Ward*, the disruption of a pheasant shoot was likely to have that result. The general tenor of these decisions has been upheld as correct by the European Court of Human Rights in *Steel v UK* (above).

The issue again fell for consideration in *Foulkes v Chief Constable of the Merseyside Police* [1998] 3 All ER 705, [1998] 2 FLR 789, [1999] FCR 98, an action for false imprisonment. The Court of Appeal held unlawful the arrest of a husband seeking to gain re-entry to the matrimonial home from which he had been excluded by his wife that morning following a dispute with two adult children. At first instance, the Recorder had considered that the arresting constable had reasonable grounds for believing that the husband might cause harm or damage to property, or might provoke it, and that there was an "imminent chance of a breach of the peace."

". . . although I am prepared to accept that a constable may exceptionally have power to arrest a person whose behaviour is lawful but provocative, it is a power which ought to be exercised by him only in the clearest of circumstances and when he is satisfied on reasonable grounds that a breach of the peace is imminent. . ."

In *Redmond-Bate v DPP* (1999) 163 JP 789, [1999] Crim LR 998, *The Times* 28 July 1998 (QBD), Christian fundamentalist preachers on cathedral steps attracted a crowd, some of whom were showing hostility. The preachers refused to leave and were arrested and charged with offences contrary to s 89 Police Act 1996. While acknowledging the difficult task of the police, the court held that there was nothing provocative about the conduct of the defendants and that the threat to the peace came from the hecklers. Sedley LJ said that:

"A police officer has no right to call upon a citizen to desist from lawful conduct. It is only if otherwise lawful conduct gives rise to a reasonable apprehension that it will, by interfering with the rights or liberties of others, provoke violence which, though unlawful would not be entirely unreasonable that a constable is empowered to take steps to prevent it."

In *Bibby v Chief Constable of Essex, The Times*, 24 April 2000 (CA), a civil case, a bailiff sought to execute a walking possession agreement with a debtor. There was a heated confrontation in the defendant's shop between the debtor and the bailiff, and the police officer asked the bailiff to leave. When he refused, he was arrested and handcuffed by the police officer. Applying principles set out in *Redmond-Bate v DPP, Foulkes v Chief Constable of the Merseyside Police*, and *Nicol and Selvanayagam v DPP,* Schiemann LJ thought it a correct statement of the law that:

(1) there must be the clearest of circumstances and a sufficiently real and present threat to the peace to justify the extreme step of depriving of his liberty a citizen who is not at the time acting unlawfully;
(2) the threat must be coming from the person who is to be arrested;
(3) the conduct must clearly interfere with the rights of others;
(4) the natural consequence of the conduct must be violence from a third party;
(5) the violence in (4) must be wholly unreasonable;
(6) the conduct of the person arrested must be unreasonable.

It remains possible that there may be circumstances in which the behaviour of the defendant, while falling short of actual violence, is so outrageous as to be likely to provoke a "not wholly unreasonable violent reaction from others". Cases such as *Wise v Dunning* and *Humphries v Connor*, although more likely to be dealt with now as substantive offences under the Public Order Act 1986, would appear to fall within the range of cases where the behaviour persisted in would be regarded as unreasonable and provocative. Even so, this sits uncomfortably with the approach set out in *Bibby v Chief Constable of Essex*. The better view is that *in extremis* the police are entitled to terminate a lawful activity where this is the only way to prevent a breach of the peace threatened, however unreasonably, by others; see the *dictum* of Lord Slynn in *R v Chief Constable of Sussex ex p International Traders' Ferry* [1999] 2 AC 418, [1999] 1 All ER 129 concerning the imposition of a restriction on lorries carrying livestock from entering a port town.

2.9 Alternative Charges

The statutory formulae for the offences contrary to ss 4, 4A and 5 of the 1986 Act, among others, and the grant of wide executive statutory powers to control processions and assemblies, reflect a line drawn by Parliament. This is implicit acceptance that criminal sanctions may be imposed on speech or activity in response to a hostile or potentially hostile audience where the behaviour falls within the scope of the relevant legislation. The statutory limits imposed in respect of these offences have not been tested against the criteria in the European Convention of Human Rights, but the additional requirement that there should be a threat or provocation to violence or harassment, alarm etc does serve to emphasise the general principle inherent in cases such as *Steel v UK*.

2.10 Preventive Action

The general proposition is that the citizen may take reasonable steps to deal with or prevent actual or reasonably apprehended imminent breaches of the peace. See *Albert v Lavin* [1982] AC 546, [1981] 3 WLR 955, [1981] 3 All ER 878 (HL), where Lord Diplock said that:

"... every citizen in whose presence a breach of the peace is being, or reasonably appears to be about to be, committed has the right to take reasonable steps to make the person who is breaking or threatening to break the peace refrain from doing so; and those reasonable steps in appropriate cases will include detaining him against his will. At common law this is not only the right of every citizen, it is also his duty, although, except in the case of a citizen who is a constable, it is a duty of imperfect obligation."

Accordingly, police officers have been held to be entitled to act in a wide variety of ways which would ordinarily involve serious interference with the liberty of the individual. The same powers may apply where a breach of the peace is likely to be renewed (see *Price v Seeley* (1843) 10 Cl & Fin 28, [1843] 8 ER 651; *Baynes v Brewster* (1841) 2 QB 375, (1841) 5 JP 799; *Timothy v Simpson* (1835) 1 Cr M & R 757, (1835) 3 Nev & MMC 127, (1835) 5 Tyr 244); or where there is fresh pursuit (see *R v Marsden* (1868) LR 1 CCR 131, 32 JP 436).

The statements in certain of the earlier cases, that the preventive action should be a matter of last resort or necessity, appear not to have been relied upon in more recent authorities, where the reasonableness of the action appears to be the major consideration in determining its lawfulness.

Two factors must be borne in mind. First, the conditions for the exercise of the powers, and in particular the objective assessment of the risk to the peace (see page 25), must be met. Secondly, as *McLeod, Steel, Redmond-Bate* and *Bibby* demonstrate, the values inherent in the European Convention on Human Rights must be borne clearly in mind and applied (see page 29). The high-profile policing of events such as state visits by foreign Heads of

State have provoked controversy in respect of perceived interferences with the proper expression of political opposition. Where the legality of the police action is an issue, then the effective testing of that action against the requirements of the European Convention is a necessary step in the proper exercise of the judicial function.

The following are general categories of commonly encountered preventive powers.

Arrest

The leading authority is *R v Howell* [1982] QB 416, [1981] 3 All ER 383, where Watkins J drew together many of the older authorities and remarked:

". . . there is a power of arrest for breach of the peace where (1) a breach of the peace is committed in the presence of the person making the arrest, or (2) the arrestor reasonably believes that such a breach will be committed in the immediate future by the person arrested although he has not yet committed any breach, or (3) where a breach has been committed and it is reasonably believed that a renewal of it has been threatened."

There is also a power to arrest in fresh pursuit of someone who has committed a breach of the peace (see *R v Light* (1857) 27 LJMC 1; *R v Walker* (1854) Dears CC 358, 23 LJMC 123; and *R v Marsden* (1868) LR 1 CCR 131, 32 JP 436).

Arrest may be with a view to taking a person before a magistrate to be bound over, or as a preliminary to a charge for a substantive offence, eg assault. A statement that the arrest is for a breach of the peace will be sufficient in either instance and will satisfy the requirements of s 28 of the Police and Criminal Evidence Act 1984 (see *R v Howell*).

Once a breach of the peace has ended and there is no danger of recurrence, the power of arrest lapses. Arrest in such an instance is not permissible under s 25(1) of the Police and Criminal Evidence Act 1984 since breach of the peace is not of itself an offence, although the facts giving rise to the breach of the peace may reveal another offence for which arrest may be permissible under s 25 of the Police and Criminal Evidence Act 1984, or under another provision.

Detention

It is permissible to restrain someone and detain him for as long as reasonable to prevent the breach of the peace or its recurrence (see *Albert v Lavin* [1982] AC 546, [1981] 3 WLR 955, [1981] 3 All ER 878). It seems that the person detained need not be the person seeking to use violence (*Albert v Lavin*; *Humphries v Connor* (1864) 17 ICLR 1) so long as the criteria set out at page 27 are satisfied.

Entry

The general common law powers in connection with entry to premises were abolished by s 17(5) of the Police and Criminal Evidence Act 1984, but the common law powers of entry without warrant to deal with or prevent breaches of the peace were expressly preserved by s 17(6). It is clear that there is power to enter premises to deal with breaches of the peace actually occurring: see *Robson v Hallett* [1967] 2 QB 939, [1967] 3 WLR 28, [1967] 2 All ER 407 (DC). Where a constable has unlawfully entered or remained on premises and, while trespassing, apprehends an actual or threatened breach of the peace on the premises, the constable need not leave the premises and re-enter lawfully; the constable may rely on the apprehension of a breach of the peace to justify his presence on the property (see *Robson v Hallett; Lamb v DPP* (1990) 154 JPN 172, (1990) 154 JP 381 (DC)).

Where a breach of the peace is not actually occurring but is apprehended as likely to occur, there is power to enter and remain on premises of any description, whether private or public (see *McLeod v Commissioner of Police of the Metropolis* [1994] 4 All ER 553 (CA); *Thomas v Sawkins* [1935] 2 KB 249, [1935] All ER Rep 655; *McGowan v Chief Constable of Hull* (1967) 117 NLJ 1138, [1967] Crim LR 34 (DC)). Although the point was not specifically in issue in *McLeod v Commissioner of Police of the Metropolis*, it seems now that the power to enter and remain on premises extends to public meetings on private premises and to private meetings on private premises. The narrowest realistic view of the ambiguous and unsatisfactory decision in *Thomas v Sawkins* is that the power to enter private premises in anticipation of a breach of the peace was restricted to public meetings. The widest view of *Thomas v Sawkins* is that it extended the anticipatory power of entry to premises of all descriptions. In *McLeod v Metropolitan Police Commissioner*, Neill LJ, delivering the judgment of the Court of Appeal, held that the power of entry in anticipation of a breach of the peace should not be dependent on the nature of the premises or on the nature of any invitation offered to the public:

" . . . I am satisfied that Parliament in s 17(6) has now recognised that there is a power to enter premises to prevent a breach of the peace as a form of preventive justice. I can see no satisfactory basis for restricting that power to particular classes of premises such as those where public meetings are held. If the police reasonably believe that a breach of the peace is likely to take place on private premises, they have power to enter those premises to prevent it. The apprehension must, of course, be genuine and it must relate to the near future . . . It may be necessary in some future case to consider how far in advance of a possible breach of the peace the right to enter arises. It will depend on the facts of the case, and on the nature and scale of the apprehended breach."

In the case of breaches of the peace actually occurring, forced entry is permitted, although it is not clear that force may be used to compel entry in the case of the anticipatory preventive power. If a constable is invited on to premises by someone with appropriate authority (see *McGowan v Chief*

Constable of Hull; *R v Thornley* (1981) 72 Cr App R 302, [1981] Crim LR 637 (CA)), then the constable may remain despite the revocation of that permission, provided that there is reasonable anticipation of an imminent breach of the peace or an actual breach of the peace. In such a case the constable may not be ejected forcibly (*Thomas v Sawkins*).

Dispersal of a Meeting
The following comments must be read subject to the general observations in relation to *Redmond-Bate v DPP* (1999) 163 JP 789, [1999] Crim LR 998, *The Times* 28 July 1998 (QBD) (see page 33), and the exercise of the statutory preventive powers to control public assemblies falling within the scope of the 1986 Act, see Chapter 5. In *Duncan v Jones* [1936] 1 KB 218, [1935] All ER Rep 710, (1935) 52 TLR 26, the holding of a meeting on the highway (although not alleged to have been an obstruction of the highway) was reasonably apprehended as likely to lead to breaches of the peace. Refusal to comply with the request of the police officer to disperse amounted to a wilful obstruction of that constable (see also *O'Kelly v Harvey* (1883) 15 Cox CC 435). *Duncan v Jones* is reconcilable with the principle in *Redmond-Bate v DPP* on the basis that the threat to the peace came from the defendant. This reconciliation should not deflect from the criticism of that case that it represents a less than strict assessment of the risk to the peace or the general direction of the threat.

Preventive powers are frequently used in the policing of pickets, in both the industrial and the non-industrial contexts. The Code of Practice on Picketing, issued under the Employment Act 1980, observes:
> "26. . . . The law gives the police discretion to take whatever measures may reasonably be considered necessary to ensure that picketing remains peaceful and orderly. . .
> 28. It is for the police to decide, taking into account all the circumstances, whether the number of pickets at any particular place is likely to lead to a breach of the peace. If a picket does not leave the picket line when asked to do so by the police, he is liable to be arrested for obstruction either of the highway or of a police officer in the execution of his duty if the obstruction is such as to cause, or be likely to cause, a breach of the peace."

For examples of cases demonstrating the application of the common law principles underlying the Code of Practice, see also *Piddington v Bates* [1961] 1 WLR 162, [1960] 3 All ER 660 (DC) (where the power was used to limit the number of pickets); *Kavanagh v Hiscock* [1974] QB 600, [1974] 2 WLR 421, [1974] 2 All ER 177 (DC) (preventing pickets from approaching vehicles); and *Tynan v Balmer* [1967] 1 QB 91, [1966] 2 WLR 1181, [1966] 2 All ER 133 (DC), a case on public nuisance; see also *Smith v Reynolds* [1986] Crim LR 559 (DC) and *Riding v Long* (19 June 1986, unreported). The principle underpinning such cases is also applicable to non-industrial pickets such as vigils.

Control of the Highway

Constables also have common law powers to control the highway. For example, during the miners' strike of 1984, the anticipatory preventive powers of
the police were held to extend to preventing pickets from journeying to certain coal mines. At what precise stage such actions are unjustifiable is a matter of fact. There may be some distinction between such directions being
given 105 miles from a site, and those given five miles from a site. In *Moss v
McLachlan* (1985) 149 JP 167, [1985] IRLR 76, (1985) 149 JPN 149 (DC),
a road check was one and a half miles from two collieries and four miles
from two other collieries. The road check was lawful because of the reasonable apprehension of a breach of the peace. The police had reason to believe
that striking miners stopped at road checks were on their way to picket *en
masse* at one or more of the collieries and that there would be a breach of the
peace should they be allowed to continue. The miners refused to obey a direction to turn back and were arrested for obstructing the police in the execution of their duty. The appellants were held to have been properly convicted
since the direction had been properly given by the police acting in the execution of their duty.

The decision of the House of Lords in *R v Chief Constable of Sussex ex
p International Traders Ferry* (1999) lends some support for the principle
under discussion. The Chief Constable in that case had taken steps to control
protests involving very large numbers of protesters and a considerable risk
of a serious breakdown in public order. In the light of the substantial drain
on resources and diversion of officers from other duties, these steps included
effectively permitting exporters to use harbour facilities on only two days
per week and restricting access to the harbour by exporters' vehicles. Lorries
seeking to gain access to the site were turned away because of the fear that
there would be breaches of the peace. Although the matter was peripheral to
their Lordships' decision (which concerned judicial review of police discretion and an application of Community law), Lord Slynn ventured to say that:

"The police, in the performance of their duty, here sought to protect people exercising a lawful trade from the acts of violent demonstrators acting unlawfully and threatening a breach of the peace. When, with their
finite resources of officers and finance, the police could do this, they did
so. Only when their resources were insufficient did they not provide the
protection and, in order to prevent a breach of the peace, on rare occasions, they told lorry drivers to turn back. I do not accept that *Beatty's*
case lays down that the police can never restrain a lawful activity if that
is the only way to prevent violence and a breach of the peace . . . It
seems to me that in the way the police behaved here, they were acting
within their discretion and taking the only steps they could, steps which
were necessary to protect lorry drivers from the violence of some of the

demonstrators."

In that case there were no instances of direct challenge to the legality of the police instructions to lorry drivers and the matter remains largely speculative, a point made by Lord Hoffmann who thought the matter might have raised interesting questions.

Seizure of Items

When appropriate, the discretion of constables may extend to the removal of articles designed or likely to lead to breaches of peace. In *Humphries v Connor* (1864) 17 ICLR 1, the seizure of an orange lily, symbolic of a particular political persuasion and deeply provocative to a crowd of a different political hue, was held to be justified because of the reasonable anticipation of a breach of the peace by the crowd (whether this case would be decided in the same way following the reasoning in *Redmond-Bate v DPP* (see page 33) is open to question). Placards, banners, flags, emblems and similar objects might be seized on this basis, or directions as to their use may be given; see, for example, *Minto v Police* [1987] 1 NZLR 374, which concerned the use of a loud hailer. Breach of these directions would amount to wilful obstruction of a constable in the execution of his duty, contrary to s 89 of the Police Act 1996. Whether or not it is lawful to take these steps must be judged in the light of the comments at page 27.

Of increasing significance is the use of masks and similar items during protests. In so far as the wearing of masks represents a legitimate form of protest there can be no doubt that it is legal to do so. But the use of masks to hide the identity of the wearer during occasions of violent criminal activity has increased, and specific powers have been invoked to deal with this; s 60 CJPOA 1994, as amended by s 25 Crime and Disorder Act 1998, grants a police officer in uniform the power to require the removal of any item which he reasonably believes is being worn wholly or mainly for the purposes of concealing the wearer's identity. Seizure is permissible under certain circumstances. This power is narrowly constrained by the requirement that there should be in force an authorisation under the CJPOA 1994, s 60. Where a breach of the peace is reasonably apprehended then the common law power would be available; it is doubtful whether the statutory preventive powers would extend as far as this.

Ejection of Trespassers

The ejection of trespassers is something of a grey area; see page 16 and the cases mentioned there. The better view is that the police are acting in the execution of their duty when engaged generally in supervising the ejection of trespassers. There is no doubt that a police officer is acting in the execution of his duty where there is an actual or threatened breach of the peace, provided that acting to eject a trespasser would be a reasonable step to take; see *Porter v Commissioner of Police of the Metropolis,* 20 October 1999, unreported (CA), although in that case the appellant had been arrested for a breach of the peace and the specific point did not arise. In addition, there may be specific powers in relation to particular types of premises, such as those within s 547 Education Act 1996 (as amended) or the Local Government (Miscellaneous Provisions) Act 1982 (as amended) (nuisance or disturbance on educational premises).

It is not always easy for the police to recognise when a citizen is a trespasser. Usually, the issue can be simplified by reference to the commonly cited cases on express or implied licence. On occasions it may be suggested that an alleged trespasser is lawfully on premises by virtue of some public or quasi-public right. For instance, in *Porter* the appellant was in an electricity showroom disputing a particular matter. It was suggested that she was not a trespasser because the showroom was open to customers to facilitate the performance by the electricity board of its statutory functions, and that the implied licence extended to customers could not be withdrawn at will. The court rejected the suggestion that there was an irrevocable licence in public or quasi-public spaces. See also *CN Properties v Rawlins* [1995] 2 EGLR, which effectively rebuts the assertion that there is in English law (the position in America is radically different) an irrevocable right for the public to use "quasi-public spaces" such as shopping malls. Presence in such areas is a matter of leave and licence. But there may be areas of some doubt, eg as to whether a particular footpath is dedicated to public use as, say, a walkway within the Highways Act 1980, see *CN Properties v Rawlins*.

On occasions, there may be raised by way of defence to a prosecution under s 89 a public law defence, eg that a particular bye-law is *ultra vires*; see *R v Reading Crown Court ex p Hutchinson* [1988] QB 384, [1987] 3 WLR 1062, [1988] 1 All ER 333 (DC); and *Boddington v British Transport Police* [1999] 2 AC 143, [1998] 2 WLR 639, [1998] 2 All ER 203 (HL). A court should be prepared to enquire into this matter, applying the normal principles of judicial review. On the other hand, it has been established that in the case of a police officer taking action under a bye-law subsequently found to be *ultra vires* the constable was nonetheless within the law: *Percy v DPP* [1955] 1 WLR 1382, [1995] 3 All ER 124, [1995] Crim LR 714 (DC).

3   Binding Over

The powers of justices to bind over are of ancient origin and apparently predate the Justices of the Peace Act 1361. For the history, see generally *Lansbury v Riley* [1914] 3 KB 229, [1911-13] All ER Rep 1059, (1911) 77 JP 440 (KBD), and Law Commission Working Paper No 103. The powers have been the subject of extensive review by the Law Commission (see page 48) and considerable adverse criticism, which throws their future into some doubt. Such criticism is not novel and there have been several attempts to repeal the Justices of the Peace Act 1361, albeit without government support.

The extensive powers to bind over to keep the peace or be of good behaviour are derived from the Justices of the Peace Act 1361 or common law and the Magistrates' Courts Act 1980, and have been unaffected by recent legislative changes to the substantive law. Like the powers of the police in connection with breaches of the peace, these powers are preventive in nature (*Veater v Glennon* [1981] 1 WLR 567, [1981] 2 All ER 304, (1981) 72 Cr App R 331 (DC)). The common law has long been concerned with preventive justice which " . . . consists in restraining a man from committing a crime he may commit but has not yet committed, or of doing some act injurious to members of the community which he may do but has not yet done . . ." (*R v Halliday* (1889) 61 LT 701).

As Blackstone said:

> "This preventive justice consists in obliging those persons, whom there is probable ground to suspect of future misbehaviour, to stipulate with and to give full assurance to the public, that such offence as is apprehended shall not happen; by finding pledges or securities for keeping the peace, or for their good behaviour."

It has been said that the justices' jurisdiction to bind over "rests on the maxim or principle *salus populi suprema lex*, in pursuance of which it sometimes happens that individual liberty may be sacrificed or abridged in the public good" (*Lansbury v Riley*).

3.1 Powers in General

Historically, justices of the peace were able to require any person before the court to enter into a recognisance, with or without sureties, to keep the peace or be of good behaviour, or both, for a specified period. Research by the Law Commission, conducted before the introduction of the Crown Prosecution Service and the 1986 Public Order Act, suggested that 79 per cent of binding over orders were made both to keep the peace and be of good behaviour; 12 per cent to keep the peace; and 9 per cent to be of good behaviour. Breach of the peace bears the same meaning as in connection with the common law preventive powers of the police. Good behaviour encompasses keeping the peace, and is the more extensive of the two; see *Hughes v Holley* (1988) 86 Cr App R 130, [1987] Crim LR 253, (1987) 151 JP 233 (QBD), where failure to be of good behaviour extended to behaviour *contra bonos mores*, contrary to a good way of life or "offensive and contrary to standards of generally accepted decent behaviour". The power to bind a person over to be of good behaviour expressed in general terms has been found to be contrary to the European Convention of Human Rights and the terms must now be more particularised; see page 47.

Breach of a recognisance may result in forfeiture of the whole or part of the sum, but is not punishable by imprisonment (*R v Finch* (1962) 106 SJ 961, (1962) 47 Cr App R 58 (CCA)). A binding over order is neither a conviction nor a punishment.

The powers to bind over to come up for judgment, and to bind over a parent or guardian to enter into a recognisance to take proper care of a child or young person, lie outside the scope of this book.

3.2 The Statutory Complaints Procedure

The statutory complaints procedure originated in the old commissions of the peace and was codified in s 25 of the Summary Jurisdiction Act 1879. It was restated in s 91 of the Magistrates' Courts Act 1952 and currently is provided for under s 115 of the Magistrates' Courts Act 1980:

"The power of the magistrates' court on the complaint of any person to enter into a recognisance, with or without sureties, to keep the peace or be of good behaviour towards the complainant shall be exercised by order on complaint."

Although this procedure has as its objective the binding over of the respondent, the justices' other powers to bind over may be employed in the course of a hearing by way of complaint. Despite the wording of s 115(1), the order may be either to keep the peace generally or to be of good behaviour towards the actual complainant.

The power to bind over on complaint lies with a magistrates' court, not individual justices; see ss 115, 121 and 148 of the Magistrates' Court Act 1980. Any person may request the issue of a summons under s 51 of the Magistrates' Courts Act 1980 to bring the respondent before the magistrates' court to seek an order binding over the respondent to keep the peace or be of good behaviour towards the complainant. A complaint may be oral. There is power in a magistrates' court, on dismissing a complaint, to order costs against a complainant: s 64 Magistrates' Courts Act 1980; see *R v Coventry Magistrates' Court ex p Crown Prosecution Service* (1996) 160 JP 741, applied in *DPP v Speede and Others* [1998] 2 Cr App R 108 (QBD), where the charge sheet expressing the requirement that the defendant should show cause why she should not be bound over, coupled with oral evidence of the main police witness, amounted to an oral complaint. Accordingly, costs could not have been awarded against the CPS, only against the complainant police officer.

The order sought under the statutory complaints procedure may not be made until the conclusion of the proceedings and after the court has heard sworn evidence (see *R v Aubrey-Fletcher ex p Thompson* [1969] 1 WLR 872, [1969] 2 All ER 846, 53 Crim App R 380 (DC)). The court must be satisfied that the allegations have been proved beyond reasonable doubt.

Section 115(3) empowers magistrates to commit to prison anyone they order to enter into a recognisance but who refuses to do so.

Where the defendant is not before a magistrates' court then, according to *DPP v Speede and Others,* the court may adopt one of two courses: either it may hear the case but may not then issue a warrant for the arrest of the defendant; or it may substantiate the case by hearing the complainant and then issue a warrant for the arrest of the defendant. In the former case the court may chose to adjourn, give notice of the adjourned hearing, and then issue a warrant should the defendant fail to attend.

3.3 Other Procedures

A person may be arrested in respect of a breach of the peace and brought before a court (for the powers of arrest, see page 35). An order may be made only upon conclusion of the case, but is not dependent upon a finding that a breach of the peace had actually occurred (*R v Morpeth Ward Justices ex p Ward* (1992) 95 Cr App R 215, [1992] Crim LR 497, (1992) 142 NLJ 312 (DC)).

The powers of justices survived intact the statutory changes in the Summary Jurisdiction Act 1879, and similar powers are enjoyed by the Crown Court and judges of the Court of Appeal. Under s 1(7) of the Justices of the Peace Act 1968:

"It is hereby declared that any court of record having a criminal jurisdiction has, as ancillary to that jurisdiction, the power to bind over to be of good behaviour, a person who or whose case is before the court, by requiring him to enter into his own recognisances or to find sureties or both, and committing him to prison if he does not comply."

3.4 Failure to Enter into a Recognisance

No penalty or conditions may be attached to the order other than the requirement to enter into a recognisance (see *Goodlad v Chief Constable of South Yorkshire* [1978] Crim LR 51; *Lister v Morgan* [1978] Crim LR 292; *R v Randall* [1987] Crim LR 254, (1986) 8 Cr App R(S) 433; *R v Ayu* [1958] 1 WLR 1264, [1958] 3 All ER 636, 43 Crim App R 31 (CCA)). The order may name the person protected by the order (*Wilson v Skeock* (1949) 65 TLR 418, (1949) 113 JP 293).

In the event of failure to comply with the order to enter into a recognisance, the respondent may be committed to custody for up to six months (s 115(3)), and the same may follow under the Act of 1361 (*Veater v Glennon* [1981] 1 WLR 567, [1981] 2 All ER 304, (1981) 72 Cr App R 331 (DC)). A refusal to enter into a recognisance is not itself contempt of court and cannot be dealt with under s 12(1) of the Contempt of Court Act 1981, but it may (particularly if repeated), be a kindred offence for the purposes of s 9(1)(c) of the Criminal Justice Act 1982. This may have important consequences, eg as regards the imposition of imprisonment on a person aged between seventeen and twenty-one: *Howley v Oxford* (1985) 81 Cr App R 246, [1985] Crim LR 724, (1985) 149 JP 363 and *Chief Constable of Surrey v Ridley* [1985] Crim LR 725 (DC).

3.5 The Subject of the Order

Any of the following participants in proceedings may be bound over without proof of any offence and at any stage of the proceedings, including upon acquittal or conviction, upon withdrawal of the prosecution case or a decision to offer no evidence, or upon adjournment:

- the complainant;
- the prosecutor or a witness (*R v Hendon Justices ex p Gorchein* [1973] 1 WLR 1502, [1974] 1 All ER 168, [1973] Crim LR 754 (DC); *R v Wilkins* [1973] 1 WLR 1502, [1974] 1 All ER 168; *Sheldon v Bromfield Justices* [1964] 2 QB 573, [1964] 2 WLR 1066, [1964] 2 All ER 131 (DC); *R v Sidhu* [1976] Crim LR 379 (CA)) – but not a witness not called upon to give evidence (*R v Swindon Crown Court ex p Pawittar Singh* [1984] 1 WLR 449, [1984] 1 All ER 941, (1984) 79 Cr App R 137 (DC); *R v Lincoln Crown Court ex p Jones* [1990] COD 15, *The Times* 16 June 1989 (DC); *R v Kingston upon Thames Crown Court ex p Guarino* [1986] Crim LR 325 (DC));
- the respondent;
- the defendant, whether convicted or acquitted (*Wilson v Skeock* (1949) 65 TLR 418, (1949) 113 JP 293; *R v Inner London Crown Court ex p Benjamin* (1987) 85 Cr App R 267, [1987] Crim LR 417 (DC); *R v Woking Justices ex p Gossage* [1973] 1 QB 448, [1973] 2 WLR 529, [1973] 2 All ER 621 (DC); *R v South West London Magistrates' Court ex p Brown* (1974) 4 Fam Law 158, [1974] Crim LR 313 (DC); *R v Marylebone Magistrate ex p Okunnu* (1988) 87 Cr App R 295, *The Times* 4 November 1987 (DC)).

Where the binding over is imposed before conviction, there is no power to impose any other penalty, such as a fine.

3.6 Nature of the Proceedings: Criminal or Civil

When acting pursuant to the statutory complaint procedure, justices of the peace exercise what is technically their civil jurisdiction, but is effectively a quasi-criminal jurisdiction (see *Everett v Ribbands* [1952] 2 QB 198, [1952] 1 All ER 823, [1952] 1 TLR 933 and *R v Bolton Justices ex p Graeme* (1986) 150 JP 129, (1986) 150 JPN 271 (CA)). It is unclear whether the criminal or civil standard of proof is to be employed; nor need the facts be proved by admissible evidence. In *Percy v DPP* [1955] 1 WLR 1382, [1995] 3 All ER 124, [1995] Crim LR 714, the Queen's Bench Division favoured the criminal standard in the light of *R v Bolton Justices ex p Graeme* and the consequences and circumstances of the proceedings, applying *Re Bramblevale Ltd* [1970] Ch 128, [1969] 3 WLR 699, [1969] 3 All ER 1062 (CA), where it was held that, to establish a civil contempt, proof beyond reasonable doubt was required.

Proceedings for forfeiture of a recognisance are civil and require the civil standard of proof (*R v Southampton Justices ex p Green* [1976] QB 11, [1976] 3 WLR 277, [1975] 2 All ER 1073 (CA) and *R v Marlow Justices ex p O'Sullivan* [1984] QB 381, [1984] 2 WLR 107, [1983] 3 All ER 578 (DC)), although that point was doubted, *obiter*, in *Percy v DPP*.

3.7   Evidence

The power to bind over requires evidence that there might be a future breach of the peace by the person concerned (*R v Aubrey-Fletcher ex p Thompson* [1969] 1 WLR 872, [1969] 2 All ER 846, 53 Crim App R 380 (DC)), and this is so even where the person concerned consents (*R v Marylebone Metropolitan Stipendiary Magistrate ex p Okunnu* (1988) 87 Cr App R 295, *The Times* 4 November 1987 (DC)). The magistrates must direct themselves properly as to the meaning of breach of the peace and the likelihood of its occurrence, and must be satisfied that there is a real risk of the conduct continuing and that a breach of the peace may occur. It is rare that a defendant acquitted on the merits should be bound over, and then only where the court is satisfied beyond reasonable doubt that that person poses a potential threat to others: *R v Middlesex Crown Court ex p Khan* (1997) 161 JP 240, [1997] COD 186, (1997) 161 JPN 212 (QBD). In that case the court added conjunctively that the person should be a "man of violence", but it is suggested that this is not required as a matter of law.

The evidence need not be sworn evidence but has "to be such as, when considered carefully and not capriciously, . . . justified a conclusion that there was a risk of a breach of the peace unless action was taken to prevent it" (*R v South West London Magistrates' Court ex p Brown* (1974) 4 Fam Law 158, [1974] Crim LR 313 (DC)). In the absence of such evidence, the power to bind over does not arise, although it seems that the violence which is anticipated may stem from the activities of others, provoked or encouraged by the acts of the person bound over (see *Wise v Dunning* [1902] 1 KB 167, [1900–3] All ER Rep 727, (1902) 85 LT 721; *R v Morpeth Ward JJ ex p Ward* (1992) 95 Cr App R 215, [1992] Crim LR 497, (1992) 142 NLJ 312 (DC); and *R v Inner London Crown Court ex p Benjamin* (1987) 85 Cr App R 267, [1987] Crim LR 417 (DC)). To prove a danger to the peace it is sufficient that the natural consequence of the behaviour persisted in would be enough to provoke others to violence (*Wise v Dunning*; *R v Morpeth Ward JJ ex p Ward* and *R v Inner London Crown Court ex p Benjamin*, above). See, generally, the discussion at page 27.

The same general principles apply to the power to bind over to be of good behaviour (*R v South Molton JJ ex p Ankerson* [1989] 1 WLR 40, [1988] 3 All ER 989, (1990) 90 Cr App R 158 (DC)), including where the person's behaviour was unlawful and where it was felt by justices to be *contra bonos mores* (*Hughes v Holley* (1987) 151 JP 233, (1988) 86 Cr App R 130, [1987] Crim LR 253 (QBD)) and a repetition is feared (*R v Sandbach JJ ex p Williams* [1935] 2 KB 192; *Hughes v Holley*).

3.8   Procedural Safeguards

The higher courts have tended to indicate that there ought to be more effective procedural safeguards, although such as do exist have been frequently criticised.

Notice of Intention to Bind Over

Complainants, witnesses or others who are before the court ought to be told when the court is considering a bind over and the reasons for it, and they or their legal representatives (if present) should be given the opportunity to make representations (see *R v South Molton JJ ex p Ankerson, R v Hendon JJ ex p Gorchein* [1973] 1 WLR 1502, [1974] 1 All ER 168, [1973] Crim LR 754 (DC); *Sheldon v Bromfield JJ* [1964] 2 QB 573, [1964] 2 WLR 1066, [1964] 2 All ER 131 (DC)). Such good practice is not required in the event of misconduct in the face of the court (*R v North London Metropolitan Magistrate ex p Haywood* [1973] 1 WLR 965, [1973] 3 All ER 50, [1973] Crim LR 442 (DC)), confirmed in *R v Clerkenwell Metropolitan Stipendiary Magistrate ex p Hooper* [1998] 1 WLR 800, [1998] 4 All ER 193, (1998) 162 JP 215 (QBD).

Where defendants (whether acquitted or not, or where an indictment is to remain on the file) have come to court aware of the case against them, they are not necessarily to be afforded an opportunity to make representations, but this may be advisable in the case of an acquitted defendant: see *R v Woking JJ ex p Gossage* [1973] 1 QB 448, [1973] 2 WLR 529, [1973] 2 All ER 621 (DC), approved in *R v Lincoln Crown Court ex p Jude* [1997] 3 All ER 737, (1997) 161 JP 589 (QBD). In *ex p Ankerson,* the reason for the proposed binding over order was not related to the circumstances of the case which had brought the party to court and the party should have been given an opportunity to be heard. Where a legal representative is present and has been consulted but no representations are made, then the court need not offer the individual the opportunity to make representations.

Where a court is relying on material such as a report, a copy of the material should be made available to the person before the court or that person's legal representative: *R v Middlesex Crown Court ex p Khan* (1997) 161 JP 240, [1997] COD 186, (1997) 161 JPN 212 (QBD).

Enquiry into Means

There must be an enquiry into means (*R v Nottingham Crown Court ex p Brace* (1990) 154 JP 161, [1990] COD 127, (1990) 154 JPN 63 (DC); *R v Central Criminal Court ex p Boulding* [1984] QB 813, [1984] 2 WLR 321, [1984] 1 All ER 766 (DC); *R v South Molton JJ ex p Ankerson* (above), although perhaps not where the sum proposed is obviously a nominal amount. The sum fixed must be reasonable, but need not be restricted to the maximum penalty available for the offence in respect of which the person appears before the court, if relevant. This approach has been confirmed by the Divisional Court in *R v Clerkenwell Metropolitan Stipendiary Magistrate ex p Hooper* [1998] 1 WLR 800, [1998] 4 All ER 193, (1998) 162 JP 215.

Requirement for a Surety

A person in respect of whom it is intended to make a binding over order subject to providing a surety should be given an opportunity to be heard on this particular matter: *R v Clerkenwell Metropolitan Stipendiary Magistrate ex p Hooper*, above.

Conditions
The order itself cannot be made subject to conditions (see page 43).

Finite Period
The order must be for a finite period (*R v South Molton JJ ex p Ankerson*, above), although the period is a matter of discretion (*R v Edgar* (1913) 77 JP 356). It should not be used to circumvent restrictions on imposing bail conditions (*R v South Molton JJ ex p Ankerson*).

Consent to the Order
The matter of consent was examined authoritatively by the Divisional Court in *R v Lincoln Crown Court ex p Jude* [1997] 3 All ER 737, (1997) 161 JP 589. The court made clear that consent is not one of the cumulative prerequisites for making a binding over order. This decision departed from the view of the law expressed in *ex p Ankerson*.

The reason for requiring consent is to relieve the court of dealing with the complaint or information before it (eg as in a typical neighbour dispute or common assault case), or to relieve the court of the obligation to give an opportunity to the person concerned to make representations. The conclusion of *ex p Jude* is that where a court intending to make a binding over order against an unconvicted person affords that person an opportunity to be heard, then the court is not also required to obtain consent before making the order.

3.9   Other Matters
Appeals against binding over orders are governed by the Magistrates' Courts (Appeals from Binding Over Orders) Act 1956, and are by way of re-hearing in the Crown Court. Forfeiture of recognisance is governed by s 120 of the Magistrates' Courts Act 1980.

A variation of a requirement for a surety may be sought under s 118 Magistrates' Courts Act 1980, and a surety may obtain discharge on application under s 116 Magistrates' Courts Act 1980.

3.10   "To be of good behaviour"
In *Hashman & Harrup v UK* [1999] EHRLR 342, 8 BHRC 104, *The Times* 1 December 1999, the European Court of Human Rights considered the power of a court to bind over to be of good behaviour. It decided that the power was contrary to the terms of art 10 of the European Convention on Human Rights (a right now to be found in the Human Rights Act 1998). The Court cited, as part of its assessment of the law, the Law Commission's Report on Binding Over, which noted that the bald requirement to be of good behaviour did not "give sufficient indication to the person bound over of the conduct which he or she must avoid in order to be safe from coercive

sanctions".

The European Court of Human Rights held that the absence of particularity in such a bind-over meant that the applicants could have no clear guidance as to what behaviour to avoid, and that the order as expressed breached the requirement of certainty inherent in the expression in art 10 that the power to interfere with art 10 rights should be prescribed by law (in contrast with its findings on this point in respect of binding over to keep the peace, see *Steel v UK,* above, page 21).

Accordingly, besides the other procedural requirements common to both types of binding over, it must now be made clear to anyone who is to be bound over to be of good behaviour, the respect(s) in which their past behaviour has been deficient, and what conduct they are being expected to refrain from in the future.

3.11 The Future

Criticism of the scheme of preventive justice is not new, but in the light of the adverse criticisms voiced by the Law Commission, the long-term future of the justices' powers to bind over may be in some doubt.

On consultation, the Law Commission found a clear preponderance of support for retaining a power to bind over, despite the objections of principle identified. Support for binding over is based largely on what are regarded as the considerable practical advantages of the present system, and the perceived lacuna should the system be abolished. Practical matters such as the ability of the courts to defuse situations without conferring the stigma of conviction, but with a warning as to future conduct, the saving of court time and money, and the additional sentencing option, all influenced those in favour of retaining the powers.

The arguments relied upon by the Law Commission related to the unconstitutionality of the powers and process arising from:
(1) the unsatisfactory nature of the current practice and procedure, regarded as irredeemable breaches of principles of natural justice;
(2) the wide range of criminal sanctions and cautioning practices currently available; and
(3) the impracticability of designing a satisfactory and new form of judicial warning system.

The unsatisfactory nature of the current practice and procedure was addressed on both an academic and a practical level, and related to:
(1) the vagueness of the meanings of breach of the peace and good behaviour and the consequent difficulty of those bound over in knowing precisely what they might or might not do;
(2) the absence of any power to impose conditions which would clarify the conduct to be avoided;
(3) the unrealistic requirement for consent and the power to punish for refusal (but not for breach of the recognisance);

(4) the absence of any limit to the duration or amount of the recognisance; and

(5) the likelihood that in many material respects the practice relating to binding over would breach the European Convention on Human Rights (supported by the rejection in the United States of binding over as a violation of the constitutionally protected right of due process).

The Law Commission concluded that the powers of binding over to keep the peace and be of good behaviour under the Justices of the Peace Act and at common law and in related legislation should be abolished without replacement.

There are no current plans to introduce legislation to meet these criticisms and implement the proposal of the Law Commission. It is not unusual for Law Commission proposals, even those couched in such strong terms, to lie dormant, although a successful challenge to the powers in the European Court of Human Rights might prove a catalyst to reform or abolition.

The fact remains that, despite the best efforts of the higher courts to impose a suitable procedure on all aspects of the binding over procedures, most recently in *R v Clerkenwell Metropolitan Stipendiary Magistrate ex p Hooper* [1998] 1 WLR 800, [1998] 4 All ER 193, (1998) 162 JP 215 (QBD) (and see *R v Lincoln Crown Court ex p Jude* [1997] 3 All ER 737, (1997) 161 JP 589 (QBD)), there is a likelihood that unfairness in procedure will be called into question as a breach of the requirements of the Human Rights Act 1998 and the procedural safeguards pursuant to the Convention.

4 Other Restriction Orders

It was recognised that the substantive statutory criminal offences, and the quasi-criminal powers to bind over following a breach of the peace, were insufficient to provide an effective framework to control criminality. The civil law was also largely ineffective (see *Hussein and Another v Lancaster City Council*, 14 May 1998, unreported (QBD)). Accordingly, in recent years innovative measures have been introduced with a view to reducing levels of crime, particularly among young people. Some of these measures are dealt with briefly here: anti-social behaviour orders; local child curfew orders; on-the-spot fines; and alcohol-related matters.

4.1 Anti-social Behaviour Orders

A small minority of young people and children require early interventions to divert them from criminality before it takes a hold on their lives. Although not exclusively aimed at young people, anti-social behaviour orders ("ASBOs") were seen as a means of bringing misbehaving youngsters before the court in circumstances where previously their conduct would have gone "unpunished". For those cases where witnesses would not give evidence because of fear of reprisals by the group, or where the conduct itself fell short of the precise definition of a particular crime, it was expected that this provision would fill some of the gaps. On the other hand, the use of an essentially civil mechanism to "brand" particular young people as anti-social was seen as flawed. In circumstances where breach of the order put them at serious risk of custody, some felt that the initial procedure should be part of the criminal process to afford them the necessary protection from the start.

Section 1 of the Crime and Disorder Act 1998 provides for the making of anti-social behaviour orders. An application for an order can be made by the local authority in respect of any person over the age of ten, where the person has acted in an anti-social manner, ie caused or been likely to cause harassment, alarm or distress to one or more persons not of the same household. The order must be necessary to protect people, in the local government area in which the harassment, alarm or distress was caused or was likely to be caused, from further anti-social acts. The defendant may prove that his actions were reasonable.

The application is made on complaint to the local magistrates' court. If the case is proved the court may make an ASBO. The order prohibits the defendant from doing anything described in the order. Such an order must last for a period of at least two years and can be the subject of an application to vary or discharge. No variation can take place within two years without the consent of the parties. Prohibitions must be necessary to protect people in the area from anti-social behaviour and the order can extend to cover neighbouring areas so long as the appropriate authorities in those areas have been consulted. Any act in breach of the prohibition can lead to conviction in the magistrates' court and to a penalty of up to six months imprisonment, but not a conditional discharge. In the Crown Court the maximum penalty is five years imprisonment or a fine or both. Successful ASBO applications may well be followed by applications to identify youths made subject to the orders.

In *McCann and Others v Manchester Crown Court*, 1 March 2001, the Court of Appeal had to consider the findings of the Crown Court in an ASBO case. The Chief Constable alleged that three boys had acted in an anti-social manner over nine months of 1999. He therefore sought orders. On behalf of the boys it was said that the title of the Act demonstrated that this was a criminal statute, and that prosecution by a "relevant" authority was the formula for prosecuting for crimes. It was also suggested that s 1 is formulated in terms very similar to the provisions of the Public Order Act 1986 and that the geographically and behaviourally limiting nature of the order is prohibitive and analogous to sentence. The Crown Court had said that, although these were civil proceedings, the standard of proof was the criminal one.

The Lord Chief Justice dismissed each of the arguments and concluded that the section created two procedures. The first was to create the anti-social behaviour order, and the second was to establish and, if appropriate, penalise, the breach. In that situation the second procedure was clearly criminal because of the risk of imprisonment or fine as a penalty. The first procedure was not criminal. It was more akin to a civil application for an injunction which imposes an order, the breach of which could lead to fine or imprisonment. An ASBO was an order designed to protect not to punish, albeit that in doing so it imposed restrictions on the youngsters. The Lord Chief Justice then reviewed the European authorities and found nothing contrary to his interpretation.

In reaching his conclusion the Lord Chief Justice was assisted by the decision in *B v Chief Constable of Avon and Somerset Constabulary* [2001] 1 WLR 340 (QBD). In this case the former Lord Chief Justice, Lord Bingham, dealt with the related question of how to approach the standard of proof in civil cases where the "allegations" were serious or the consequences for the appellant were serious. Lord Bingham made it clear that the civil standard was the appropriate standard, but that:

"the civil standard did not mean a bare balance of probability . . . the civil standard is a flexible standard to be applied with greater or lesser strictness according to the strictness of what has to be proved and the implications of proving those matters . . . in a serious case such as the present the difference between the two is, in truth, largely illusory."

Because there is so much at stake in the anti-social behaviour order application, there is no material difference between the civil and the criminal standard.

The precise level of efficacy of such orders remains to be seen. There is the risk that they simply move problem behaviour by the same people to a different location. There is understandable concern about publicising the names of very young people against whom such orders are made, and there is anxiety about the serious consequences of breach.

4.2 Local Child Curfew Orders

Another area of anxiety related to difficulties sometimes caused by children below the age of criminal responsibility. Children roaming the streets in certain areas into the early hours of the morning were perceived as responsible for criminal activity, including public disorder. They were regarded as causing disturbance to the community and contributing to harassment of neighbours and on the streets. It was thought that their ability to "get away with it" meant that they were acclimatised at a very young age to dealing with the public authorities. There was a need to intervene to keep them off the streets, both for the prevention of crime and for the protection of public order. Sections 14 and 15 of the Crime and Disorder Act 1998 were designed to address this problem.

Section 14, as amended by s 49 of the Criminal Justice and Police Act 2001, provides for local authorities or chief officers of police to make schemes for a notice imposing, for a specified period (not exceeding 90 days), a ban on children under sixteen being in specified places during specified hours between 9 pm and 6 am otherwise than under the effective control of a parent or responsible person aged eighteen or over.

The local authority is required to consult the police (s 14(3)) before making such a scheme. Chief officers of police are required to consult relevant local authorities before making such a scheme. Schemes require the consent of the Secretary of State (s 14(4)). Notice of such schemes must be posted in a conspicuous place or places within the specified area and in such other manner as the authority thinks desirable to achieve publicity.

Section 15 provides that where a constable has reasonable cause to believe that a child under ten is in breach of the ban imposed by a curfew notice, he shall as soon as practicable notify the local authority. He may remove the child to the child's place of residence unless he has reasonable cause to believe that if removed to that place the child would be likely to suffer significant harm.

Whether these provisions perform a genuine role in the range of legislative tools to protect the public from disorder and/or crime generally will be shown with time. It may be that they focus attention on a particular need. In practical terms most breaches will lead to police officers taking children home. The impact of the provision will then depend on the attitude of the child's parents. The risk is that a curfew order relating to a particular area may simply reinforce local views that there is something wrong with the people living in that area, exacerbating problems rather than reducing them.

4.3 On-the-Spot Fines

Using "on-the-spot" fines was originally seen as a means of dealing with "yob" culture. The Criminal Justice and Police Act 2001 puts in place the mechanisms for imposing such fines. They were not scheduled for immediate implementation, but for regional piloted schemes.

The Penalty Offences

Section 1 of the Act contains a schedule of offences defined as "penalty offences". This list can be amended by the Secretary of State but for the moment contains ten offences:

- being drunk in a public place;
- throwing fireworks in a thoroughfare;.
- trespassing on a railway;
- throwing stones at trains;
- buying alcohol for persons under eighteen;
- sending a false message to cause annoyance;
- being drunk and disorderly;
- consuming alcohol in a designated public place;
- wasting police time;
- giving a false alarm to a fire brigade.

Any constable in uniform may give a person over the age of eighteen a "penalty notice" if the officer has reason to believe that the person has committed a penalty offence (s 2). If the penalty notice is given in a police station there is no requirement for the constable to be in uniform but the constable must be authorised on behalf of the chief constable for the area. In the case of a person who is drunk and disorderly, the uniformed police officer would see his behaviour and might, in theory, elect to give him the penalty notice on the spot and leave matters at that. In reality, the nature of public disorder arising from drunk and disorderly behaviour usually requires the constable to arrest the offender to take him out of the offending situation. Having arrested him and taken him to the police station and allowed him to become sober it would then be quicker, and cheaper on the public purse, to issue the penalty notice and leave the defendant to pay the penalty in due course.

The procedure will doubtless follow the common pattern where numbers of petty offenders are charged and then, because of their drunkenness, forget to attend court on the adjourned date. This leads to the issuing and execution of many warrants at real expense. It will be cheaper overall, when the defendant forgets, through drunkenness, to pay the penalty, because he will simply be registered as a fine defaulter for an increased amount, although there is then the cost of enforcement.

Police officers will have to be ready for the defendant who takes the penalty notice and then pleads not guilty. In such cases courts may be in difficulties if the officer does not have reliable and detailed notes to refresh his memory when giving evidence. These cases will involve more work than fixed penalty motoring cases, but less than cases that have led to charge or summons. There will be cases where it is both appropriate and possible for the penalty notice to be served at the scene because, for example, public order does not require the defendant to be arrested and removed.

The Penalty Notice
It is for the Secretary of State to specify in each case the amount of the penalty in respect of each offence. He can specify up to a quarter of the maximum fine for the particular offence. It is to be expected that he will specify figures that reflect current sentencing levels. He will probably take into account the approach taken in fixed penalty motoring cases. It is likely that the penalties payable in response to the notices will be well below the quarter maximum.

The penalty notice is in a prescribed form describing both the offence and its circumstances. It must specify the penalty and the suspended enforcement period for it. It must identify the justices' chief executive to whom payment should be made and inform the recipient of his right to ask for trial and how to exercise that right. If he wants a trial, he is required to request it in the manner set out on the form and within the suspended enforcement period (twenty-one days). If he fails to pay the penalty within the suspended enforcement period and fails to request trial, then a sum which is one and a half times the penalty will be registered against him for enforcement as a fine.

Payment of the Penalty

Any person who decides to pay the penalty is to be regarded as having paid the penalty at the time at which an ordinary letter would have been delivered by ordinary post. He must claim to have paid it by properly addressing, pre-paying and posting a letter containing the amount of the penalty. He must show that his letter was posted, but if he does then it has to be proved against him that payment was not actually received. If he does not pay then the po-lice will certify the position, pass the information to the court and the court will enforce the certified figure as a fine, giving the defaulter notice of the registration of the sum. Ultimately there is a risk of imprisonment for non-payment of the penalty.

This procedure has the capacity to prove a useful means of dealing promptly with some minor offenders who otherwise take up a great deal of court time. Although it does not involve marching offenders to the cashpoint for payment on the spot, it has a certain immediacy and the potential to en-able some offenders to avoid an embarrassing court appearance.

4.4   Alcohol-Related Disorder

Sections 12 to 32 of the 2001 Act relate to the combating of disorder due to drunkenness. They amount to detailed changes to the legislation to address particular problems. Historically, some local authorities have used bye-laws to curb public drinking in particular locations; others have not. Now, local authorities have a standard permissive power to designate particular areas where consuming intoxicating liquor may lead to a direction from a police officer. Non-compliance will be an offence. There are changes to the under-age drinking regime to define more precisely the defence to a charge of sell-ing liquor to a person under eighteen.

Alcohol Consumption in Designated Public Places

If a constable reasonably believes that a person is or has been consuming in-toxicating liquor in a designated public place, or intends to consume it in such a place, he may require the person not to consume in that place any-thing which is or which the constable reasonably believes to be intoxicating liquor (s 12(1) and (2)(a)). He may require the person to surrender anything in his possession which is, or which the officer reasonably believes to be, in-toxicating liquor or a container for such liquor, except a sealed container (s 12(2)(b)). The constable may dispose of anything thus confiscated in any manner he considers appropriate (s 12(3)). Non-compliance with such a re-quirement, without reasonable excuse, is an offence. The maximum penalty is a level 2 fine. The constable making the requirement must tell the person that failure to comply without reasonable excuse is an offence.

The procedure for designating public places is set out in s 13, and designation is a matter for the local authority. Licensed premises are not designated public places (s 14). Section 15 deals with pre-existing bye-laws of similar effect and s 16 defines intoxicating liquor as having the same meaning as under the Licensing Act 1964.

Closure of Licensed Premises
Sections 17 to 27 detail the mechanisms for the closure of licensed premises where disorderly behaviour on or in the vicinity of licensed premises is reasonably believed to exist by a senior police officer.

Alcohol and Young People
Section 29 amends s 1(1) of the Confiscation of Alcohol (Young Persons) Act 1997 to enable a constable to require the surrender of "a container for such liquor", in addition to his powers in relation to intoxicating liquor itself.

Section 30 amends s 169A Licensing Act 1964 with regard to the sale of intoxicating liquor to a person under eighteen. The person alleged to have sold to such a person has a defence if he can prove:

(a) that he believed that the person was not under the age of eighteen; and
(b) either that he had taken all reasonable steps to establish the person's age or that nobody could reasonably have suspected from his appearance that the person was under the age of eighteen.

"All reasonable steps" are taken if a person is asked for evidence of age, unless it is shown that the evidence is such that no reasonable person would have been convinced by it.

Chapter 3

Riot, Violent Disorder and Affray

1 The Public Order Act 1986

The Public Order Act 1986 provides for the most serious public order offences:

"1.–(1) Where 12 or more persons who are present together use or threaten unlawful violence for a common purpose and the conduct of them (taken together) is such as would cause a person of reasonable firmness present at the scene to fear for his personal safety, each of the persons using unlawful violence for the common purpose is guilty of riot.

(2) It is immaterial whether or not the 12 or more use or threaten unlawful violence simultaneously.

(3) The common purpose may be inferred from conduct.

(4) No person of reasonable firmness need actually be, or be likely to be, present at the scene.

(5) Riot may be committed in private as well as in public places.

(6) A person guilty of riot is liable on conviction on indictment to imprisonment for a term not exceeding ten years or a fine or both.

2.– (1) Where 3 or more persons who are present together use or threaten unlawful violence and the conduct of them (taken together) is such as would cause a person of reasonable firmness present at the scene to fear for his personal safety, each of the persons using or threatening unlawful violence is guilty of violent disorder.

(2) It is immaterial whether or not the 3 or more use or threaten unlawful violence simultaneously.

(3) No person of reasonable firmness need actually be, or be likely to be, present at the scene.

(4) Violent disorder may be committed in private as well as in public places.

(5) A person guilty of violent disorder is liable on conviction on indictment to imprisonment for a term not exceeding five years or a fine or both, or on summary conviction to imprisonment for a term not exceeding six months or a fine not exceeding the statutory maximum or both.

3.– (1) A person is guilty of affray is he uses or threatens unlawful violence towards another and his conduct is such as would cause a person of reasonable firmness present at the scene to fear for his personal safety.

(2) Where two or more persons use or threaten unlawful violence, it is the conduct of them taken together that must be considered for the purposes of subsection (1).

(3) For the purposes of this section a threat cannot be made by the use of words alone.

(4) No person of reasonable firmness need actually be, or be likely to be, present at the scene.

(5) Affray may be committed in private as well as in public places.

(6) A constable may arrest without warrant anyone he reasonably suspects is committing affray.

(7) A person guilty of affray is liable on conviction on indictment to imprisonment for a term not exceeding three years or a fine or both, or on summary conviction to imprisonment for a term not exceeding six months or a fine not exceeding the statutory maximum or both.

6.– (1) A person is guilty of riot only if he intends to use violence or is aware that his conduct may be violent.

(2) A person is guilty of violent disorder or affray only if he intends to use or threaten violence or is aware that his conduct may be violent or threaten violence. . .

(5) For the purposes of this section a person whose awareness is impaired by intoxication shall be taken to be aware of that of which he would be aware if not intoxicated, unless he shows either that his intoxication was not self-induced or that it was caused solely by the taking or administration of a substance in the course of medical treatment.

(6) In subsection (5) "intoxication" means any intoxication, whether caused by drink, drugs or other means, or by a combination of means.

(7) Subsections (1) and (2) do not affect the determination for the purposes of riot or violent disorder of the number of persons who use or threaten violence.

7.– (1) No prosecution for an offence of riot or incitement to riot may be instituted except by or with the consent of the Director of Public Prosecutions.

(2) For the purposes of the rules against charging more than one offence in the same count or information, each of sections 1 to 5 creates one offence.

(3) If on the trial on indictment of a person charged with violent disorder or affray the jury find him not guilty of the offence charged, they may (without prejudice to section 6(3) of the Criminal Law Act 1967) find him guilty of an offence under section 4.

(4) The Crown Court has the same powers and duties in relation to a per-

son who is by virtue of subsection (3) convicted before it of an offence under section 4 as a magistrates' court would have on convicting him of the offence.

8. – In this part –

"dwelling" means any structure or part of a structure occupied as a person's home or as other living accommodation (whether the occupation is separate or shared with others) but does not include any part not so occupied, and for this purpose "structure" includes a tent, caravan, vehicle, vessel or other temporary or movable structure;

"violence" means any violent conduct, so that—

(a) except in the context of affray, it includes violent conduct towards property as well as violent conduct towards persons, and

(b) it is not restricted to conduct causing or intended to cause injury or damage but includes any other violent conduct (for example, throwing at or towards a person a missile of a kind capable of causing injury which does not hit or falls short).

9.– (1) The common law offences of riot, rout, unlawful assembly and affray are abolished . . .

10.–(1) In the Riot (Damages) Act 1886 and in section 515 of the Merchant Shipping Act 1894 (compensation for riot damage) "riotous" and "riotously" shall be construed in accordance with section 1 above.

(2) In Schedule 1 to the Marine Insurance Act 1906 (form and rules for the construction of certain insurance policies) "rioters" in rule 8 and "riot" in rule 10 shall, in the application of the rules to any policy taking effect on or after the coming into force of this section, be construed in accordance with section 1 above unless a different intention appears.

(3) "Riot" and cognate expressions in any enactment in force before the coming into force of this section (other than the enactments mentioned in subsections (1) and (2) above) shall be construed in accordance with section 1 above if they would have been construed in accordance with the common law offence of riot apart from this Part.

(4) Subject to subsections (1) to (3) above and unless a different intention appears, nothing in this Part affects the meaning of "riot" or any cognate expression in any enactment in force, or other instrument taking effect, before the coming into force of this section."

Riot (s 1), violent disorder (s 2) and affray (s 3) replaced the common law offences of riot, rout, unlawful assembly and affray, which were abolished by s 9(1) of the 1986 Act. There are overlaps between offences but two features are common to each of the serious offences. The first is unlawful violence, and the second is the degree of that violence, judged from the standpoint of a hypothetical bystander, "a person of reasonable firmness present at the scene".

2   Violence

In defining the conduct which will satisfy the *actus reus* of these serious offences, and the lesser offence in s 4, the 1986 Act relies on the concept not of
breach of the peace, but of unlawful violence. Any conduct which amounts
to violence may also amount to a breach of the peace (*R v Howell* [1982] QB
416, [1981] 3 All ER 383), and, if so, activates the common law powers discussed in Chapter 2. The use or threat of unlawful violence may also amount
to other offences, such as criminal damage or one of the range of assaults.

2.1   Definition

"Violence" is defined in s 8 of the Act as:

> "any violent conduct, so that—
>
> (a)   except in the context of affray, it includes violent conduct towards
>   property as well as violent conduct towards persons, and
>
> (b)   it is not restricted to conduct causing or intended to cause injury or
>   damage but includes any other violent conduct (for example,
>   throwing at or towards a person a missile of a kind capable of caus-
>   ing injury which does not hit or falls short)."

The partial definition, adopted in s 8, was that offered by the Law Commission but is not satisfactory since it includes the adjective "violent". The Law
Commission wished to avoid a definition based on specific offences against
the person or property, taking the view that where such offences are committed then they may properly be charged, although in many instances of disorder it may be difficult to prove the requisite intent of the individual, the result of his action or the identity of the victim. Accordingly the Law Commission, at para 5.33 of its report, *Criminal Law – Offences Relating to Public
Order* (Report 123), observed:

> "The definition . . . emphasises the nature of violent conduct rather than
> its consequences . . . [V]iolence is not limited to physical damage or in-
> jury . . . and . . . it must in some way be violence towards persons or
> property; and the example is given of the throwing of a missile towards a
> person, capable of causing injury (a paper dart would thus not qualify)
> whether that missile falls short or wide of the mark. Many other exam-
> ples of violence will amount to violent conduct upon these criteria, such
> as the wielding of a lethal instrument or the discharge of a firearm in the
> direction of another. The example is given because it explains the con-
> cept without the difficulties of a detailed list or extended definition. The
> conduct must be such that it can be regarded as violence towards persons
> or property and the jury must be sure that it was of such a character."

Statutory definitions of violence elsewhere are rare, although since
"violence" is an ordinary word of the English language it ought to be interpreted in such a way as to be given its ordinary meaning; thus an ordinary

sensible man will know violence when he sees or hears it (see *Brutus v Cozens* [1973] AC 854, [1972] 3 WLR 521, [1972] 2 All ER 1297 (HL)).

Support for this approach is found in *R v Criminal Injuries Compensation Board ex p Webb, Warner and Others* [1987] QB 74, [1986] 3 WLR 251, [1986] 2 All ER 478 (CA). In deciding whether a crime was a "crime of violence" for the purpose of the criminal injuries compensation scheme, the court had imposed no special construction; since the words were ordinary words it took the view that "the ordinary or generally understood meaning of the words must prevail". This approach was approved by the Court of Appeal. And in *Dino Services Ltd v Prudential Assurance Co Ltd* [1989] 1 All ER 422, [1989] 1 Lloyd's Rep 379 (CA), in the context of the interpretation of "violent" in an insurance policy, Kerr LJ observed that:

> "The word 'violent' is an ordinary English word, which here appears in a common commercial document. It seems to me that there is no reason why its meaning should be in any way different from what an ordinary person would understand."

See also the definition of "violent offence" in s 31 of the Criminal Justice Act 1991: "an offence which leads or is intended or likely to lead, to a person's death or to physical injury to a person". This definition, which is narrower than that in the 1986 Act, was considered in *R v Palin* (1995) 16 Cr App R(S) 888, [1995] Crim LR 435 (CA); *R v Khan Touriq* (1995) 16 Cr App R (S) 180, [1994] Crim LR 862 (CA); and *R v Cochrane* [1993] Crim LR 48 (CA). The Court of Appeal called for the definition to be amended in *R v Richart* (1995) 16 Cr App R(S) 977, [1995] Crim LR 574, *The Times* 14 April 1995 (CA) and *R v Ragg* [1995] 4 All ER 155, [1995] Crim LR 664, *The Times* 13 May 1995 (CA).

In Law Commission Report No 76, *Conspiracy and Criminal Law Reform*, it was said that "violence will cover any application of force to the person, but carries a somewhat restricted meaning in relation to property". In relation to s 2(6) of the Criminal Law Act 1967, force, in the context of entry to premises, was said to be the application of energy to an object with a view to moving it (*Swales v Cox* [1981] QB 849, [1981] 2 WLR 814, [1981] 1 All ER 1115 (QBD)). In the context of the serious public order offences, it seems possible to argue that whereas force may be involved in violent conduct, the converse is not true, ie not every use of force involves violence, and violent conduct would suggest a substantial degree of force, whether applied to the person or to property, and deriving the tenor of violence from all the surrounding circumstances. Some assistance for this approach is to be found in the interpretation of insurance policies where a distinction is often drawn between an entry which is merely forced and an entry where violence was used (see *Dino Services Ltd v Prudential Assurance Co Ltd*, above).

In any event, there are occasions where violence does not involve contact either with the person or property. As the Law Commission explained, it would be wrong to restrict violence to cases where force is actually applied;

a punch thrown but which misses its target is just as much the use of violence as a punch which finds its target. Waving a weapon so as to cause a person fear of injury or concern may properly be described as violent conduct; see s 8: ". . . it is not restricted to conduct . . . intended to cause injury . . .".

The fact that damage or injury results should not be a decisive factor in deciding whether violence was used. Throwing a rotten tomato at a politician may well be described as the use of violence, but that emerges from the throwing rather than the fact that it happens to hit and necessitates clothing to be cleaned. By contrast, daubing a politician's clothing with paint may be criminal damage and assault, but is probably not violent behaviour.

2.2 Unlawfulness

During the early stages of the passage of the 1986 Act, the definition of violence included "violence not justified by law, for example, the law relating to self-defence or the prevention of crime or disorder". At a late stage the epithet "unlawful" was adopted in ss 1, 2, 3 and 4 and the above definition was omitted. Commentators have suggested that the word "unlawful" is superfluous, and that it might safely be ignored since Parliament could not be taken to have intended to exclude the application of the general defences to criminal charges (for examples of mere surplusage see *McMonagle v Westminster City Council* [1990] 2 AC 716, [1990] 2 WLR 823, [1990] 1 All ER 993 and *R v R (Rape; Marital Exemption)* [1992] 1 AC 599, [1991] 3 WLR 767, [1991] 4 All ER 481 (HL)).

Certainly, the word "violence" tends to be used in a pejorative fashion to describe behaviour of which the speaker disapproves. Force is more often used to describe behaviour in a more neutral or even approving fashion. Thus, the Police and Criminal Evidence Act 1984, s 117 legitimises the use of reasonable force by a constable where necessary in carrying out a power granted by that Act, and that presumably would include conduct which in another context might be described as violence, for example, breaking down a door using a sledge-hammer.

It could be argued that the use of the word "force" in s 31 of the Criminal Law Act 1967 might suggest that "violence" should be read as extending only to unreasonable force, but this view would fail to give sufficient weight to the epithet "unlawful". There is a natural reluctance to describe as violent conduct such as the use by police of riot shields and truncheons in the suppression of a riot, and the term force is often substituted. Equally, in such an instance, where it is sought to criticise the deployment of that tactic or the degree of force employed, there may well be a tendency to describe the force used as violence.

The view of the Court of Appeal is that "unlawful" must have some meaning, and accordingly the general law applies and the use of violence justified by law is not an offence under ss 1, 2, 3 and 4. In *R v Rothwell and*

Barton [1993] Crim LR 626 (CA), the recorder had directed the jury that self-defence, reasonable defence of a friend and force used to prevent a breach of the peace were not defences to a charge of violent disorder. The Court of Appeal held that the prosecution had to demonstrate the unlawfulness of the violence used or threatened, and quashed the verdict.

In *R v Bane* [1994] Crim LR 135, the Court of Appeal held that, no matter how weak the defence, a defendant is entitled to have it considered by the jury, and that self-defence was a defence to a charge of affray. Judges ought to deal adequately with the meaning of unlawful violence. In *R v Pulham and Pulham* [1995] Crim LR 296 the judge failed to leave the issue of self-defence to the jury and the appeal against conviction was allowed.

For the effect of a misdirection on the issue, see page 88.

It is for the prosecution to satisfy the jury (or magistrates in the case of violent disorder or affray tried summarily) that the force used by the defendant was unlawful, although the defence has the evidential burden of raising that as an issue (*R v Rothwell and Barton*, above).

Commonly, the issue of the unlawfulness of force arises in the context of the use of reasonable force in self-defence or in the defence of others or of property, and is decided by applying the usual principles. Given the difficulties inherent in self-defence, it has been said, in a case of affray, that when self-defence is an issue, it is desirable that the judge should follow the words of Lord Morris in *Palmer v R* [1971] AC 814, [1971] 2 WLR 831, [1971] 1 All ER 1077 (PC) when addressing the jury, and that a summing up which omitted those or similar words would be defective (*R v Rivolta* [1994] Crim LR 694 (CA)).

Any person may use reasonable force in the prevention of crime, or in arresting or assisting in the arrest of an offender or suspected offender (Criminal Law Act 1967, s 3(1)).

Where the alleged offence occurs in the context of an exercise by the police or officials of their powers, eg of arrest or entry to premises, there may be difficult questions of both fact and law relating to the legality of police conduct. There must be sufficient proof of the legality of the police exercise of their powers.

Violence may be used in the prevention of actual or apprehended breaches of the peace. On other occasions violence may be justified by way of self-help, for example, to bring to an end or prevent an unlawful detention; or to remove demonstrators from a site, or trespassers from property (although the trespassory conduct may now be caught by other provisions of the 1986 Act, as amended; see Chapter 6). There are strict constraints on self-help in the civil context of the law of nuisance and trespass to land or goods; see, eg, *Burton v Winters* [1993] 1 WLR 1077, [1993] 3 All ER 847 (CA) and *Lloyd v DPP* [1992] 1 All ER 982, [1992] Crim LR 904, [1992] RTR 215 (DC), where, in the context of a charge of criminal damage for the removal of a wheel clamp, the court observed that "self help involving the use of force can only be contemplated where there is no reasonable alternative".

Where necessity is pleaded, the law relating to trespass to land places strict limits on self-help, although a jury may be persuaded in a particular case of a more generous application of the principles in the light of the objectives of the defendants.

There may be other examples of lawful violence, eg in the specific defence provided by s 5 of the Criminal Damage Act 1971. Duress and necessity may provide defences in appropriate cases.

2.3 Threats

In violent disorder and affray, both those who threaten unlawful violence and those who use unlawful violence are guilty (ss 2(1), 3(1)). For the purposes of riot, only those who use unlawful violence are guilty (s 1(1)); those who threaten unlawful violence are not guilty, except perhaps of incitement or as secondary parties. For the purposes of riot and violent disorder those who threaten unlawful violence, whether by verbal or other means, are included when assessing the required number of participants (see page 75).

Threats of any description may also fall within s 4, 4A or 5, or if of a racial character, s 18 or 19 (see Chapter 4).

At times there may be doubt whether conduct constitutes violence or the threat of violence. For example, X waves a fist in the air in the direction of Y. That behaviour may be described as violence since it is violent conduct towards a person and is not prejudiced by virtue of the fact that it neither causes injury nor was intended to cause injury. On the other hand, it may be better described as a threat of violence. In any event, unless the necessary degree of apprehension is engendered (see below) it may be better to proceed under s 4 or 5 of the 1986 Act.

As regards conduct which amounts to a threat of violence, there is still some scope for doubt. In the context of mass picketing or a disturbance during a march or assembly, it is not clear whether large numbers alone may constitute a threat of violence, although it seems unlikely.

Will a chanting crowd be said to be using violence? See the comments in *Thomas v NUM*, page 154. The emphasis in s 8 is on violent conduct and it seems reasonably clear that verbal threats alone, whether oral or written, cannot fall within the meaning of "violence" as explained in s 8.

Since violence is said to be "any violent conduct" it is difficult to accept that oral or written threats, unaccompanied by separate acts, could fall within the meaning of "conduct". This is especially so as the Act, like its predecessor, draws a distinction elsewhere between words and behaviour. The distinction in ss 1, 2 and 3 between those who threaten violence and those who use violence would militate against a contrary view. Thus, a purely verbal threat, unaccompanied by any other activity, is unlikely to fall within the meaning of violence, but may amount to a threat of violence for the purposes of ss 1–3.

For the purposes of ss 1, 2, 4, 4A and 5, a threat may be made by words alone; but for the purposes of affray, "a threat cannot be made by the use of words alone" (s 3(3)). Section 3(3) has been examined on two occasions, in *R v Robinson* and *R v Dixon* (see page 83).

2.4 Person of Reasonable Firmness Present

In the cases of the serious offences (ss 1, 2 and 3) the standard by which the violence or threats of violence are to be judged is objective. What must be established is that a reasonably firm bystander would have been caused to fear for his personal safety.

It need not be shown that such a person either was present or was likely to have come on to the scene. This person may conveniently be described as the hypothetical bystander. The hypothetical bystander is not regarded as fearing for the safety of others, whether male or female, aged or infant, and is a hypothetical and objectively assessed individual; this corresponds to the approach taken in connection with the common law in *R v Plastow* (1989) 88 Cr App R 48, [1988] Crim LR 604 (CA).

Proof of the degree of fear does not appear to have caused juries any problems. The feelings of anyone actually involved as victim or as participant or as bystander cannot be used as the measure of the required level of fear, although evidence from such a person may be relevant to the nature of the fear which would have been engendered in the hypothetical bystander.

Actual Bystanders

There may be instances, probably relatively few, where the surrounding circumstances are such as to persuade the arbiters of fact that violence, for example a fight, was limited to those involved and that others, perhaps close by, were not affected by what happened. Direct evidence of the inactivity or equanimity of actual bystanders might then lead to the conclusion that, viewed objectively, a hypothetical reasonable bystander would equally not have been affected.

In *DPP v Cotcher and Cotcher* [1993] COD 181, *The Times* 29 December 1992 (DC), magistrates had taken the view that the defendants "assaulted three persons clinically and no other persons were involved or likely to be involved in violence". As the Court of Appeal pointed out, such cases are rare. The inactivity or passivity of actual bystanders is simply one factor to assist the arbiters of fact in applying the objective criterion, in the same way as excitability or fear will not be decisive of the objective question. Actual bystanders may exhibit no apprehension simply because they have been cowed into that state, or they may have become accustomed to the exhibition of violence so that it no longer concerns them.

DPP v Gormley, 18 May 1992, unreported (QBD, CO/342/91) is another case where magistrates were held to have applied the law correctly in concluding that, in the circumstances of the case (including evidence that the actual bystanders, two women in a car who intervened to deter the fighters, were not afraid), a hypothetical bystander would not have been caused to fear for his personal safety.

Victims as Bystanders

In *DPP v Gormley* the Divisional Court adverted to the problem, stemming from the common law, of whether or not the victim of violence was capable of being a bystander (see *Attorney-General's Reference (No 3 of 1983)* [1985] QB 242, [1985] 2 WLR 253, [1985] 1 All ER 501 (CA)). Although that point may have been a matter of some relevance to the common law, for the purposes of the statutory offence of affray as drawn by the 1986 Act, actual bystanders, whether or not participants, are not required, and the question left open at common law is irrelevant to the statutory offences of riot, violent disorder and affray. The only question for the court is whether, on the facts, a person of reasonable firmness would have been caused to fear for his personal safety, and that is a question for all the circumstances, including consideration of the victim if there were such a person. This point has been confirmed by the Court of Appeal in *R v Sanchez* (1996) 160 JP 321, [1996] Crim LR 572 (CA), approving the earlier decision in *R v Davison* [1992] Crim LR 31 (CA), and was itself applied in *R v Thind (Hardeep Singh)*, 27 April 1999, unreported (CA).

Present at the Scene

The violence must be of such a degree as would have put the hypothetical bystander in fear for his personal safety had he been there. For riot (s 1(4)), violent disorder (s 2(3)), or affray (s 3(4)), it need not be shown that such a person was actually there or would have been likely to have come on to the scene. This is so even where the offence is committed in a private place to which the public does not have access. Use of the word "would" rather than "might" indicates that the question is one of probability rather than possibility.

The common law also relied on the concept of bystander in the context of affray. In *Attorney-General's Reference (No 3 of 1983)* (above), it was said:

"We have employed the word 'bystander' . . . as a convenient abbreviation and in deference to what seems to have become common usage. The word has however connotations which make it not altogether apt. We use it in the sense of 'innocent members of the public within sight or earshot of the fighting'. We reject as impracticable the distinction which counsel . . . seeks to draw between persons who are the intended victims of those unlawfully fighting on the one hand and those on the other hand who are . . . 'merely sucked into the melee'."

In *R v Davison* (above) the Court of Appeal had regard to the Law Commission's explanation of "present at the scene" (at para 3.38):

"As regards 'presence at the scene', there may be some degree of uncertainty as to what is meant by 'presence', but we doubt whether it is possible or desirable to be more specific as to how far away from or how near to the disturbance the hypothetical person must be. Every case will to this extent depend on its circumstances, but we believe that a jury will sufficiently understand what is meant by 'present at the scene', that is anyone who would have been in real danger of becoming involved in the disturbance."

The advantage of this approach is to demonstrate that the entirety of the circumstances must be taken into account by the magistrates or jury for the purposes of evaluating the degree of violence involved. Most important is the type of conduct. The use of weapons, the numbers of participants and the nature of the premises are all relevant. For example, where conduct occurs in a confined space it may well be that a relatively slight degree of violence will suffice to render the hypothetical bystander fearful for personal safety given that he would be unable to manoeuvre himself to a place of safety; yet were that same degree of violence to be employed in the open, then the relevant standard would not be satisfied.

3 Riot

Checklist
- twelve or more persons must be present together using or threatening unlawful violence;
- there must be a common purpose;
- the behaviour must cause a person of reasonable firmness present at the scene to fear for his personal safety;
- the violence must be unlawful;
- the defendant must have intended to use violence or been aware that his conduct may have been violent;
- location is irrelevant;
- consent to prosecution is needed;
- triable on indictment only;
- an arrestable offence.

3.1 Definition
The common law offence of riot was hedged about with uncertainties and was rarely charged. It was generally accepted that the constituents of the offence were as set out in the following extract from *Field v Receiver of the Metropolitan Police* [1907] 2 KB 853, [1904–7] All ER 435:
"(1) number of persons three at least; (2) common purpose; (3) execution or inception of the common purpose; (4) an attempt to help one another by force if necessary against a person who may oppose them in the execution of their common purpose; (5) force or violence . . . displayed in

such a manner as to alarm at least one person of reasonable firmness and courage."

The 1986 Act retains many of the features of the common law offence. Section 1(1) provides:

"Where 12 or more persons who are present together use or threaten unlawful violence for a common purpose and the conduct of them (taken together) is such as would cause a person of reasonable firmness present at the scene to fear for his personal safety, each of the persons using unlawful violence for the common purpose is guilty of riot."

The following indictment approved by the Court of Appeal (see *R v Tyler* (1993) 96 Cr App R 332, [1993] Crim LR 60, (1992) 156 JPN 762 (CA), and *R v Jefferson & Others* [1994] 1 All ER 270, (1994) 99 Cr App R 13, [1993] Crim LR 880 (CA)) is to be found in *Blackstone's Criminal Practice* (Blackstone Press, 1993), para B 11.19:

". . . on or about the . . . day of . . ., being one of 12 or more persons present together at . . . and using [or threatening] unlawful violence for a common purpose, namely . . ., used unlawful violence for the said common purpose by assaulting members of the public, the conduct of the 12 or more persons aforesaid, taken together, being such as would cause a person of reasonable firmness present at the scene to fear for his personal safety."

In the past, proof of common purpose often turned out to be a serious stumbling block to the successful prosecution of the more serious public order offences. No doubt this will continue to demand careful consideration before prosecutions are launched.

3.2 Use or Threat of Unlawful Violence

Generally, see pages 59 to 64 above. Section 1 of the 1986 Act has been judicially described as consisting of two parts (*R v Tyler (above)*; *R v Jefferson (above)*; *R v Mandair* [1995] 1 AC 208, [1994] 2 WLR 700, [1994] 2 All ER 715 (HL)). The first part indicates the context of the offence and predicates twelve or more persons present together using or threatening unlawful violence for a common purpose and which would have the appropriate effect on the mind of a hypothetical bystander. It should be noted that those who use or threaten violence are counted in for the purposes of establishing the required number of participants (see page 75).

The second part specifies the precise offence, which comprehends only the use of violence; threats of violence are not an alternative. A person using unlawful violence, but not a person threatening it, may be convicted of riot, subject to the law relating to secondary parties (*R v Tyler* and *R v Jefferson*, above).

An indictment which alleges that the defendant used or threatened unlawful violence will be flawed but may be amended during the course of trial. In *R v Tyler* Farquharson LJ said:

"The statement of offence clearly and accurately referred to riot. The particulars disclosed the correct offence but widened its ambit to include 'threaten' as well as the 'use' of violence. In our judgment, that is not in the same category as alleging an offence which does not exist, as in *Gastor*. It gives an imperfect description of one that does. In those circumstances, the defect is capable of amendment on the basis laid down in *McVitie*."

In *R v Jefferson* the Court of Appeal applied the principle in *R v Tyler* to a similarly badly framed indictment. Even though there had been no amendment, the prosecution case and the judge's directions had made it clear that the case against the defendants was that they had encouraged and intended to encourage, and thereby aided and abetted, those who had used unlawful violence.

Those who threaten unlawful violence (as well as those who encourage it by other means) may, in appropriate instances, be guilty of aiding and abetting or inciting riot (or guilty of other offences under ss 2–5). The 1986 Act contains nothing to exclude the application of the normal common law principles (*R v Jefferson*, see page 72).

3.3   Common Purpose

There must be a purpose common among the alleged participants. The retention of this prerequisite (and its absence from violent disorder and affray) marks the special seriousness of behaviour committed collectively by a group. Before the 1986 Act it was remarked that riot is an offence "which derives its great gravity from the simple fact that the persons concerned were acting in numbers and using those numbers to achieve their purpose" (*R v Caird* (1970) 114 SJ 652, [1970] Crim LR 656 (CA)).

Individual motives are irrelevant to the proof of the offence. Prior agreement or planning is not necessary. Common purpose may be shown by admissions of the defendant; by evidence of planning; or by the circumstances as a whole, eg the object of the attack or the presence of banners; see s 1(3), "the common purpose may be inferred from conduct".

The common purpose is often an unlawful purpose, but it seems it may also be a lawful purpose. What renders the activity open to condemnation is the use of violence during the course of, or in order to achieve, the common purpose. The purpose must be shown to be common to at least the minimum number of participants (ie twelve). An accurate assessment of the activity upon which the defendant and others were engaged is all that need be shown, and such activity may be stated as the common purpose, eg that they were attempting to prevent the police from gaining access to a particular place, or to use unlawful violence to celebrate a football victory (*R v Jefferson*, above).

Although it may be preferable to state the common purpose in the indictment, in *R v Jefferson*, the Court of Appeal upheld a conviction for riot where the prosecution case establishing the common purpose was clear from the outset, and where the judge summed up on the basis of the alleged common purpose.

3.4 Twelve or More Persons Present Together

The minimum number of persons who must be present together has been increased to twelve from the common law requirement of three. Despite the historical significance in this figure (the Riot Act 1714), it remains somewhat arbitrary, although the large number does indicate the gravity attached to the offence.

The meaning of "present together" is a question of fact for the jury. There must be violence, or the threat of violence, from each of the twelve, although the violence or threats need not be simultaneous (s 1(2)). Where there is sporadic disorder it may be difficult to establish that there were twelve persons present together at the specific time violence was used or threatened. Where there is doubt as to the number of participants or whether they are present together, a charge of violent disorder might be appropriate (provided that three or more can be shown to be present together), or affray, or threatening behaviour contrary to s 4.

Where there are exactly twelve defendants and it is not alleged that there were any more participants then, in the unlikely event of a prosecution, the acquittal of one should inevitably lead to the acquittal of the remainder on the riot charges if the evidence was that there had been exactly twelve participants in the riot and that they were all before the court. Most commonly, the allegation is that some of the participants only are being prosecuted and that others who participated are not before the court.

Where it is alleged that there were more than twelve participants, then the acquittal of one defendant will not be fatal if the jury is satisfied that the overall number involved amounted to twelve or more. This was explored in *R v Beach and Morris* (1909) 2 Cr App Rep 189, a case on the common law. The computation of the number of participants has proved difficult in several reported cases on violent disorder and the principles identified in those cases apply equally to the offence of riot (see page 75).

The *mens rea* required for the offence is not taken into account in the computation of the twelve required (s 6(7)); the prosecution need only show the use or threat of unlawful violence by the other participants.

3.5 Public or Private Place

There is no restriction on the location in which the ingredients of a riot may occur. This affirms the common law approach; see, for example, *Pitchers v Surrey County Council* [1923] 2 KB 57, (1923) 128 LT 337, (1923) 87 JP 39, where the riot occurred in an army camp.

3.6 Mens Rea

Section 6 states the *mens rea* required for all the offences under Part I of the Act. For the purposes of riot, s 6(1) is relevant. Section 6(5) and (6) are common to all the offences. For the application of s 6(7), see page 75. According to the Law Commission's explanatory note to its draft Bill, the effect of s 6(7) is that:

> "when a person is charged with an offence where proof of a number of participants is required . . . the mental element . . . requires to be proved only in relation to that person: the mental element of the other participants . . . is irrelevant."

It follows that the self-induced intoxication of the others is also irrelevant for the purposes of calculating the number present. However, where intoxication is alleged there may be difficulties in establishing a common purpose.

It must be shown that the defendant intended to use violence or that he was aware that his conduct may have been violent. While stressing that *mens rea* is relatively unimportant from a practical point of view, the Law Commission deliberately effected a move away from the view of recklessness as applied in *R v Caldwell* [1982] AC 341, [1981] 2 WLR 509, [1981] 1 All ER 961 (CA), and preferred the approach taken in the case of *R v Cunningham* [1982] AC 566, [1981] 3 WLR 223, [1981] 2 All ER 863. The *mens rea* is therefore either an intention to do the harm, or foresight of the type of harm and a decision to take the risk.

Generally, where awareness is impaired by intoxication, the defendant is taken to have been aware of that of which he would have been aware if he had not been intoxicated (s 6(5)). Where the defendant alleges that the intoxication was not self-induced or was as a result of medical treatment, the burden of proving this is on the defendant, on the balance of probabilities.

Where the defendant is so intoxicated that he cannot form the common purpose necessary, then he is entitled to be acquitted, since, according to the Law Commission, para 6.28:

> "the element of common purpose . . . amounts in substance to a further mental element of intent . . . [I]f there were sufficient evidence to indicate that a defendant accused of riot was too intoxicated to have the common purpose, he could not be found guilty of riot."

In such a case the defendant could, however, be found guilty of violent disorder which does not depend on any element of common purpose.

3.7 Arrest

Riot is an arrestable offence (by virtue of the possible term of imprisonment), and the provisions of the Police and Criminal Evidence Act 1984 apply; see s 24 (arrest without warrant for an arrestable offence) and s 28 (statement of reasons). A statement that arrest is for rioting may be preferable, but an indication that the arrest is for using violence may suffice since it indicates the nature of the offence. In any event, the power at common law to arrest for breach of the peace exists, and a statement that the arrest is for breach of the peace would serve for the time being, although a full statement of reasons and arrest on the charge of riot would have to follow in accordance with the 1984 Act.

3.8 Consent to Prosecutions

Prosecutions for riot or incitement to riot must be by, or with the consent of, the DPP (s 7(1)). Consent is now governed by ss 25 and 26 of the Prosecution of Offences Act 1985 and is effectively a matter for the Crown Prosecution Service. Consent need only be lodged at the court of trial with the clerk and need not be proved (see *R v Dexter* (1899) 19 Cox CC 360, and now s 25 of the 1985 Act). A consent in broad terms, eg where the charge is not specified, is nonetheless sound; see *R v Cain and Schollick* [1976] QB 496, [1975] 3 WLR 131, [1975] 2 All ER 900, where the consent read:

"In pursuance of my powers under the . . . Act I hereby consent to the prosecution of [name of address] for an offence or offences contrary to the provisions of the said Act."

In *R v Pearce* (1981) 72 Cr App R 295, [1981] Crim LR 658, consent in the above form sufficed for a prosecution under s 5A of the 1936 Act but did not constitute consent to prosecution for conspiracy to commit s 5A offences since it did not refer to any Act but the 1936 Act (as amended).

3.9 Trial

A charge of riot is triable only on indictment. The maximum sentence is ten years' imprisonment, a fine or both (s 1(6)).

3.10 Alternative Verdicts

Section 7(3) applies only to violent disorder and affray, and conviction under s 4 as an alternative to riot is not available. Conviction for violent disorder or affray as an alternative to riot may be available in an appropriate case under s 6 of the Criminal Law Act 1967 (see page 79).

3.11 Avoidance of Duplicity

Section 1 is to be treated as creating one offence only (see s 7(2)).

3.12 Dispersal of Rioters

The powers and duties to disperse rioters have already been dealt with (see Chapter 2). At various times there have been calls for the return of the Riot Act 1714. The former Act, repealed in 1967, had long fallen into obsolescence and was a draconian mechanism developed in a time of great emergency, mainly for the purposes of increasing the penalty on conviction for riot to death, and granting an indemnity to peace officers in respect of the use of lethal force in the dispersal of rioters. A specific power to compel dispersal was not created in the 1986 Act, in part because of the practical difficulties in making an appropriate announcement. In the light of the power to make directions under ss 12 and 14 it may be doubted whether this argument alone justifies the absence of a power to order dispersal.

3.13 Riot by Involvement in Other Offences

In *R v Sharp and Johnson* [1957] 1 QB 552, [1957] 2 WLR 472, [1957] 1 All ER 577 (CCA), Lord Goddard remarked that:

> "The term riot is a term of art and, contrary to popular belief, a riot may involve no noise or disturbance of the neighbours though there must be some force or violence. For instance if three men enter a shop and forcibly or by threats steal goods therein technically they are guilty not only of larceny or robbery but also of riot."

In *J W Dwyer Ltd v Metropolitan Police District Receiver* [1967] 2 QB 970, [1967] 3 WLR 731, [1967] 2 All ER 1051 (CA), a case on the Riot (Damages) Act 1886, where four hooded men armed with iron bars raided a jeweller's shop and robbed the owner, it was held that there had been a riot.

Under the terms of the 1986 Act, provided there are sufficient participants, there is no reason why this result should not follow, eg a large gang raid on a warehouse or security van. Violent disorder might also be charged, but with a relatively low maximum penalty, this may not be appropriate.

3.14 Secondary Parties

The general law of aiding and abetting and incitement applies to the offences under ss 1–5 of the Public Order Act 1986 (see *R v Jefferson & Others* [1994] 1 All ER 270, (1994) 99 Cr App R 13, [1993] Crim LR 880). In that case, the Court of Appeal considered that the conclusion that the ordinary law relating to aiding and abetting was unaffected by the 1986 Act was supported by the preparatory material for the 1986 Act, ie the Law Commission Report and the White Paper.

Mere presence at the scene does not suffice for conviction as a secondary party. There must be a sufficient degree of participation or active encouragement (for an extreme example in the public order context see *Devlin v Armstrong* [1972] NI 13, CA); or promotion by words, signs or other actions, supported by an intention to participate or encourage. For the application of the relevant law in other public order cases, see *Allen v Ireland* [1984] 1 WLR 903, (1984) 128 SJ 482, (1984) 79 Cr App R 206 (DC), a case on s 4 of the 1986 Act.

3.15 Riot under Other Legislation

Riot and cognate expressions occur in numerous statutes. The effect of s 10 of the 1986 Act is clear with regard to the Acts specified, ie the Riot Damages Act 1886, the Merchant Shipping Act 1894 and the Marine Insurance Act 1906. Thus in the first two Acts the words "riotous" and "riotously" are construed in accordance with s 1. In the third Act, policies are construed in accordance with s 1 unless the contrary intention appears. In marine insurance policies, the word "riot" bears the meaning given to it by the common law so that the provisions of s 1 are now appropriate. In *The Andreas Lemos* [1983] QB 647, [1983] 2 WLR 425, [1983] 1 All ER 590, Staughten J construed the word "riot" in an insurance policy according to the common law. Thus, a clandestine theft was not a riot and "nobody but a Sloane Ranger would say . . . 'it was a riot'".

The effect on other legislation is less clear. It appears that most legislation is construed in accordance with the common law view of riot and is therefore now to be interpreted in the light of s 1. Examples would be the Licensing Act 1964, the Representation of the People Act 1983 and the Ecclesiastical Courts Jurisdiction Act 1860.

The Riot (Damages) Act 1886 provides a scheme for compensation in respect of damage to property flowing from riots. In the case of personal injury a claim might be made under the Criminal Injuries Compensation scheme. The 1886 Act replaced earlier Acts which had themselves consolidated and amended the laws relating to remedies against "the hundred". The Act deals only with injury to property, ie "house, shop or building", and property therein. Motor cars in the street would not be within the scope of the Act.

To fall within the terms of the 1886 Act, the assembly must be not only riotous but also tumultuous. A crime of stealth is not covered: *J W Dwyer Ltd v Metropolitan Police District Receiver* (above), referred to in *D H Edmonds Ltd v East Sussex Police Authority, The Times* 15 July 1988 (CA), as "an instance of a quiet riot". According to *Dwyer*, there must be rioters:

> "in such numbers and in such a state of agitated commotion and . . . generally so acting, that the forces of law and order should have been well aware of the threat which existed . . .".

"Riotous" and "tumultuous" are not the same thing. Although not spelled out by the court in the *Edmonds* case, there must be substantial noise; a substantial number of participants (inherent now in the definition of "riot"); an open, not secret, gathering; an assembly over a considerable period of time; and widespread commotion from those involved in the riot.

The Act provides for a form of contributory negligence. Where the applicant provoked or contributed to the riot or his own loss, the compensation may be reduced. The procedures for claiming are governed by regulation (see the Riot (Damages) (Amendment) Regulations 1986, SI 1986 No 36) and the claim should be made to the relevant police authority, or the receiver in the Metropolitan Police District.

4   Violent Disorder

Checklist

- three or more persons who are present together use or threaten unlawful

violence;
- common purpose irrelevant;
- would the conduct have caused a person of reasonable firmness present at the scene to fear for his personal safety?
- did the defendant use or threaten unlawful violence?
- location is irrelevant;
- did the defendant intend to use or threaten violence, or was he aware that his conduct may be violent or may threaten violence;
- triable on indictment or summarily;
- an arrestable offence.

4.1 Definition

Violent disorder is the successor to the common law offence of unlawful assembly. The offence of unlawful assembly was generally regarded as made out where there was "an assembly of three or more persons with a common purpose either to commit a crime of violence or to achieve any other object, lawful or not, in such a way as to cause a reasonable man to apprehend a breach of the peace".

When considering the replacement of unlawful assembly, the government chose not to follow the recommendation of the Law Commission to create two offences, one of which (using violence) would be triable on indictment, while the other (threatening violence) would be triable summarily. Under the Act both those who use, and those who threaten, unlawful violence may be tried for the same offence and jointly. It is upon sentence that distinctions may be drawn between levels and manner of involvement.

Section 2(1), POA 1986, states:

"Where three or more persons who are present together use or threaten unlawful violence and the conduct of them (taken together) is such as would cause a person of reasonable firmness present at the scene to fear for his personal safety, each of the persons using or threatening unlawful violence is guilty of violent disorder."

The new offence differs from the common law in one important respect: it lacks the element of common purpose. It relies on the fear of an individual for his personal safety where that fear is induced by actual use or threats of violence. Assembled individuals who intend either to commit a crime by open force, or to further a common purpose by methods which would cause apprehension of breaches of the peace, do not commit the offence of violent disorder. Previously, such an assembly would have been an unlawful assembly. This may be of importance where there is evidence of an assembly at which is planned a series of attacks on different targets one after another, but the participants are prevented by arrest from carrying out any or all of the attacks; here the offence of violent disorder is not constituted.

An allegation of violent disorder commonly amounts to an allegation of affray where the assertion is that the violence was used or threatened towards another person and the threats are not made by words alone.

4.2 At Least Three Persons

There must be at least three persons present together. There is no need to establish a common purpose, although it must be possible to say that the participants were "present together". This seems to be a requirement for at least knowledge of each other's presence, but it is not a requirement that they should be acting in concert. In most cases there is no difficulty in establishing that the participants are present together, eg a gang of youths on a street corner hurling missiles at a police car or bus. In some cases the facts may not allow of such easy interpretation, eg sporadic violence or threats from a few people in a large crowd. In such instances charges of threatening behaviour contrary to s 4 would be appropriate or, in extreme instances, affray contrary to s 3. As to difficulties of computation, see below.

The use or threats of violence need not be simultaneous (s 2(2)), but there must presumably be something more than sporadic or infrequent acts or threats of violence. Sporadic acts or threats of violence are unlikely to generate the degree of fear necessary to establish the offence.

Unlike riot, both those who threaten and those who use unlawful violence are guilty of violent disorder.

Computation of the Number

For the purposes of riot and violent behaviour the mental element required by s 6(1) and s 6(2) of the 1986 Act respectively "does not affect the determination for the purposes of riot or violent disorder of the number of persons who use or threaten unlawful violence" (s 6(7)). It may be possible to envisage circumstances where a participant, whether or not he is also a defendant, uses or threatens violence but does not have the relevant mental element of intending to use violence or of being aware that his conduct may be violent. In such a case, that person may be counted in for the purposes of riot and violent disorder, but as a defendant he could not be convicted, subject to the provisions of s 6(5) and (6), which deal with the effect of intoxication.

Given the unlikelihood of this situation, the more frequent suggestion is that among the participants some were using or threatening not unlawful, but lawful, violence, eg in self-defence, and were intending so to act. If such an account is accepted, it reduces the numbers who may be counted in, and in a marginal case may reduce the number below the relevant threshold.

There has been a number of cases dealing with this difficult issue. In *R v Mahroof* (1989) 88 Cr App R 317 (CA), the particulars in the indictment read:

"EB, AM and TS on the 29th day of June 1987 being present together did use or threaten unlawful violence and the conduct of them was such as would cause a person of reasonable firmness present at the scene to fear for his personal safety."

Both EB and TS were acquitted of violent disorder and the jury did not convict on s 4 (see s 7(3), below). Evidence was given during the trial that two unnamed individuals had also been present at the scene and had participated. The judge directed the jury that they had to consider each defendant separately but at the same time to bear in mind the need to convict only if they were satisfied that there had been three persons using or threatening unlawful violence.

The Court of Appeal concluded that, subject to two important qualifications, the indictment contained a sufficient allegation despite the omission of any reference to the involvement of others. The qualifications were that there should be evidence of the involvement of others in the unlawful violence, and that the defence should be properly informed of any allegations which they would have to meet. In *R v Mahroof*, the second qualification had not been met. The Court of Appeal observed that the most obvious way to inform the defence is to make the allegation clear in the indictment.

In *R v Fleming and Robinson* (1989) 153 JP 517, [1989] Crim LR 658, (1989) 153 JPN 530, the allegation was that only four persons had been involved in a fight. Two were convicted, one was acquitted and in respect of the remaining one the jury failed to agree. The Court of Appeal concluded that, subject to very rare instances of someone present using or threatening unlawful violence, but not having the relevant *mens rea*, the conviction could not stand. There was no one else present who could be counted in as the necessary third person. The Court of Appeal observed that:

"On a charge under s 2 of the Public Order Act 1986, where the only persons against whom there is evidence of using or threatening unlawful violence are those named in the indictment, the jury should be specifically directed that if it cannot be sure that three or more of the defendants were using or threatening violence, then it should acquit every defendant even if satisfied that one or more particular defendants were unlawfully fighting."

R v Mahroof and *R v Fleming and Robinson* were applied in *R v Worton* (1990) 154 JP 201, [1990] Crim LR 124 (CA). In this case there was evidence of participation in violence by a large number. Of the four charged with violent disorder only three were tried, and of these one was acquitted. The evidence of participation by others meant that *R v Fleming and Robinson* could be distinguished and that the first qualification in *R v Mahroof* was satisfied. The second qualification in *R v Mahroof* was satisfied since the defence had been apprised, by the way the evidence was led, of the allegation that others were involved. The Court of Appeal upheld the appeal against conviction on the basis that in the circumstances the trial judge misdirected the jury. He had to do more than describe the offence in general terms; he had to:

". . . go on and warn the jury specifically that if any of the three defendants should be acquitted of violent disorder, then they must necessarily acquit the other two, unless satisfied that some other person not charged was taking part in the violent disorder."

In *R v McGuigan and Cameron* [1991] Crim LR 719, the Court of Appeal made it clear that a direction from the judge, that aiders and abetters might be counted in for the purposes of violent disorder, amounted to a misdirection. Before a person can be guilty of aiding and abetting, the prosecution must show that the substantive offence has been committed, and that requires at least three independent participants using or threatening unlawful violence. If two persons use or threaten unlawful violence, a third person cannot, by aiding and abetting them, render them guilty of violent disorder.

4.3   Unlawful Violence

"Unlawful violence" has the meaning attributed to it in s 8, and is discussed in greater depth at page 61 above. For the purposes of violent disorder, violence includes violent conduct towards property as well as the person. Violent conduct does not necessarily involve injury or damage, and throwing a missile will suffice.

4.4   Person of Reasonable Firmness Present

This has been discussed generally at page 64 above. No such person need actually be on the scene or likely to come on the scene. The "hypothetical bystander" is simply the standpoint from which the relevant degree of violence is to be established.

4.5   Private or Public Place

As with riot and affray, the offence may be committed in either a public or a private place (s 2(4)), eg in a public house, on a road or at a private party. There is no reason why the offence should not be committed in a dwelling house, although it would be necessary carefully to consider whether it would be proper to charge violent disorder in relation to a purely domestic incident occurring within a dwelling house. By way of contrast, offences contrary to ss 4 and 5 do not normally extend to conduct occurring in a dwelling house.

4.6   Mens Rea

See generally page 70 *et seq* above. For violent disorder the *mens rea* required is:

"6(2) A person is guilty of violent disorder or affray only if he intends to use or threaten violence or is aware that his conduct may be violent or threaten violence. . .

(5)   For the purposes of this section a person whose awareness is impaired by intoxication shall be taken to be aware of that of which he would be aware if not intoxicated, unless he shows either that his intoxication was not self-induced or that it was caused solely by the taking or administration of a substance in the course of

medical treatment.

(6) In subsection (5) "intoxication" means any intoxication, whether caused by drink, drugs or other means, or by a combination of means."

4.7   Secondary Parties
See page 72.

4.8   Continuing Offence
Unlawful assembly was a continuing offence, and the offending activity might have been one event or a series of acts taking place in different locations, provided always that the common intention was not lost. In *R v Jones* (1974) 59 Cr App R 120 it was suggested that a count in an indictment disclosed more than one offence since it, and further particulars, referred to several sites at which similar incidents of violence occurred on the same day. The defence suggested that the incidents at each site were isolated and separated from each other by journeys and meal breaks during which no violence took place. The court rejected this:

> ". . . The ingredients of the offence are (i) the *actus reus* of coming together and (ii) the *mens rea* involved in the intention of fulfilling a common purpose in such a manner as to endanger the public peace. These ingredients have to be co-existent. There is nothing . . . which indicates that, at any time between the arrival at Shrewsbury and the departure from Telford, those charged with the offence ceased to be an assembly or ceased to have the intent of making an unlawful assembly."

With the statutory relaxation of the common law requirement of assembly for a common purpose, a different conclusion would now be reached. Separate counts for each such incident would have to be preferred in cases like *R v Jones* since each of the incidents would be separated by a period of inactivity during which no bystander would be put in fear.

In cases of public disorder, which may comprise distinct episodes over a prolonged period, there is a danger that the jury may convict without having achieved unanimity (or majority if relevant) in respect of either the defendant's participation or the necessary level of violence in a particular incident. There may be a danger that a jury will convict on different bases. Where there is such a danger it is appropriate for the judge to give a direction consistent with the requirement in *R v Brown (Kevin)* (1984) 79 Cr App R 115, [1984] Crim LR 167 (CA). The point arose in *R v Houlden* (1994) 99 Cr App R 244 (CA), where there were three separate incidents amounting to what the Crown argued was an offence of violent disorder. The judge failed to direct the jury that they had to be sure that at least one of the incidents involved the defendant and that it amounted to violent disorder, and that the jury had to be agreed about the same and not different incidents. In *R v Keeton* [1995] 2 Cr App R 241, *The Times* 21 July 1994 (CA), there was only one incident which was alleged to be capable of giving rise to an offence of violent disorder, and the jury had been properly directed that they had to be satisfied as to that specific incident. Accordingly there was no need to give a *Brown* direction.

For an example arising from affray see page 84.

4.9 Arrest

Violent disorder is an arrestable offence by virtue of the possible sentence (see s 2(5)), and the powers to arrest without warrant under s 24 of the Police and Criminal Evidence Act 1984 apply. The appropriate statement of reasons required by s 28 of the Police and Criminal Evidence Act 1984 should refer to violent disorder, although it may be that the use of the word "violence" would adequately indicate to the defendant the reasons for the arrest. Since the offence contains the elements of a breach of the peace, an arrest or other preventive action would be permissible.

4.10 Avoidance of Duplicity

Although s 2 may be read as creating two offences, s 7(2) provides that for relevant purposes it is to be treated as creating one offence only.

4.11 Trial and Alternative Verdicts

Violent disorder is triable on indictment (with a maximum penalty of five years' imprisonment) or summarily (maximum penalty, six months' imprisonment, a fine or both) (s 2(5)). As to mode of trial, the Practice Note [1990] 3 All ER 979, which provides guidance, not direction, to magistrates deciding on mode of trial for offences triable either way, concludes that cases of violent disorder should generally be committed for trial.

The National Mode of Trial Guidelines were produced in 1990 and updated in 1994 to reflect case law developments. Essentially, until 1994, mode of trial had been important in the sense that if a case was retained in the magistrates' court, it could not subsequently be sent to the Crown Court for sentence under s 38 of the Magistrates' Courts Act 1980 unless the character and antecedents of the defendant called for a greater sentence than the magistrates had power to impose. The problem arose in cases where, at the mode of trial stage, the magistrates underestimated the gravity of the case, kept it in the magistrates' court and then, after trial, realised its true seriousness. In such a case, if the defendant had no previous convictions, the court could not commit to the Crown Court for sentence.

The 1995 guidelines reflect the terms of s 25 of the Criminal Justice Act 1991 in relation to committals for sentence (see *R v Sheffield Crown Court & Sheffield Stipendiary Magistrate ex p DPP* (1994) 158 JP 334, (1994) 158 JPN 274; *R v North Sefton Magistrates' Court ex p Marsh* [1994] Crim LR 865, (1995) 159 JP 9, [1995] COD 27 (QBD); and *R v Dover Magistrates' Court ex p Pamment* (1994) 15 Cr App R(S) 778, (1994) 158 JP

665, [1994] COD 292 (QBD). It is now established that there is no need to review the character of the defendant before committing for sentence. It is sufficient if, at any time, the magistrates feel the offence is so serious that their sentencing powers are inadequate. Essentially, now, if an error has been made on determination of mode of trial, the court is able to remedy it by committing a convicted defendant to the Crown Court for sentence.

A person tried on indictment may, if found not guilty of violent disorder, be found guilty of an offence under s 4 (s 7(3)), and punished accordingly (s 7(4)). Section 6(3) of the Criminal Law Act 1967, which also allows for alternative verdicts, is unaffected by s 7. See further page 87.

4.12 The Policy

Both the Law Commission and the Government in its White Paper indicated their views of prosecution policy and, in the light of the large degree of overlap between the offences in ss 2–5, their comments remain significant:

"Of course, not every case in which three or more people participate in the specified conduct will necessarily be regarded as appropriate to be dealt with under this offence. Prosecutors may well feel that some cases are not sufficiently serious to warrant proceedings for a 'combination' offence and that this offence will be appropriate for use only when the extra gravity of the circumstances of the group's conduct is such as to justify prosecution for such an offence." (Law Commission, para 5.29)

"Like the Law Commission, the Government anticipates that it will be used in the future as the normal charge for serious outbreaks of public disorder. But it will be capable of being applied over a wide spectrum of situations ranging from major public disorder to minor group disturbances involving some violence. The proposal to make it triable either way will give it a useful degree of flexibility for dealing with lesser outbreaks of group violence, such as those commonly associated with football hooliganism." (White Paper, para 3.13)

5   Affray

Checklist

- may be committed by one person alone;
- did the defendant use or threaten unlawful violence towards another?
- threats of unlawful violence cannot be by words alone;
- the conduct of a group as a whole must be considered;
- common purpose irrelevant;
- would the conduct have caused a person of reasonable firmness present at the scene to fear for his personal safety?
- location is irrelevant;
- did the defendant intend to use or threaten violence or was he aware that his conduct may be violent or may threaten violence?

- triable on indictment or summarily;
- limited power of arrest.

5.1 Definition

The common law offence of affray consisted of unlawful fighting or display of force in such a manner that a person of reasonably firm character might be likely to be terrified. Although charges of affray had dwindled, there was a rejuvenation in the 1950s. The Law Commission observed:

"Affray is typically charged in cases of pitched street battles between rival gangs, spontaneous fights in public houses, clubs and at seaside resorts, and revenge attacks on individuals. It is sometimes charged on its own, but is often accompanied by charges of one or more offences, most of them falling within the general rubric of offences against the person."

The higher courts emphasised that there should be a high degree of fear and that this requirement should not be watered down. The retention of an offence of affray which reflects much of the common law marks the seriousness of the offence, not so much because of the extent of the injuries inflicted but rather because of the nature of the offence, ie the participation in acts of violence causing alarm and terror to the public. The government was able to accept the recommendations of the Law Commission and to give effect to them in the POA 1986.

Although affray is said to be essentially an offence against public order and not an offence against the person, it is capable of being a species of the latter. Unless the governing factor of the violence needed to threaten a hypothetical bystander is rigorously and realistically applied, then the offence will certainly lose its character as an offence against public order. On occasions, the higher courts have cautioned against inappropriately charging affray and have cited two reasons. First, an allegation of affray tends to introduce complexity and legal difficulty into what are often very simple events, and this may tend to confuse or distract the jury. Secondly, it is bad practice to charge simple assault cases as public order offences: see *R v Davison* [1992] Crim LR 33 (CA) and *R v Connor,* 13 March 2000, unreported (CA). The House of Lords has commented upon the increasing tendency to charge the offence of affray; see *I and Others v DPP, The Times* 9 March 2001.

Section 3(1) POA 1986 states:

"A person is guilty of affray if he uses or threatens unlawful violence towards another and his conduct is such as would cause a person of reasonable firmness present at the scene to fear for his personal safety."

5.2 Unlawful Violence Towards Another

A person must use or threaten unlawful violence; see above, pages 59 and 63. For the purposes of affray, the word "violence" does not include violence to property (s 8). In *Cobb v DPP* (1992) 156 JP 746, (1992) 156 JPN 330 (DC), an information alleging affray referred to the threat or use of violence "by causing damage to property, fighting and assaulting C". The reference to causing damage to property was irrelevant and immaterial to the charge of affray, and did not vitiate the charge.

The unlawful violence must be used or threatened "towards another"; violence offered to passers-by generally would be sufficient; there is no reason why the victim should be restricted to the singular. The phrase "towards another" is found in s 4 and it suggests that the defendant must be aware of, or perhaps reckless as to, the presence of the other person or persons.

Relying on the Law Commission Report, the House of Lords has confirmed that, as under s 4 of the Act (see page 94 and *Atkin v DPP* (1989) 89 Cr App R 199, [1989] Crim LR 581, (1989) 153 JP 383 (DC)), there must not only be another person actually present but it must be possible to say that the violence was used or threatened against that person, ie the offence requires a victim; see *I and Others v DPP* (above). In that case, the defendants were in possession of petrol bombs (without brandishing them), and when a police carrier drew up, they discarded the bombs. The defendants did not thereby use or threaten unlawful violence towards either the police officers or anyone else. It is not sufficient that the threats are made in respect of or concerning someone not present at the scene.

Although there must be a victim (in the sense of a person towards whom violence has been used or threatened), a participating opponent in a fight would suffice for these purposes. But any fear actually induced in the victim (or other participant) does not replace the fear of the hypothetical reasonable bystander as the gauge of the violence. Instead, the reaction of the participants will be one of the matters to be taken into account in assessing the likely impact on the hypothetical reasonable bystander (see above and *R v Sanchez* (1996) 160 JP 321, [1996] Crim LR 572 (CA)). How such a hypothetical reasonable bystander would react is a matter for the arbiters of fact.

Possession of a Weapon
The circumstances in which possession of an item may amount to a threat of unlawful violence was discussed in *I and Others v DPP* (above). The brandishing of a weapon, whether or not accompanied by words, suffices for the purposes of affray as a threat of unlawful violence but, of course, in addition, the threats must be made towards another person present at the scene (see page 64). In *I and Others*, a group of youths carrying primed petrol bombs congregated outside a residential block. When the police arrived, the group dispersed and discarded the bombs. Applying the common law cases (*R v Sharp and Johnson* [1957] 1 QB 552, [1957] 2 WLR 472, [1957] 1 All ER 577 (CCA) and *R v Taylor* (1992) 13 Cr App R(S) 466), the House of Lords held that the carrying of dangerous weapons such as petrol bombs can in law constitute a threat of violence. Whether or not in any particular case it does so is a matter of fact for all the circumstances. Thus, in this particular case, the visible carrying in public of primed petrol bombs by a gang out for no

good was capable of amounting to threats of violence. On the other hand, the mere possession of a weapon is insufficient without these aggravating features.

In respect of the carrying of weapons it may be apt to prefer a charge under a statutory provision designed for the purpose, such as s 1 of the Prevention of Crime Act 1953.

Words Alone

Threats of unlawful violence cannot be made by words alone (s 3(3): "a threat cannot be made by words alone"). This reflects the approach of the common law (*R v Sharp and Johnson* (above); *Taylor v DPP* [1973] AC 964, [1973] 3 WLR 140, [1973] 2 All ER 1108 (HL)). Care in summing up is needed to avoid inadvertent suggestions that words alone might be sufficient to constitute the offence; for example in *R v Robinson* [1993] Crim LR 581 (CA), a reference by the judge to spoken words was probably not enough of itself to amount to a misdirection. It would seem to be appropriate for the judge to direct the jury in every case that a threat cannot, for these purposes, be made by words alone: see *R v Dackers*, 23 November 2000, unreported (CA).

In *R v Cullen* (1984) 51 Cr App R 17, [1985] Crim LR 107 (CA), the defendant was alleged to have thrown a coin at a police officer causing injury, and to have shouted abuse. The jury acquitted of assault occasioning actual bodily harm but convicted of affray. The judge had directed the jury to the effect that the ". . . throwing of a coin, if that is proved, and any words used by the defendant would cause a person . . . to fear for his safety". The Court of Appeal held that, bearing in mind the inconsistent verdicts, the direction had indicated to the jury that it was open to them to convict on the basis of words alone.

In *R v Robinson*, there was no evidence of anything other than words alone, even where the context was that the manner in which they were spoken was aggressive and the atmosphere tense, and the events occurred in the middle of the night.

In *R v Dixon* [1993] Crim LR 580 (CA), two police officers cornered the defendant and his Alsatian dog on the driveway of a house. The dog was in an excitable state, barking and snarling. The defendant told the dog "go on, go on" repeatedly. The dog bit the police officers and returned to the defendant, who said "go on, kill", whereupon the police officers retired to a safe distance to await assistance. The defendant denied affray on the basis, *inter alia*, that the threat was verbal only and that there was no evidence that the dog had responded to his words or had been trained to respond. The prosecution case was based on events leading up to but excluding the biting of the police officers.

The Court of Appeal held that the defendant had been properly convicted of affray. It was not the prosecution case that the dog had responded to the words, but that the words constituting the threats had been issued while the dog was in an excitable state and as a means of using the dog to create fear. Even on this view, it is not easy to see what the defendant did except for speaking words. It seems possible that the case may be viewed as an example of the use of violence deriving from the context as a whole.

5.3 A Group

Where a group is involved, an individual defendant is still guilty of affray even if his own actions taken alone would not amount to an offence, eg by not causing the necessary degree of terror. It is the conduct of the group as a whole, and the terror which is induced by that conduct, which must be considered. Section 3(2) states that:

> "Where two or more persons use or threaten the unlawful violence, it is the conduct of them taken together that must be considered for the purposes of subsection (1)."

5.4 Sequence of Events

Although affray is not strictly a continuing offence, often the conduct amounting to an affray derives from a more or less continuous sequence of events, some of which may have the necessary character of terrifying the hypothetical reasonable bystander and some of which may not. In this type of instance it is important for the prosecution to demonstrate the overall impact of the behaviour, rather than that each separate element had the necessary character.

On the other hand, where it is possible to distinguish separate sequences or episodes then different considerations arise. Here the prosecution should make clear which episodes are being relied upon and the judge should direct the jury on the need to be satisfied, in respect of the same incident or incidents, that the conduct had the necessary character and that the defendant was involved.

Similar considerations may arise in respect of the other serious offences (see page 78 and the cases of *R v Houlden* (1994) 99 Cr App R 244 (CA) and *R v Keeton* [1995] 2 Cr App R 241, *The Times* 21 July 1994 (CA)). In the context of affray Lord Bingham CJ observed, in *R v Smith (Paul Dennis)* (1994) 15 C App R(S) 106 (CA):

> "[Affray] typically involves a group of people who may well be shouting, struggling, threatening, waving weapons, throwing objects, exchanging and threatening blows and so on. Again, typically it involves a continuous course of conduct, the criminal character of which depends on the general nature and effect of the conduct as a whole and not on particular incidents and events which may take place in the course of it. Where reliance is placed on such a continuous course of conduct it is not necessary for the Crown to identify and prove particular incidents. To require such proof would deprive section 3(1) of the 1986 Act of its in-

tended effect, and deprive law-abiding citizens of the protection which this provision intends that they should enjoy. It would be asking the impossible to require a jury . . . to be satisfied beyond reasonable doubt that each or any incident in an indiscriminate mêlée such as constitutes the typical affray was proved to the requisite standard.

Different considerations may, however, arise where the conduct which is alleged to constitute an affray is not continuous but falls into separate sequences. The character of the conduct relied on in each sequence may in such a case be quite different and so may the effect on persons who are (or might hypothetically be) present at the scene. The possibility then arises that half the jury may be persuaded that the first sequence amounted to an affray and the second did not, and the other half of the jury may be persuaded that the second sequence amounted to an affray and the first did not. The result would then be that there was no unanimous jury verdict in support of conviction based on either sequence."

5.5   Secondary Parties
See page 72.

5.6   Private and Public Places
The offence may be committed in public and in private, according to s 3(5), which reflects the common law.

5.7   Person of Reasonable Firmness Present
See generally page 64. Neither the actual nor the likely presence of a person of reasonable firmness need be shown (s 3(4)). This confirms the approach of the common law to attacks in public places (see *Attorney General's Reference (No 3 of 1983)* [1985] QB 242, [1985] 2 WLR 253, [1985] 1 All ER 501 (CA)), although it is wider than the common law approach to violence in a private place where it had to be shown that a person was likely to come across the violence.

Since the offence may be committed by one person only it would be possible to convict of affray in a wide variety of instances, eg an attack by a youth on his parents in the home. Whether it would be proper to bring a charge of affray on such an occasion is another issue; see the comments at page 81. The Law Commission remarked:

". . . it seems unlikely . . . that a personal quarrel between two people involving mutual assaults without the danger of the involvement of others . . . would fall within the offence . . . such incidents can hardly be said to give rise to the serious disturbance to public order with which the offence is intended to deal." (para 3.38).

5.8 *Mens Re*a

See page 70.

5.9 *Arrest*

Affray is not an arrestable offence since it does not fall with the criteria in s 24 of the Police and Criminal Evidence Act 1984. There is, however, a power for a constable to arrest without warrant (s 3(6)), which power is expressed in limited terms. It is restricted to arrest on reasonable suspicion that the person is committing affray. In *Dhesi v Chief Constable of the West Midlands Police, The Times* 9 May 2000, the Court of Appeal, without reference to authority, adopted a broad approach to the phrase. It is essentially a question of fact whether or not it can properly be said that an affray has terminated, but it should be borne in mind that, commonly, the facts underpinning an affray may span a considerable period of time.

A similar point on the continuous conduct underpinning an affray was made in *R v Smith* [1998] 1 Cr App R 14, although this was in a different context, see page 84.

Where the activity has terminated then there is no power to arrest without warrant unless the general arrest conditions in s 25 of the Police and Criminal Evidence Act 1984 apply, as they might in cases where there is a need to prevent further violence or damage from a recurrence of the affray or by way of retaliation. A statement of reasons using the words "affray" or "violence or threat of violence" would be sufficient to explain the ground for the arrest where it is arrest for affray.

The common law power to arrest or restrain to prevent apprehended breaches of the peace would be available in appropriate circumstances, eg if a renewal was feared (see page 35); again the appropriate words would be required.

5.10 *Trial*

Affray is triable either way with a maximum sentence following trial on indictment of three years or a fine or both (s 3(7)). As to mode of trial, see the Practice Note (above) in which it is concluded that cases of affray should be committed for trial at the Crown Court only where they involve:

(1) organised violence or use of weapons;

(2) significant injury or substantial damage;

(3) clear racial motivations; or

(4) an attack on police officers, ambulancemen, firemen or the like.

The list is not exhaustive and is subject to the general proviso that the courts' sentencing powers are felt to be insufficient. Additional factors which may influence the mode of trial decision might be the complexity of the evidence; the fact that the trial may last a substantial time; a large number of defendants; the likelihood that issues of self-defence may be raised; and violence which was extreme or premeditated or not spontaneous. In these cases trial on indictment may be appropriate (see also *R v Crimlis* [1976] Crim LR 693). In other cases summary trial may be appropriate.

The possibility of summary trial enables the prosecution both to indicate the nature of the violence and to draw a clear distinction between that conduct and conduct within s 4. There is a large degree of overlap between ss 4 and 3, and in some instances a charge under s 3 will be appropriate. At the same time, a trial on indictment might seem too heavy-handed and yet a charge under s 4 might not reflect the degree of criminality. In this instance a charge under s 3 and summary trial would be appropriate.

The general considerations at page 79 are relevant to committal for sentence after conviction for affray.

5.11 Avoidance of Duplicity

Section 3 might be read as creating two offences. To avoid doubt or difficulties, s 7(2) provides that for relevant purposes it creates only one offence. Once the fighting ceases, the offence terminates. Should fighting recommence, then a new offence starts. Should the fighting spill from one place to another without ceasing, then one offence only is committed (see *R v Woodrow, Cooper and Harrington* (1959) 43 Cr App R 105 (CCA)).

6 Alternative Verdicts

A person tried on indictment for an offence of violent disorder or affray, may, if found not guilty, be found guilty of an offence under s 4 (using threatening, abusive or insulting words or behaviour etc (POA 1986 s 7(3); see Chapter 4), and may be punished accordingly (s 7(4)). For s 4 see page 93. There are material differences between the serious offences and the offence in s 4. In particular, for the purposes of s 4 there is no test of the (hypothetical) reasonably firm person present at the scene. And, although the serious offences may be committed in any place, public or private, including a dwelling house, the offence in s 4 cannot be committed in a dwelling house.

Section 7(3) is expressed to be without prejudice to s 6(3) of the Criminal Law Act 1967. On trials on indictment, except murder and treason, s 6(3) of the 1967 Act permits the jury, if it finds the accused not guilty, to find him guilty of an alternative offence which is within the jurisdiction of the trial court (see *R v Collison* (1980) 71 Cr App R 249, [1980] Crim LR 591 (CA)). The allegations in the indictment must amount to or include (expressly or by implication) an allegation of the alternative offence (see also *R v Wilson, R v Jenkins* [1984] AC 242, [1983] 3 WLR 686, [1983] 3 All ER 448 (HL)).

It has been held that s 6(3) of the 1967 Act is unaffected by s 7 (*R v O'Brien (David)* (1992) 156 JP 925, [1993] Crim LR 70, (1992) 156 JPN 538 (CA)). Section 6(3) continues to be relevant to the serious public order offences, since in appropriate circumstances it permits someone charged with riot or violent disorder to be found guilty in the alternative of affray, even where the jury was not specifically directed on the alternative charge (see *R v Fleming and Robinson* (1989) 153 JP 517, [1989] Crim LR 658, (1989) 153 JPN 530 (CA)); or someone charged with riot to be found guilty in the alternative of violent disorder. The Court of Appeal, on an appeal against conviction, may substitute an offence under s 3 for that of which the jury convicted under s 2 (see *R v Fleming and Robinson*).

When applying the general law to the serious public order cases in particular, there may be instances where it is not possible to substitute a conviction on one serious offence for another. In *R v McGuigan and Cameron* [1991] Crim LR 719 (CA), the defendant was acquitted on a charge of violent disorder, but the conviction was overturned on appeal on the basis that there had not been three or more persons involved (see page 75). A conviction for affray could not be substituted because the circumstances of the violence included violence directed at property. Accordingly, it would have been wrong to conclude that the jury must have been satisfied that the appellant had used or threatened violence to the person. For the same reason, conviction for the lesser offence contrary to s 4 could not be substituted under s 7(3) of the Public Order Act 1986.

The importance of s 7(3) is that it permits the summary offence under s 4 of the 1986 Act to be dealt with by a court trying a charge on indictment, contrary to the expectation in s 6(3) of the 1967 Act. Section 7(3) applies where the jury, of its own volition, having considered the evidence, has found the defendant not guilty, or where it has been directed by the judge to acquit (*R v Carson* (1991) 92 Cr App R 236, (1990) 154 JP 794, [1990] Crim LR 729 (CA)).

Where a defendant on arraignment, without pleading to the indictment alleging affray or violent disorder, has tendered a plea of guilty to a s 4 offence, that plea may be accepted under s 6(1) of the Criminal Law Act 1967 and there is no need for a jury to be empanelled (*R v O'Brien*, above). If the plea is unacceptable to the prosecution, then it is deemed to have been withdrawn (*R v Hazeltine* [1967] 2 QB 857, [1967] 3 WLR 209, [1967] 2 All ER 671 (CA); *R v Notman* [1994] Crim LR 518 (CA)). Where the plea of guilty has been withdrawn, as in *R v Notman*, then a jury which acquits of the offence contrary to s 2, or s 3, can convict of an offence contrary to s 4 only where it has been directed on the elements of s 4 and told that it was open to it to convict; or where the defendant has made a formal admission of an offence contrary to s 4 (*R v Notman*).

A direction to a jury on an indictment alleging violent disorder, which properly dealt with the issue of the unlawfulness of violence in respect of violent disorder, and affray as an alternative verdict, but which failed to emphasise unlawfulness in respect of the violence necessary to support the alternative of threatening behaviour, was a material misdirection. Accordingly, a conviction for the alternative of threatening behaviour was quashed (*R v*

Afzal (1992) 13 Cr App (S) 145, [1991] Crim LR 722, *The Times* 25 June 1991 (CA)). On the other hand, a failure to direct the jury properly on the issue of the intent required in order to convict of threatening behaviour as an alternative to affray, but where the direction on affray was correct, was not a material irregularity and appeal against conviction was dismissed (*R v Stanley and Knight* [1993] Crim LR 618 (CA)). The jury had been properly told to consider the alternative only if it acquitted of affray.

Where the offence in respect of which there has been an acquittal or in respect of which an appeal is upheld, involves violence to property, it may not always be possible to substitute a conviction under s 7(3) since the offence under s 4 involves using towards another person threatening, abusive or insulting words or behaviour (*R v McGuigan and Cameron,* above).

Alternative verdicts are not available in magistrates' courts, although it is permissible, within the guidelines laid down by the House of Lords in *Chief Constable of Norfolk v Clayton* [1983] 2 AC 473, [1983] 2 WLR 555 [1983] 1 All ER 984 (HL), for a magistrates' court to try two or more informations charging different offences.

Chapter 4

Summary Offences and Racial Hatred

This chapter deals with ss 4, 4A and 5 of the Public Order Act ("POA") 1986, the racially aggravated public order offences under the Crime and Disorder Act 1998, and provisions relating to racial hatred. It also deals with harassment and malicious communications. Section 4A of the POA 1986 (enacted by the Criminal Justice and Public Order Act 1994) increased the maximum penalty for what would previously have been an offence under s 5 POA, when committed with intent, thereby creating the danger that in cases where intent is demonstrated, s 5 will fall into disuse in favour of s 4A, for which imprisonment is available.

1   The Summary Offences under the Public Order Act
The Human Rights Act impacts on summary public order offences both at trial and on appeal. Disclosure issues need careful analysis by the courts when setting down for trial. In public order cases, the names of witnesses are sometimes confirmed by the police without statements being taken. Such names should be made available to defendants who require them to pursue their own enquiries. Video tapes and CCTV footage should be treated with particular care. It is not sufficient to rely on a police officer's word that he has seen the video/CCTV and that there was nothing relevant on it. If it exists, it has to be made available to the defendant: *DPP v Chipping (David Frederick)*, 11 January 1999, unreported (QBD). In that case an abuse of process argument was upheld after the disappearance of "not relevant" video footage. Summary only non-disclosure is now a thing of the past. The guideline case on the subject is *R v Feltham Magistrates' Court ex p Ebrahim; Mouat and DPP*, 21 February 2001, unreported (QBD). That case sets out the approach to be taken when video evidence is not available to the defence, a problem common to a significant number of public order cases. The court is now required to review the investigating authority's duties to obtain or retain video tapes. If there is no duty, then there can be no unfairness. If the duty exists and the authority fails to comply with it, then in serious cases the trial should be stayed. If it will not create unfairness, or if it would not be unfair, to require the defendant to stand trial, then the trial should proceed.

Some summary only cases involve balancing the rights of defendants to protest against the conflicting rights of other members of the public as a group or as individuals. These issues have been visited by the courts, but following the Human Rights Act there will be more argument about them, until resolved on appeal. The trend of cases thus far suggests less dramatic change than some commentators predicted. Public order law features a number of situations in which the burden of proof is transferred, as a result of which the defendant has had to prove the matter in question on a balance of probabilities. There have been no appeals on public order transferred burdens yet, but in *R v Lambert and Other Appeals* (5 July 2001), the House of Lords reviewed the question of transferred burden in the context of a drugs case. It seems likely that the same approach will be taken in relation to transferred burden in public order cases. The House of Lords decided that transferring the burden of legal proof to the defendant breached art 6 of the European Convention on Human Rights because the defendant should not have to prove his innocence. Although the legal burden could not be transferred, the evidentiary burden could. The defendant had to provide evidence of whatever the particular statute required him to prove. If he provided that evidence, then it was for the prosecution to disprove it, ie to make the tribunal of fact sure that the thing which he claimed was not the case. In essence the decision means that transferred burden issues will be dealt with in court just as self-defence is. The defendant raises the point, and the prosecution must disprove it beyond reasonable doubt. However, it remains possible that a distinction may be drawn between transferred burden in cases where the penalties include long terms of imprisonment and cases where the penalty range is much lower. Public order transferred burdens will have to be considered as they arise.

1.1 The Choice Between Section 4 and Section 5

Sections 4 and 5 of the Public Order Act 1986 are different in nature; they are not points on a sliding scale of seriousness. Prosecutors must pitch prosecutions correctly. Defence advocates must tell magistrates if and why the wrong charge has been brought. Magistrates should not seek to convict merely because something untoward has happened, and if the wrong count is before them they should acquit.

Most public order cases are dealt with in the magistrates' courts as summary only matters under s 4 or s 5 of the POA 1986. There is often an overlap between the statutory provisions, making it difficult for the courts to determine whether a particular case is an offence at all, a serious s 5 case, or, more accurately, a s 4 case. Courts face a dilemma if they find facts which amount to a s 5 case but the defendant has been charged under s 4; the court has no power to make an alternative finding of guilt if the wrong charge has been brought.

The choice available to both police and prosecutors is significant in that their interpretation of a set of facts, which may fit all three provisions equally well, determines the range of penalties available on conviction. To that extent the police and the prosecutor exercise a discretion which is difficult to challenge save by negotiating an alternative plea or resolving the case in court by showing that the wrong alternative has been chosen. In the *Mag-*

istrates Association Sentencing Guidelines, the guideline penalty for a s 5 offence is a fine or discharge; the guideline penalty for a s 4A offence is custody, while the guideline for a s 4 offence is a community-based penalty.

Home Office Research Study 135 (Brown and Ellis, *Policing Low Level Disorder*, 1994), reported that one quarter of the cases brought under s 5 arose out of insults directed solely at the police and not, as the Government had intended, to deal with rowdy youngsters disturbing the public:

> "from many of the section 5 cases and from interviews with arresting officers, the impression comes across very strongly that what is at issue in many of the cases is the enforcement of respect for the police".

There is no evidence that this has changed in more recent times. Although the study showed that one-fifth of all s 5 cases ended in the defendant's agreeing to be bound over, in cases where the police were the target, the usual outcome was conviction followed by a fine:

> ". . . in the absence of authoritative guidance, local police have gone their different ways – a clear managerial failure to structure discretion; about the speed with which s 5 came to be used frequently for a purpose for which it was not intended ie as a resource for the police to use in order to maintain respect when their authority is challenged."

Given the above analysis, it would be interesting to compare the use of ss 4, 4A and 5 to see how far they have been implemented in accordance with the express intentions of Parliament. (See also pages 8 and 9 on group disorder and policing.) It will also be interesting to see whether Parliamentary intention will be invoked in arguments about abuse of process and the European Convention on Human Rights.

1.2 Reasons for the Provisions

The rationale for these provisions should be remembered. It may not always be proper to adduce information as to background in court, although when it is, magistrates ought to be receptive to indications that the allegation goes beyond what was intended by Parliament. The research into the use of s 5 undertaken by Brown and Ellis may still be used in court argument alongside the following.

The Law Commission and the government identified, in *Offences Relating to Public Order*, Law Commission Report 123, the following points from the case law on s 5 of the 1936 Act, highlighting the difficulties inherent in summary public order matters:

(a) the need, in so far as practicable, to maintain the principle in *Beatty v Gillbanks* (1882) 9 QBD 308, [1881–5] All ER Rep 559, (1882) 47 LT 194 (QBD), that provided a person's conduct is not threatening, abusive or insulting he commits no offence even if it provokes others to violence;

(b) the need to avoid the concept of "breach of the peace";

(c) theoretical difficulties which arose from the issue of causation in s 5 of the 1936 Act, including the need to protect those who are disinclined to react to threatening, abusive or insulting conduct by themselves having recourse to violence (*Parkin v Norman* [1983] QB 92, [1982] 3 WLR 523, [1982] 2 All ER 583 (DC); *Marsh v Arscott* (1982) 75 Cr App R 211, [1982] Crim LR 827 (QBD)). Section 5 of the 1936 Act was concerned with cause and effect and the effect required to make out the offence was a breach of the peace; it was not enough that the conduct of the defendant should itself amount to a breach of the peace;

(d) the offence was restricted to public places and there was a major need to avert difficulties apparently encountered at major public disorder incidents, and in other cases (eg *Marsh v Arscott, R v Edwards and Roberts* (1978) 122 SJ 177, (1978) 67 Cr App R 228, [1978] Crim LR 564 (CA)) where the offending activity occurred on private premises to which the public did not have access;

(e) s 5 of the 1936 Act was not designed to deal with minor acts of hooliganism falling short of the criteria of threatening, abusive or insulting, or which engendered not fear of violence but a more generalised sense of unease or apprehension.

1.3 Aiding and Abetting

It is possible to aid, abet, counsel or procure an offence under the POA 1986, even though the words "only if he intends" appear in s 6. In *R v Jefferson and Others* [1994] 1 All ER 270, (1994) 99 Cr App R 13, [1993] Crim LR 880 (CA), the court analysed whether anything in the 1986 POA excluded the general common law principles of aiding and abetting:

"In our judgment, the offences created by the 1986 Act may be committed by aiders and abettors as well as by principals . . . In our view s 6 is concerned only with identifying . . . the requisite *mens rea* . . . It does not exclude or cut down in relation to any of those offences the liability of an aider or abettor." (*per* Auld J)

2 Threatening, Abusive or Insulting Words or Behaviour (Section 4)

Checklist

- no victim required but conduct must be directed at a person present;
- section 4 applies to both public and private places;
- no offence is committed if both people are inside a dwelling (or one of them is in another dwelling);
- "intent" has a complex meaning, covering four states of affairs (see ss 4 and 6(3));
- "such violence" means immediate unlawful violence;
- "threatening" has its ordinary meaning;
- "display" includes displaying on a tee-shirt.

Section 4 of the Public Order Act 1986 states:

"(1) A person is guilty of an offence if he—

    (a) uses towards another person threatening, abusive or insulting words or behaviour, or

    (b) distributes or displays to another person any writing, sign or other visible representation which is threatening, abusive or insulting,

with intent to cause that person to believe that immediate unlawful violence will be used against him or another by any person, or to provoke the immediate use of unlawful violence by that person or another, or whereby that person is likely to believe that such violence will be used or it is likely that such violence be provoked.

(2) An offence under this section may be committed in a public or a private place, except that no offence is committed where the words or behaviour are used, or the writing, sign or other visible representation is distributed or displayed, by a person inside a dwelling and the other person is also inside that or another dwelling.

(3) A constable may arrest without warrant anyone he reasonably suspects is committing an offence under this section.

(4) A person guilty of an offence under this section is liable on summary conviction to imprisonment for a term not exceeding six months or a fine not exceeding level 5 on the standard scale or both."

The offence is punishable with imprisonment for up to six months or a fine up to level 5 (s 4(4)). There is a power of arrest where a constable reasonably suspects that a person is committing an offence under the section (s 4(3)). The offence is triable summarily only, although in certain cases a defendant can be convicted of this offence as an alternative verdict in the Crown Court (ss 4(4)) and 7(3)).

2.1   Place Where the Offence is Committed

Section 4 is not restricted to public places and the offence may, with one exception, be committed anywhere. There is no need to decide whether a place is a public or a private place, although the authorities on "public place" may be helpful (see POA 1986 s 57(1); *Anderson v Miller* [1976] Crim LR 743 (DC); *Knox v Anderton* (1983) 76 Cr App R 156, (1983) 147 JP 340 (QBD)). The only restriction is where the conduct occurs in a dwelling (s 4(2)); here no offence is committed. "Dwelling" is defined in s 8 of the POA 1986 (see page 58). Where the conduct occurs in a garden or on a driveway or in the staircase of a block of flats, then the offence may be committed. The communal landing of a block of self-contained flats does not form part of "a person's home" as defined in s 8 and therefore the offence may be committed there (*Rukwira v DPP* (1994) 158 JP 65, [1993] Crim LR 882, (1993) 157 JPN 709 (DC)). Where a person inside a dwelling uses threatening, abusive or insulting conduct towards someone outside, eg in the street, at the front door or in the garden of that or another house, then the offence may be committed (*R v Va Kun Hau* [1990] Crim LR 518 (CA) and see *Atkin v DPP* (1989) 89 Cr App R 199, [1989] Crim LR 581, (1989) 153 JP 383 (DC)).

In *Atkin v DPP* the appellant had been convicted of a s 4(1)(a) offence. Customs officers had gone to his farm. A bailiff stayed outside the farmhouse while the customs officers went inside to speak to the appellant. The appellant said that the bailiff would be a "dead 'un" if he came in. As the appellant had a gun in the room, his statement was taken seriously. A customs officer went out and told the bailiff, who naturally felt threatened. The justices held that the appellant intended the threat to be conveyed to the bailiff outside; they convicted the appellant. The Divisional Court, in allowing the appeal, held that the words "uses towards another person" in the section meant "uses in the presence of and in the direction of another person directly". It follows that for a s 4 offence to be proved, the words must be addressed towards a person present. Since the relevant persons were inside the dwelling house, no offence contrary to s 4 had been committed (s 4(2)). The court did not have to consider the situation if the conversation had occurred in a different part of the farm buildings.

The trespassing hooligan no longer has a defence (*R v Edwards and Roberts* (1978) 122 SJ 177, (1978) 67 Cr App R 228 (CA)), provided he is not in a dwelling house. A person who posts offensive literature through a letter box is guilty of an offence since the distribution does not occur *in* the dwelling (see also *Chappell v DPP* (1989) 89 Cr App R 82, [1989] COD 259 (DC), and the Malicious Communications Act 1988, page 123).

2.2   Words or Behaviour; Distribution or Display
The prohibited conduct consists of the use of words or behaviour, or the distribution or display of any writing, sign or other visible representation.

The display of a flag, badge, emblem, armband or tee-shirt may be caught, depending on the context. The words "display" and "distribute" are not defined for the purposes of s 4 and are to be given their ordinary meanings. Whether the orange lily in *Humphries v Connor* (1864) 17 ICLR 1 (see page 39) would be caught by the words "writing, sign or other visible representation" is debatable.

The word "distribute" in the POA 1986, Part III, dealing with racial hatred, is restricted to distribution to the public or a section of the public. This qualification does not appear in s 4, and any distribution suffices for offences under s 4, whether to the public or an individual or group of people. Distribution has been held to include leaving pamphlets in the front porch of an MP's house, which was to an individual, not to a section of the public (*R v Britton* [1967] 2 QB 51, [1967] 2 WLR 537, [1967] 1 All ER 486 (CA)).

2.3   Threatening, Abusive, Insulting
To constitute the offence, the conduct must be threatening, or abusive or insulting. These words have a long history, going back to s 5 of the POA 1936,

and their interpretation is largely governed by cases following that Act. Synonymous expressions, such as "behaviour evidencing a disrespect or contempt for the rights of others" are not interchangeable with the words of the section. Conduct which is annoying is not enough (*Brutus v Cozens* [1973] AC 854, [1972] 3 WLR 521, [1972] 2 All ER 1297 (HL)); and it must be more than disgusting or offensive behaviour (*Parkin v Norman* [1983] QB 92, [1982] 3 WLR 523, [1982] 2 All ER 583 (DC)). The words "threatening, abusive or insulting" were described as "very strong words" in *Jordan v Burgoyne* [1963] 2 QB 744, [1963] 2 WLR 1045, [1963] 2 All ER 225. *Brutus v Cozens* is the leading case on the interpretation of the words and the House of Lords declined to define them:

> ". . . an ordinary sensible man knows an insult when he sees one . . . Parliament has given no indication that the word is to be given any unusual meaning. Insulting means insulting and nothing else." (*per* Lord Reid)

The essential element of *Brutus v Cozens* is that it is for the tribunal of fact to determine whether given behaviour is insulting. In *Vigon v DPP, The Times* 9 December 1997 (DC) the court considered the implications of covert surveillance cameras in changing rooms, and determined that "insulting" was not confined to actively rowdy behaviour but could be applied to the passive activity of the covert use of cameras (see also page 113).

2.4 No Victim Required

There is no requirement that any person should actually feel insulted or threatened or abused. In *Parkin v Norman* (above), McCullough J remarked:

> ". . . if the conduct in question is of this character it does not, in our judgement matter whether anyone feels himself to have been threatened abused or insulted. Insulting behaviour does not lose its insulting character simply because no one who witnessed it was insulted. . ."

In *Parkin v Norman*, the activity had not and would not have been witnessed by anyone who would have been insulted; nonetheless it could be classed as "potentially insulting". That potentiality characterised the behaviour as insulting, but this referred only to the capacity of words to be insulting and did not deal with the other requirements of s 4 of the POA 1986.

The approach of the court in *Brutus v Cozens* and *Parkin v Norman* was of general application and has been applied to the meaning of "threatening" (*Ewart v Rogers*, 1985, unreported), where the need for an element of menace in order to constitute a threat was recognised. The judgment in *Parkin v Norman* also included useful observations on the nature of an insult. This approach should be applied equally to threats and abuse:

> "One cannot insult nothing. The word presupposes a subject and an object and, in this day and age, a human object. An insult is perceived by someone who feels insulted. It is given by someone who is directing his words or behaviour to another person or persons."

2.5 *"Directed towards"*

The above *dictum* in *Parkin v Norman* introduced the idea that for there to be an insult, the conduct had to be directed at a specific person or persons. In *R v Newham Justices ex p Sadiku*, 15 January 1985, unreported, the Divisional Court took this approach, and concluded that urinating on the public highway could not be said to be "insulting" in the circumstances of that case: "There was no question here of the behaviour being in any way directed at the persons who were present".

Parkin v Norman has been explained on the basis that:

"what the . . . passage must be understood to mean is that words or behaviour cannot be insulting if there is not a human target which they strike, whether they are intended to strike that target or not . . . The magistrates were perfectly entitled to infer that the two appellants must have known that other people would be likely to be present . . . Their conduct . . . if in the ordinary sense it was capable of being insulting, would be likely to make some impact on anybody who was nearby. . . [I]t can properly be said that the conduct could be insulting albeit it was not deliberately aimed at a particular person." (*Masterson v Holder* [1986] 1 WLR 1017, [1986] 3 All ER 39, (1986) 83 Cr App R 302 (DC))

The significance of the words "directed towards" or "aimed at" can now be seen in the opening phrase of s 4(1)(a). In practice the criteria may not have been applied strictly. The decisions indicate that the issue is one of fact and the Divisional Court will not interfere with a finding of fact unless no court properly directing itself could have made that finding.

In *Rogers Blake and Others v DPP*, 22 July 1999, unreported (QBD), appellants had been part of a large scale demonstration against a particular activity at a farm. The crowd attempted to get past police and into the farm. They were arrested and charged with offences contrary to s 4. They claimed that as there was no evidence that they knew the farmer was at his farm, it could not be said that they intended to cause him harassment etc. On appeal it was held that the real question was simply whether it could be inferred that they intended, through the medium of the crowd, to cause harassment etc. In the context of such a demonstration the only answer was "yes", and therefore no detailed analysis of their precise thought processes was required.

2.6 *Intention or Awareness*

A difficulty inherent in s 4 is that there are two separate mental elements. The first is that s 6(3) requires proof by the prosecution of a mental element concerning the description and character of the behaviour. The second is in the description of the offence itself, ie the *intention* to provoke violence or cause fear. The first is always required. The second is required only where the prosecution seeks to establish intention rather than the objective likelihood of provocation or fear.

The question of intent in s 4 allegations is dealt with both in s 4 itself and in s 6(3), which provides that the defendant must have intended the conduct described to have the proscribed character, or be aware that it was likely to have that character. He must intend his words or behaviour, or the writing, sign or representation, to be threatening, abusive or insulting; or be aware that it may be any of those things. The defendant's intent is a matter of fact for the magistrates. By incorporating awareness into the provision, the intention was that the court should be able to determine whether there were obvious consequences from a defendant's conduct, which he should have been aware of, independently of his actual intent.

In *Swanston v DPP* (1996) 161 JP 203, [1997] COD 180, (1997) 161 JPN 212 (QBD), it was decided that it is not a requirement of s 4(1) that the court should hear from the person who was "threatened", and that it was sufficient that the court acted upon the evidence of a bystander and drew an inference that the victim perceived what was said and done by the defendant. Any admissible evidence could be used to demonstrate intent.

In *Kelleher v DPP*, 1994, unreported (QBD), it was argued that the necessary intent could not be attributed to a defendant shouting threats at another man if that other man was surrounded by police. Obviously, it was said, that man would not feel threatened because of the protection provided by the police. The court determined that by analysing the defendant's mind at the time it was clear that in this case his intention was to make the man feel threatened and therefore that the intent element of the offence was made out, whether or not the man in fact felt threatened.

In *DPP v Wilmot and Another*, 1991, unreported (QBD), a magistrates' court dealing with a s 4 allegation had formulated the view that under s 6(3) they could not be satisfied beyond reasonable doubt that the defendants had intended their words to be threatening, and therefore dismissed the allegation. Two men had run into premises shouting "get him" and then chased a man. The defendants had said the meeting was spontaneous and the words may have been provocative and frightening to others in the premises but that was not their intention. The magistrates also felt that the defendants were not aware of the threatening nature of the behaviour. The Divisional Court found as follows (*per* Hodgson J):

> "it is impossible to conclude that either defendant can have been unaware that his conduct might have been threatening abusive or insulting. For words like these to be shouted and for a law abiding citizen to be chased through a shop and out into the street speaks for itself."

While this conduct "spoke for itself" in the view of the High Court, it had not said the same thing to the magistrates, who perhaps tried to delve too deeply into the actual thought processes of the defendants rather than applying ordinary meaning to the expression "is aware that it may be threatening".

Prior to the POA 1986, various observations about intent were canvassed. They remain of interest as a demonstration of the higher courts' interpretation of words still forming part of public order law, but since 1986 the statutory position has been clear. Either intent or awareness is required, and these words have not led to significant numbers of requests to the higher courts to define their meaning.

2.7 "Another person"

Section 4 comes into play only if the conduct is specifically used towards another person. These words were not found in the 1936 Act, nor are they found in s 5 of the 1986 Act. They are reminiscent of McCullough J's comment in *Parkin v Norman* [1983] QB 92, [1982] 3 WLR 523, [1982] 2 All ER 583 (DC) that ". . . the defendant's conduct was aimed at one person and one person only".

The words in s 4(1)(a) introduced a requirement that the defendant must be shown to have deliberately directed his conduct at a specific person or persons and must therefore be shown to have been aware of the presence of the person(s). It must then be shown that the conduct falls within one of the three categories proscribed by the Act. The person towards whom the conduct is directed must be present, in the sense that he must be in earshot, for this element of the offence to be made out, as set out in *Atkin v DPP* (see page 95). There remains the possibility that the conduct need not be threatening, abusive or insulting to that particular other person (or persons), but it usually is. The other person is usually a victim, but not always. In some cases the other person is an associate of the defendant, and the threat, abuse or insult has been directed to him with a view to encouraging him to violence against another. If the intended or likely effect of the conduct is to encourage any person to indulge in violence, then the offence is made out.

Suppose that on a picket line one picket uses threatening behaviour towards a person passing through the picket line on a bus. The picket may be convicted of a s 4 offence if the likelihood is that the worker will believe that immediate violence (eg throwing stones or banging on the side of the bus) will be used, or if the threats are likely to provoke violence. Such violence need not necessarily be by the person towards whom the threats were made, but by other persons present at the scene who are likely to be provoked to violence. A man who makes threats to a person about another person who is present but does not hear the threats is caught by the provision, because he uses the threats to the first person intending to provoke violence towards him by another person who may be provoked by the words used.

2.8 Intention and Likelihood

The issues of intent are set out at page 97. Section 4 of the POA 1986 is concerned with conduct which is intended or likely to cause fear or to provoke unlawful violence. The word "fear" does not appear in the section itself, only in the marginal note. Terror is not an ingredient of the section; belief that violence will be used is. Section 4 is not concerned with conduct which is itself violent unless that conduct is supported by the necessary intention or likelihood. Nor is s 4 concerned with the actual effect of the behaviour; its intended or likely consequences are what matter. To establish an offence, it must be shown either that the person at whom the conduct was aimed was intended, or was likely, to be made to believe that unlawful violence would be inflicted on him or another, or that the person at whom the conduct was aimed, or someone else, was intended or likely to be provoked to unlawful violence. One of four alternative states of affairs must be shown: *Kelleher v DPP*, 1994, unreported (QBD) and *Winn v DPP* (1992) 156 JP 881 (1992) NLJ 527, (1992) JPN 554 (DC):

> "That the defendant intended to cause the person at whom he directed the conduct to believe that immediate unlawful violence would be used against him or another person by any person, ie by the defendant or anyone else. Or
>
> That the defendant intended to provoke the person at whom he directed the conduct or any other person to use immediate unlawful violence. Or
>
> That it was likely that the person at whom he directed the conduct would be likely to believe that immediate unlawful violence would be used (presumably against him or any other person). Or
>
> That it was likely that immediate unlawful violence by the person at whom he directed the conduct or by any other person, would be provoked."

Likelihood

Although intention may frequently be inferred from the nature of the conduct, on other occasions it may be difficult to prove. It may be easier to prove the likelihood of the conduct either causing the other person to believe that violence will be used, or provoking violence whether on the part of that person or some other person. In neither case is there any need to demonstrate actual belief that violence would occur or actual provocation to violence. The Act uses the word "likely". Regard must always be had to the circumstances. "Likelihood" is a higher burden to overcome than "liable" (*Parkin v Norman*, above). Police officers are not "likely" to react by using unlawful violence, but they are likely to believe that unlawful violence will be used against them. Whether or not conduct has the necessary character is decided by reference to the ordinary man, who may take into account the actual audience or victim or participants. It is not decided by asking whether the audience or victim *was* threatened. But the likelihood of fear or provocation of violence can be assessed only by reference to the actual audience or victim or participants. The speaker who uses what are objectively assessed as threats to an audience which has special susceptibilities, or even a predisposition to violence, must take that audience as he finds it. He cannot plead for his actions to be tested against a "reasonable audience" (*Jordan v Burgoyne* [1963] 2 QB 744, [1963] 2 WLR 1045, [1963] 2 All ER 225). Nor is it possible to argue that conduct should be tested in the context of a "reasonably firm bystander". The section is intended to protect both the public peace and the timid citizen. In *DPP v Ramos* [2000] COD 287, the court determined that letters containing bomb threats were likely to cause a person to believe that violence would be used, whether or not that was the author's intention.

Belief and Immediacy

The belief of the person towards whom the conduct is directed need not be reasonable; it may be entirely unreasonable or irrational. The perpetrator of such conduct must take his victim as he finds him. If, given the character of the victim, it is likely that the victim will anticipate the infliction of violence, then that is an end of the matter. There need not actually be such a belief; intention to cause such a belief is sufficient, as is likelihood that such belief will be caused.

In *Marsh v Arscott* (1982) 75 Cr App R 211, [1982] Crim LR 827 (QBD), the charge failed on two grounds:
(a) the car park in question was not a public place;
(b) even though the behaviour may have been threatening, abusive or insulting, it was not likely to occasion a breach of the peace since the only people who witnessed it were police officers. Police officers could not be said to be likely to react in such a way as to occasion breaches of the peace.

Under s 4 a conviction would have followed since:
(a) the s 4 offence can be committed on private property; and
(b) the person towards whom the conduct had been directed, the police officer, might be likely to believe that unlawful violence would be used against him (*DPP v Orum* [1989] 1 WLR 88, [1988] 3 All ER 449, (1989) 88 Cr App R 261 (QBD)).

In *DPP v Ramos*, the Divisional Court had to consider the meaning of "immediate" in the context of the section. A series of letters had been sent, containing the threat of a bombing campaign at an unspecified future date. The magistrate found that the absence of any date meant that the requirement for immediacy had not been met. On appeal, the court emphasised that it was the state of mind of the recipient of the letter that counted. It was open to be inferred that the recipient of the letter could believe that something could happen at any time. This was found to satisfy the test of immediacy contained in the section; the appeal was therefore upheld and the case remitted to the magistrate (see also above). Butterfield J said:

> "It is the state of mind of the victim which is crucial rather than the statistical risk of violence actually occurring within a very short space of time."

This develops the concept set out in *Swanston v DPP* (1996) 161 JP 203, [1997] COD 180, (1997) 161 JPN 212 (QBD), where the defendant was charged with using threatening words etc with intent to cause another to fear immediate violence. It was held that the offence is made out not by demonstrating what the other person believed, but by demonstrating what the defendant *intended* the other person to believe. This could be shown by any admissible evidence from which inferences could be drawn.

The use of the word "immediate" was taken by the Law Commission, in its report and Working Paper, to correspond closely to the concept of "imminence" in the common law breach of the peace preventive powers (cf *Moss v McLachlan* (1985) 149 JP 167, [1985] IRLR 76, (1985) 149 JPN 149 (DC)), although in the usual case there is no real difficulty in establishing the immediacy of the violence.

In *R v Horseferry Rd Magistrates' Court ex p Siadatan* [1991] 1 QB 280, [1990] 3 WLR 1006, [1991] 1 All ER 324, the Divisional Court reviewed a decision by a magistrate to refuse to issue a summons against Penguin Viking, the publishers of *The Satanic Verses* by Salman Rushdi. The summons had been sought on the basis that the publishers were distributing abusive and insulting writing whereby it was likely that unlawful violence would be provoked contrary to s 4 of the POA 1986. The magistrate refused to issue the summons because "such violence" had to be "immediate". The applicant contended that the prospective violence need not be immediate but only unlawful, and where violence was likely to be provoked, the section provided: "or whereby that person is likely to believe that such violence will be used or it is likely that such violence will be provoked". His claim was that because the drafting of the provision did not incorporate the word "immediate" in the second limb, the violence need not be immediate. The court took the view that the two expressions, "immediate unlawful violence" and "immediate use of unlawful violence" meant the same thing, and that "such violence" meant immediate unlawful violence. The court's interpretation was questioned in the commentary in *Criminal Law Review*:

> "There is much force in the applicant's argument that the proper grammatical meaning of the section is that the phrase 'such violence' refers back to the most proximate previous use of the word 'violence' and that is in the phrase 'unlawful violence' not 'immediate unlawful violence'. . .". [1990] Crim LR 99.

Where one group of football supporters aims threats or insults at an opposing group on the other side of the ground, it is easy to envisage the belief in, or provocation of, immediate violence. The threat might be of violence after the match, which might still have the quality of imminence in the sense of proximity in time and space.

Conduct Affecting a Non-victim
Where the conduct is intended, or likely, to encourage persons other than the "victim" to react violently, then the offence is made out. In *Simcock v Rhodes* (1978) 66 Cr App R 192, [1977] Crim LR 751 (DC), an abusive remark by one youth to a police officer was not likely to cause the police officer to

react by causing a breach of the peace. But other youths were present at the scene and it was likely that they would be encouraged to breaches of the peace. In terms of s 4, abusive language had been used towards another person (the police officer), whereby it was likely that unlawful violence would be provoked (by the youths). The defendant had also used towards another person (the police officer) abusive language whereby he was likely to believe that violence on the part of any of those present would be used against him. That case also demonstrates the difficulties inherent in the formulation "uses towards another person". It could be said that the language had been used towards everyone present and not simply the police officer.

Officer Not Acting in Execution of Duty

In *Woodhouse and Others v DPP*, 1991, unreported (QBD) the court was asked whether the necessary intent existed where a police officer was acting otherwise than in the execution of his duty. At a railway station two youths were seen to headbutt a barrier. They did not show their tickets (although they had them). Officers approached them, but the youths declined to stop and an officer prevented one from moving away while he made enquiry. This led to the youths and their appellant friends becoming threatening towards the officers, and an arrest for threatening behaviour was made. The question was whether the officer had the right to prevent the youths from walking away. If not, could the threatening behaviour be threatening, or was it merely a permitted use of force? In the event the court was able to sidestep the issue because it found the threatening behaviour began at a point in time effectively preceding the issue of the lawfulness of the stop. The court did allow for the possibility, in an appropriate case, of the threats being negatived by preceding unlawful conduct. The court did not analyse the prospective significance of the threat of lawful violence because, on the particular facts, it was not required. Nevertheless, intemperate language, even in the context of the use of lawful violence, might be expected to lead a court to the view that unlawful violence by others would be provoked.

The unwillingness of the higher courts to extend the scope of conduct, whether violent or insulting, which falls within the meaning of reasonable and is therefore not an offence, is shown in the unreported case on s 5, *Lewis v DPP*, 1995 (DC), where Keene J said: "That would lead to situations where the more extreme were the opinions of the defendant, the more readily would his conduct be regarded as reasonable". Nevertheless, in *Woodhouse and Others v DPP* (above), Watkins LJ set out the general principle that ". . . the citizen who is wrongly treated by the officer is entitled to go to the extent of using force, if need be, to resist what it is the officer does to him".

In *Collins v Wilcock* it was held that, except when exercising his power of arrest or some other statutory power, the police officer had no greater right that any other citizen to restrain another. Thus, if he used more than normal force to attract the attention of a person to whom he wished to speak, then he committed a battery which would take him outside the execution of his duty. The question of the extent to which a policeman using degrees of force may be acting outside his duty has been reviewed in other cases (see *Bentley v Brudzinski* (1982) 75 Cr App R 217, [1982] Crim LR 825 (DC); *Kenlin v Gardiner* [1967] 2 QB 510, [1967] 2 WLR 129, [1966] 3 All ER 931 (DC) and Chapter 7).

It remains likely that the issue of intent will continue to give rise to this category of defence to s 4 allegations, despite the principle that the law should not readily recognise new claims to justify the use of force, and that reasonable excuse is given a restricted meaning in the interests of policy (*R v Ball* (1990) 90 Cr App R 378, [1989] Crim LR 579 (CA)).

Those Threatened at a Distance

A more difficult case might be where threats are aimed at, say, a religious or ethnic group living predominantly on the opposite side of a town. That other group might be intended, or likely, to anticipate unlawful violence, but it might not be easy to establish that the violence they would anticipate could properly be termed immediate. That situation might be regarded as comparable with that in *Siadatan* (above, page 102).

In *R v Ambrose* (1973) 57 Cr App R (CA) 538, a case on the POA 1936, the appellant addressed to a girl aged twelve words which did not fall within the Act, being at worst rude and offensive. The girl reported the words to her father who, together with another man, became very angry and indicated that they felt like assaulting the appellant. Because of the finding on the language, the court felt that there was no need to enquire further into the question whether insulting words are likely to cause a breach of the peace if the breach of the peace is likely to occur some time later and in different circumstances. In this sort of case, where the victim is not likely or intended to be caused to fear the infliction of violence, no offence is made out since the violence likely to be provoked cannot be described as immediate.

In *R v Richmond Magistrates' Court ex p White*, 1989, unreported (QBD), the court was asked to review another decision of a magistrate not to issue a summons against the publishers of *The Satanic Verses* by Salman Rushdie. The court analysed the process whereby the magistrate had reached his decision and reviewed the law: "He came to the conclusion . . . that he was not satisfied that the distribution in the area for which he was responsible . . . was such as to be likely to give rise to violence" (Kennedy J). The court acknowledged that another view might have been taken by others. Clearly the prospect of violence had to be sufficiently proximate and likely, to enable proceedings to issue. The magistrate had formed the view that it "was anyone's guess" whether the publication would lead to violence (see also *R v Horseferry Rd Metropolitan Stipendiary Magistrate ex p Siadatan* above, page 102).

2.9 Avoidance of Duplicity

Section 7(2) provides that s 4 creates one offence only. This was the position under s 5 of the 1936 Act.

2.10 Arrest

Whether a police officer had, as grounds for an arrest, a genuine and reasonable suspicion that a person was committing an offence may be challenged in court. Public order cases demand instant decisions by police officers faced with difficult individuals and groups and an obligation to protect the peace. It may be right to challenge the reasonableness of the suspicion leading to the arrest, but courts will make allowances for the emergency nature of the circumstances. In practice it may be difficult to persuade courts, except in obvious cases, that reasonable suspicion did not exist (*G v Chief Superintendent of Police, Stroud* (1988) 86 Cr App R 92, [1987] Crim LR 269 (DC); see also Chapter 7).

3   Harassment, Alarm or Distress (Section 4A)

Checklist
- the offending conduct must be aimed at a person;
- a person must be harassed, alarmed or distressed;
- intent – to cause harassment, etc only;
- harassment, alarm and distress have their ordinary meanings;
- there is no offence where both accused and harassed person are in the same dwelling;
- defence – inside a house and no reason to believe conduct can be seen or heard outside.

Although there is no reference to race in the provisions on harassment, alarm or distress in s 4A, it targets a range of offending which often has a racial motive. If the power to charge this offence is aimed at that particular category of offender, it may function as intended by the Government which enacted the legislation. If it is used as an alternative to "ordinary" s 5 cases with the greater penalty, then all that will be achieved is to increase the likely penalty for relatively minor breaches of public order law. The risk is that the law will fail to achieve the proper balance between limiting individual rights and protecting the public peace. It will not be playing a useful role in the fight against racial harassment.

    In the Home Office *Guide to the Criminal Justice and Public Order Act 1994*, the provision is described as "designed to deal more effectively with cases of serious racial harassment, particularly where the behaviour is persistent". While that may have been the intention, there is nothing in the provision to focus it on racial cases, and the law has since moved on to the "racially aggravated" provisions (see page 121). The operation in practice of s 4A depends on the view taken by the prosecuting authorities and the police, and the research findings are not especially hopeful.

Section 4A provides:

"(1) A person is guilty of an offence if, with intent to cause a person harassment alarm or distress, he—

(a) uses threatening, abusive or insulting words or behaviour, or disorderly behaviour, or

(b) displays any writing sign or other visible representation which is threatening abusive or insulting, thereby causing that or another person harassment, alarm or distress.

(2) An offence under this section may be committed in a public or private place except that no offence is committed when the words or behaviour are used, or the writing sign or visible representation is displayed, by a person inside a dwelling, and the person who is harassed alarmed or distressed is also inside that dwelling."

3.1 Venue

This offence may be committed in a public or a private place. A private place is exempted only if it is a dwelling (see page 58) and both the victim and the offender are inside it. A person who affixes posters to his window or dwelling which are capable of being seen by passers-by or neighbours is capable of committing the offence.

3.2 The Victim

The offence under s 4A is committed only if the intention is to cause "a person" harassment, alarm or distress, and the conduct actually causes "that or another person" harassment, alarm or distress. The offence is therefore quite different from that under s 5. Section 5 merely requires the conduct to be in the hearing or sight of a person likely to be caused harassment, alarm or distress thereby. Under s 4A, the conduct must be aimed at a person capable of identification. That person, or another who is actually caused harassment, alarm or distress, must also be identified. It may be difficult to say that a person has been caused distress by particular conduct unless the person gives evidence to that effect. Mere evidence of distress may not link the distress to the particular conduct. However, if the evidence of distress is sufficiently compelling the court may well be able to draw the inference that the conduct caused the distress. A set of remarks directed at a person followed by that person's being reduced to floods of tears might well lead a court to the obvious inference that the tears were the consequence of the remarks. Conduct aimed at one person who remains unaffected by it is still an offence if it affects a third party against whom it is not directed, whether or not there is any connection between the intended victim and the third party. Section 4A is also different in this respect from s 4, which focuses on conduct towards an individual, with the exception of provocation which can have the effect on "that or another person".

3.3   Intent

The specific intent required by s 4A is less complex than the four components of intent under s 4. All the defendant has to intend is "to cause a person harassment, alarm or distress". In most cases the intention is obvious and deliberate. In other cases it is for the court to draw proper inferences from the circumstances of the case. It is only a *positive* intention which will render a person guilty. To that extent, proving the case may be more difficult, which is perhaps surprising given that the penalties on conviction under ss 4 and 4A are the same. Although the decision in *DPP v Wilmot and Another* (above, page 98), related primarily to findings under s 6(3), it was made clear that intention speaks for itself where the conduct is clear. The number of cases where the difficulty in the application of s 6(3) arises may be small. It is possible to behave in a threatening way without intending to cause a person harassment, alarm or distress, particularly if the behaviour occurs when the defendant thinks no one else is present. The most likely resolution of this issue is that courts will adhere to the view that intent is made out by the nature of the conduct in question.

Section 6(3) of the POA 1986 (see page 98) appears not to apply to s 4A, because s 4A was inserted into the Act *after* s 4 and not within it. If this somewhat inconsistent position is confirmed as correct, it means that awareness that conduct "may be threatening, abusive or insulting" will not suffice to make out the offence. An alternative view is that s 4A is *part* of s 4, and therefore subject to s 6(3) and (4) in the same way as the remainder of the section. This issue awaits a decision on appeal.

3.4   "Harassment, alarm or distress"; "Threatening, abusive or insulting"; "Disorderly"

These words are not defined in the statute and should be given their ordinary meanings. They are strong words, indicating a level of extreme concern, going beyond "annoyance", "disturbance" or "aggravation" (*Brutus v Cozens* [1973] AC 854, [1972] 3 WLR 521, [1972] 2 All ER 1297 (HL)). A police officer *may* be harassed, alarmed or distressed, although whether he is in fact harassed, alarmed or distressed is a question of fact (*DPP v Orum* [1989] 1 WLR 88, [1988] 3 All ER 449, (1989) 88 Cr App R 261 (QBD)).

The words "threatening, abusive or insulting" are discussed in relation to s 4 at page 93 *et seq.* In so far as they relate to writing, signs or other visible representation, it is only the display that is caught by the provision. There is no reference to distribution in s 4. It might also be argued that distribution may involve a display in certain contexts, depending on the surrounding circumstances and precisely how the distribution took place. In an appropriate case, given that s 4 is expressed in wider terms, it might be that distribution would be caught by that provision.

"Disorderly" is examined below in relation to s 5; it has been the subject of a number of references to the higher courts, although rarely in relation to the 1986 Act. For the purposes of s 4A it has the same meaning as in s 5.

3.5 Defences

The offence is not committed by one person against another inside the same dwelling (s 4A(2)). The definition of "dwelling" is set out in s 8 of the POA 1986 (see page 58). It is a defence for the accused to prove that he was inside a dwelling and had no reason to believe the words or behaviour used, or the writing, sign or other visible representation displayed, would be heard or seen by a person outside that or any other dwelling. The burden appears to be on the defence to raise the above matters; it would then be for the prosecution to disprove them (see page 91 and *R v Lambert*). The defence is not made out by simply showing the accused's state of mind and that he genuinely did not believe his conduct would be heard or seen outside the dwelling. The test is objective. Was there reason for him to believe that it would not be heard or seen? *DPP v Wilmot and Another*, 1991, unreported (QBD) indicates that courts are expected to take a common sense view of events that speak for themselves. The reference in this defence to "outside that or any other dwelling" may appear to be surplusage, given that s 4A(2) excludes an offence by a person in one dwelling against a person in another dwelling, but it is not. If a defendant telephones a victim and harasses him or her over the telephone in the belief that the victim was in the house answering the telephone, but the victim was in fact outside using a cordless telephone, then the potential for an offence exists. This is a matter for analysis of the particular facts of the case. The defence that the accused's conduct was reasonable (s 4(3)(b)) is discussed in relation to s 5 below at page 118. Rights under the European Convention on Human Rights and the history of rights of protest are set out in Chapter 1.

3.6 Arrest

A constable may arrest without warrant a person he reasonably suspects is committing the offence under s 4A. When the officer does not himself see the offending behaviour, he may utilise s 25 of the Police and Criminal Evidence Act 1984. The additional requirements in s 5(4), that the officer should warn the person to stop before arresting him in connection with continuing offensive conduct, do not apply to s 4A.

3.7 Avoidance of Duplicity

Section 7(2) provides that s 4A creates only one offence, despite the multiplicity of elements in the section.

4 Offensive Conduct (Section 5)

Checklist
- the original focus of the section was minor hooliganism;

- conduct must be in the presence of the person affected;
- a person must be likely to be caused harassment, alarm or distress;
- a police officer may be harassed;
- Home Office research shows widespread use of s 5 to deal with insults directed at the police themselves (see page 92);
- what the accused is aware of may be a matter of common sense;
- displaying a true photograph may amount to insulting or abusive behaviour;
- a warning must precede arrest under s 5, but the arrest need not be by the officer who gave the warning;
- where the s 5 offence is charged after arrest for another offence, a warning is not needed;
- defence of reasonable conduct.

Section 5 is a widely expressed "catch-all" provision designed to provide the prosecuting authorities, and the police in particular, with the means to deal with a wide range of less serious public order disturbances. After the appropriate warning has been given, if the misbehaviour continues, then the police may arrest. This enables the officer to intervene relatively promptly to prevent a difficult situation becoming worse.

When determining whether to prosecute under s 5, and when determining whether to convict, public authorities – whether the prosecution or the court – must keep in mind art 10 of the European Convention on Human Rights. Article 10 protects not only ideas that are favourably received but also those which shock or disturb the State or any section of the population. It is important to give effect to s 5 in a manner which is compatible with art 10: *Handyside v UK* [1976] 1 EHRR 737.

The apparent generality of the offence, which may contradict the principles of due process, was tempered at one stage in the Parliamentary process leading to the Act by a requirement that someone should actually have been harassed, alarmed or distressed to a substantial degree. This dual requirement was not enacted despite anxiety that the threshold of criminality was being lowered by the provision. But such a requirement has been incorporated in s 4A of the 1986 Act to the extent that the behaviour must be intended to cause a person harassment, alarm or distress and must actually do so. Section 5 has been reviewed in the higher courts, but enforcement seems not to have proved the problem that was envisaged in 1986.

The intention was to create an offence encompassing minor acts of hooliganism not otherwise falling within s 4 of the Act. The White Paper described the mischief:

"3.22 . . . Instances of such behaviour might include: hooligans on housing estates causing disturbances in the common parts of blocks of flats, blockading entrances, throwing things down the stairs, banging on doors, peering in at windows, and knocking over dustbins; groups of youth persistently shouting abuse and obscenities or pestering people waiting to catch public transport or to enter a hall or cinema."

Section 5(1) provides:

"A person is guilty of an offence if he—

(a)   uses threatening, abusive or insulting words or behaviour, or disorderly behaviour, or

(b)   displays any writing, sign or other visible representation which is threatening, abusive, or insulting,

within the hearing or sight of a person likely to be caused harassment, alarm or distress thereby."

Although there are clear similarities between s 4 and s 5 (eg the criteria of threatening, abusive or insulting, and the venue) there are important distinctions:

(a) the criteria in s 5 are extended by the addition of "disorderly" to the list of prohibited behaviour (but not words);

(b) fear or provocation of violence in s 4 is replaced by likelihood of harassment, alarm or distress in s 5;

(c) the words "towards another person" appear in s 4 but not in s 5;

(d) section 5 extends only to the display, and not the distribution, of writing, signs etc. Thus it does not extend to letters, eg poison pen letters, or the posting of leaflets through a door.

4.1   The Victim

It is tempting to say that there is no victim of a s 5 offence, but it is not an offence which can occur in a vacuum. The simple requirement is that the proscribed conduct occurs within the hearing or sight of a person who is likely to be caused harassment, alarm or distress by it (s 5(1)(b)). That person would normally be perceived as the victim. There is no requirement that the conduct should be directed towards that or any other person in particular. In *DPP v Orum* [1989] 1 WLR 88, [1988] 3 All ER 449, (1989) 88 Cr App R 261 (QBD), it was made clear that a policeman could be harassed, alarmed or distressed by particular conduct. Glidewell J said:

"I find nothing in the context of the 1986 Act to persuade me that a policeman may not be a person who is caused harassment, alarm or distress by the various kinds of words and conduct to which s 5(l) applies . . . However . . . it is not to say that every police officer in this situation is to be assumed to be a person who is caused harassment. Very frequently, words and behaviour with which police officers will be wearily familiar will have little emotional impact on them save that of boredom."

Each case depends on its own facts and is a matter for the tribunal of fact. In *R v Ball* (1990) 90 Cr App R 378, [1989] Crim LR 579 (CA), the Court of Appeal looked at a case where a police officer had arrested a person for a s 5 offence where he was the only person present and had not been harassed, alarmed or distressed. The case established that a police officer was capable of being "likely to be" harassed, alarmed or distressed, and that it is a matter of fact in each particular case whether he would have been likely to be so affected.

4.2   The Requisite Intent

In *DPP v Clarke and Others* (1992) 94 Cr App R 359, (1991) 135 SJ 135, [1992] Crim LR 60 (DC), a group of people opposed to abortion had gathered outside an abortion clinic carrying a picture of an aborted foetus; they refused to stop displaying the pictures when requested to do so by the police. They were charged with offences contrary to s 5(1)(b) of the POA 1986. The justices found that the display was abusive or insulting; and that it was in the sight of someone likely to be caused harassment, alarm or distress by it, namely one of the police officers. Applying an objective test to s 5(3) they found the behaviour unreasonable. They then applied a subjective test to s 6(4) and concluded, on a balance of probabilities, that the defendants did not intend, nor were they aware, that the display might be threatening, abusive or insulting. They therefore dismissed the charges.

On appeal, the Divisional Court found that the component parts of s 5(1) were to be distinguished, and that the intent or awareness requirement in s 6(4) did not relate to the "within the sight" part of s 5(1). Dealing with the defence, the Divisional Court found that the s 5(3)(a) defence had to be proved by the defence on a balance of probabilities and that the s 6(4) intent, being part of the offence, had to be proved by the prosecution beyond reasonable doubt:

> "So far as the defence provided by s 5(3) is concerned, the section makes it clear that the burden of proof rests upon the defendant . . . the standard of proof is the balance of probabilities. So far as s 6 is concerned, the burden of proving that the defendant had the requisite mental element rests upon the prosecution . . . the standard required is proof beyond reasonable doubt. The section plays an important role in the protection of freedom of speech." (*per* Nolan LJ)

While *DPP v Clarke* sets out the position in relation to intent and the related defences in a case where the court upheld a decision of justices to acquit, in *DPP v Wilmot and Another*, 1991, unreported (QBD), the court made the point that what a person is aware of is a matter of common sense. Provided some evidence is called by the prosecution, it would be for the court to draw proper inferences about the defendant's "awareness" from the evidence before it.

In *Lewis v DPP*, 1995, unreported (DC), the court was again called upon to deal with issues relating to abortion clinics. In that case a placard showing a baby lying in a pool of blood and titled "21 weeks abortion", held aloft, was found to be abusive and insulting. The issue of awareness and intent was more readily resolved against the defendant because others had put down placards on being requested to do so by the police. The defendant had picked up and continued to display his placard when again asked not to. It followed that he intended the placard to be abusive and insulting, and was aware that the representation on the placard was abusive or insulting.

The court's comment in *Lewis v DPP* on the capacity of a truthful representation to be abusive is instructive. It is probably also a logical development of the common sense approach to awareness determined in *DPP v Wilmot and Another*:

"The point taken is that the photograph on the placard was an accurate representation of the result of abortion, and that what is truthful cannot be abusive or insulting . . . A patient may be abused in having the activities (lawful activities in this case) depicted in the way they were on that placard." (*per* Pill LT)

4.3   Arrest

An arrest under s 5 may be made of a person who has engaged in offensive conduct, been warned by the officer about his conduct and then engaged in further offensive conduct, either immediately afterwards or shortly after the warning. The arrest may be made by any officer, not just the one who gave the warning (Public Order Amendment Act 1996, reversing the effect of *DPP v Hancock and Tuttle* [1995] Crim LR 139, [1995] COD 32 (QBD)).

The position is different in the case of a person arrested for an offence other than the offence under s 5, eg common assault or breach of the peace, but who is subsequently charged with an offence contrary to s 5. Here the warning is not required, as the arrest is not pursuant to s 5; only the elements of s 5 and the intent in s 6 need be made out.

In any event, whether or not the arrest is lawful has no bearing on whether the offence under s 5 is made out. The s 5 behaviour precedes the arrest and an invalid arrest cannot retrospectively affect the criminality of the behaviour. In *DPP v Hancock and Tuttle* the offence charged was under the more technical s 51 and related to behaviour during the arrest.

In *Groom v DPP* [1991] Crim LR 713, [1991] COD 362, the Divisional Court reviewed how courts should deal with the warnings required by s 5. In that case, following an incident of racial abuse outside a town hall, a police officer followed the abuser into the building and an exchange took place during which the officer told the person that he had harassed someone outside and that he should apologise. The appellant said "Or else you'll nick me?" She replied, "yes". The appellant continued in his aggressive manner and told her to "get stuffed", whereupon she arrested him for an offence contrary to s 5. The question was whether or not her words constituted the required warning. Bingham LJ, supporting the view that she had given sufficient warning, said:

"It is also a salutary principle that in analysing the effects of what people say and do in confused and violent, or potentially violent, situations, tribunals of fact should concentrate in a common sense way on the sub-

stance of what was said and done and not indulge in a nice analysis more appropriate to academic debate than to the crude realities of life."
It would thus appear that it is the substance of the warning and not its form that is essential.

4.4 Venue

Section 5 penalises conduct which occurs in private or public places subject to the same restriction in respect of dwellings (see page 58) as now appears in s 4A. There is no offence if the "other person" is inside the same dwelling as the offender or in another dwelling. It was observed in *Chappell v DPP* (1989) 89 Cr App R 82, [1989] COD 259 (DC) that:

> "[a] person yelling or gesturing to persons in the street . . . would not commit an offence vis-à-vis another person within his own house or a neighbouring house across the street".

4.5 The Constituents of the Offence

To constitute the offence, threatening, abusive or insulting words must be used (s 5(1)(a)); or threatening, abusive or insulting or disorderly behaviour must occur (s 5(1)(a)); or there must be a display of any writing, sign or visible representation which is threatening, abusive or insulting (s 5(1)(b)). This conduct is collectively referred to here as "offensive behaviour", a description which is not used in s 5 except in the context of arrest for the offence (s 5(4)). Display only is prohibited, not distribution. The distribution of literature might be dealt with under s 4; or it might be argued that the distribution of offensive literature amounts to disorderly conduct.

"Threatening, abusive or insulting"

The words "threatening, abusive or insulting" have been considered earlier, but in the context of s 5, in *Herrington v DPP*, 1992, unreported (QBD), the court went through the definitions in *Brutus v Cozens* [1973] AC 854, [1972] 3 WLR 521, [1972] 2 All ER 1297 (HL) for the meaning of "threatening". In the *Herrington* case the Divisional Court upheld magistrates. They had found that a man who had "gone down the garden, turned and stared for a period of time at the lady's kitchen window when standing nude and facing his genitals towards her" was engaging in threatening behaviour within the meaning of s 5. See also *Lewis v DPP*, 1995, unreported (DC), page 103 above, where the showing of a placard with a picture of a foetus in a pool of blood, and the accompanying wording, was held to be abusive or insulting.

In *Vigon v DPP, The Times* 9 December 1997, the Divisional Court had to resolve whether the use of a partially concealed camera in the changing area of a stall holder selling swimming costumes could satisfy the requirements of s 5. Was it insulting? The court took the view that if the stall holder had been peeping into the changing area directly that would have been conduct satisfying s 5. By the same token, if he peeped via a video camera the same should apply. Customers who noticed the camera would be distressed by it and it was therefore proper to convict him of the offence. The court has yet to consider the implications of a fully concealed camera not within the hearing or sight of the person being filmed (see also page 96).

"Disorderly"

"Disorderly" has been used to describe different types of conduct. In *Martin v Yorkshire Imperial Metals Ltd* [1978] IRLR 440 (EAT), it was referred to as:

> "rather a weasel word; it might mean disorderly in the sense of riotous or the sort of conduct which is inferred in the well known phrase 'disorderly house'; or it might mean . . . any conduct which is contrary to orders".

It is best known in the offence of "drunk and disorderly" (Criminal Justice Act 1967, s 91) which is of ancient origin. Much of the conduct which falls within s 91 may also fall within s 5. The meaning of "disorderly" is derived from its context, ie its relationship to the remainder of the list (threatening, abusive and insulting), and the impact upon people who witness the behaviour; ie there must be conduct which is conducive to creating extreme concern in victims. "Disorderly" is an ordinary English word and needs no definition (see *Brutus v Cozens*, above, page 96). Regard must be had to the circumstances in which conduct occurs to determine whether or not it merits the appellation "disorderly". Some conduct of a football crowd would be disorderly if it were to be repeated in a theatre during a performance. While the words listed in ss 4 and 5 are often taken to be in descending order of seriousness, they are really no more than different types of conduct which are penalised because of their likely or intended impact on others, ie the threat of violence or harassment.

In *Chambers and Edwards v DPP* [1995] Crim LR 896, the Divisional Court looked at aspects of the word "disorderly". In that case, during 1993, the defendants interfered with a land engineer by standing in front of his theodolite, preventing him from taking measurements. One defendant kept his hand in front of the machine when warned by the police that his conduct was disorderly and was causing harassment, alarm or distress. The defendants were convicted by magistrates. They appealed to the Crown Court where they were again convicted. The Crown Court found, among other things, that they had been disorderly. The Divisional Court applied the *Brutus v Cozens* principle that "disorderly" is a word whose ordinary meaning should be used and left to the tribunal of fact:

> "For my part, I can see no reason why one should conclude that the word 'disorderly' is being used in some unusual or narrower sense than normal in the context of s 5(1) . . . whether behaviour on any occasion is characterised as disorderly is a question of fact for the trial court to determine. That decision can be upset if the trial court has misdirected itself or has

reached a decision which no reasonable tribunal could properly reach."
(*per* Keene J)

Cases under the Public Order Act 1936

Conduct which may fall within s 5 was the subject of many cases where prosecutions were brought under the 1936 Act. For example in *Ewart v Rogers*, 1985, unreported, a group of youths disturbed a householder by banging on the front windows and door and smashing milk bottles. In *R v Newham Justices ex p Sadiku*, 15 January 1985, unreported, urinating in public might have been classed as disorderly. In *R v Venna* [1976] QB 421, [1975] 3 WLR 737, [1975] 3 All ER 788 (CA), the conduct of youths in shouting and singing and dancing in the street and banging dustbin lids was described by the court as unruly and disgraceful and anti-social. It might equally have been described as disorderly.

Noisy Parties

Whether s 5 can be invoked to deal with noisy parties is not clear. If the only people likely to suffer harassment, alarm or distress are people within their houses then the offence cannot be made out. Equally, it may be difficult to class such parties as disorderly. This was the view of the government during debate in the House of Commons (Hansard, Parliamentary Debates, vol 96, No 104, para 967). In practice it appears that s 5 has not been used as a means of dealing with noisy parties, which were still the subject of debate leading up to, and indeed legislation in, the Criminal Justice and Public Order Act 1994.

"Within the sight or hearing of . . ."

The conduct must occur within the hearing or sight of a person likely to be caused harassment, alarm or distress. There is no requirement that a victim should give evidence or that someone be shown to have been harassed, alarmed or distressed. It must be shown that the conduct did in fact occur within the sight or hearing of a person and that the person was likely to be caused harassment, alarm or distress by such conduct. The offence is based upon *likely* consequences, not intended or actual consequences. Should there be witnesses who can relate their feelings, the task of the prosecution will be easier. Even if such witnesses cannot be found or are unwilling to give evidence, the prosecution may still succeed, although the difficulties inherent in this are apparent. The absence of a requirement to produce a victim who was actually harassed, alarmed or distressed was a deliberate step to avoid cases where a victim would be too nervous or frail to give evidence. The Minister of State at the Home Office observed that:

> "The prosecution will not necessarily have to produce the victim in court, but it will have to identify in each case who it was who was likely to be alarmed . . . The court's mind will be concentrated upon the impact or likely impact of the defendant's behaviour on those who were around

at that time. (HC Debates, vol 96, No 104, col 964)."

That the offensive conduct was within the sight or hearing of such a person is an inference which may be drawn from the facts as a whole, eg offensive conduct in a shopping precinct where it is likely that a police officer will be able to relate only that there were shoppers who hurried away, apparently upset or annoyed. Where there is noise late at night in the vicinity of an old people's home, then the burden of showing that a person is likely to be harassed, alarmed or distressed should be relatively simple to discharge.

In *Lodge v Andrews, The Times* 26 October 1988, the Divisional Court analysed a number of the issues relating to "within the sight or hearing". In this case a young man who had just engaged in a minor confrontation with two police officers chose to walk down the middle of a road towards a bridge; a car was about to pass over the bridge and there was a risk of accident. Two issues were canvassed. Could the car driver be a person within whose sight or hearing the misconduct occurred? And could the police officer suffer harassment, alarm or distress other than by reference to his own personal position, ie not on behalf of either the motorist or the disorderly young man who might be at risk? The Divisional Court took the view that the car driver was likely to have been alarmed by the disorderly young man in the middle of the road. In relation to the police officer, having considered *DPP v Orum* [1989] 1 WLR 88, [1988] 3 All ER 449, (1989) 88 Cr App R 261 (QBD), the court went on to say that the apprehension he feels need not relate to himself or a close relative. By way of example, the court raised the possibility of disorderly behaviour adjacent to a child. They would expect such conduct to distress or alarm an observing police officer.

The defendant would appear to have to take his victims as he finds them, and if they are especially timid and easily harassed, then, upon proof of this fact (which may mean they have to give evidence, for example where a person would not normally be adversely affected), the defendant can properly be convicted. He may be able, however, to maintain a defence under s 5(3)(a) of the POA 1986 (see page 117).

"Harassment, alarm or distress"

"Harassment", "alarm" and "distress" are not defined. Since they are ordinary words of the English language and are not intended to have any special meaning they should be given their ordinary meanings (see *Brutus v Cozens* [1973] AC 854, [1972] 3 WLR 521, [1972] 2 All ER 1297 (HL)). They are strong words and should not be equated with "annoyance" or "disturbance" or "aggravation"; they indicate a level of extreme concern. Just as a police officer may fear the use of unlawful violence, so too may he be likely to be harassed, alarmed or distressed. But the level of tolerance which may be expected of a police officer may be rather higher than that of the ordinary citizen (*DPP v Orum*, above).

4.6 Defences

Each of the three defences set out in s 5(3) of the POA 1986 must be considered in the light of *R v Lambert* (see page 91). It is likely that it will now be for the defendant to provide evidence of the existence of the elements of the defence, and then for the prosecution to disprove the elements of the defence beyond reasonable doubt. Each defence applies to all offences under s 5.

No Reason to Believe Any Person in Hearing or Sight

The first possible defence is that the defendant "had no reason to believe that there was any person within hearing or sight who was likely to be caused harassment, alarm or distress" (s 5(3)(a)). Not only must the absence of belief be genuine, but the defendant must also, objectively, have had no reasonable grounds for the belief. Mr Giles Shaw, Minister of State, remarked in the committee stage of the Bill:

> "We wanted to provide a defence for the defendant who is not aware and has no reason to be aware that his behaviour is likely to cause alarm, harassment or distress, and we wanted to bring within the offence people whose behaviour would be unlikely to harass a normal victim but who used their knowledge of the victim's weakness to make life miserable for a vulnerable person (HC, SC G, col 236)."

In *Masterson v Holder* [1986] 1 WLR 1017, [1986] 3 All ER 39, (1986) 83 Cr App R 302 (DC), the activity occurred in the presence of people who were distressed and roused to anger. It might be a defence to a charge under s 5 to demonstrate that there was no reason to believe that there was anyone in the vicinity who was likely to be harassed, eg because of the cosmopolitan nature of the particular district. In the absence of an authority on this point, it is difficult to be sure, because of changing views of society. This illustrates an important difference between s 4 and s 5. Under s 4, conduct must be used towards another person. These words do not appear in s 5, and the conduct need not be aimed at anyone; having no reason to believe that a person who will be affected is present provides a defence.

The prosecution must establish an intention to use offensive behaviour, and the proximity of other people may also be relevant to that point.

Inside Dwelling

Section 5(3)(b) provides that it is a defence if the person concerned "was inside a dwelling and had no reason to believe that the offensive conduct would be heard or seen by a person outside that or any other house". This defence is likely to be of limited application since the offence is rarely committed when the defendant is inside a dwelling.

Reasonable Conduct

Section 5(3)(c) provides that it is a defence that the person's "conduct is reasonable". The circumstances indicate when conduct can be said to be offensive in the first place, and if it can be said to be offensive then it is difficult to see how it can at the same time be reasonable. Thus the scope of this defence is uncertain, not least because, for the prosecution to succeed, it will have to establish an intention to use offensive conduct (s 5(4)), but also because the relationship between this provision and the "right to protest" in demonstration cases is relevant. It may not be possible, on particular facts, to use the defence, but there may be conduct which is, arguably, reasonable in the general context of lawful protest; the defence should not therefore be discarded entirely.

Little guidance was given during the passage of the bill on the likely scope of this defence. In committee it was said that it was intended as "a general safety net". There was some suggestion that high jinks might "induce a modest level of offence" and that it would be wrong to invoke s 5 in respect of that type of activity. Unfortunately no examples were given which might explain these ambiguous observations. In addition it was suggested that there were examples of behaviour which might be reasonable on the basis that they came close to lawful authority, eg "if firemen or police officers use strong language when they want people to get out of the way, that may be deemed unreasonable to some but in the context would probably be acceptable". The practicality of the examples may be doubted. More to the point might be cases where offensive behaviour is used by an occupier in an attempt to rid himself of trespassers. Will the use of offensive conduct be "reasonable"? Would it make any difference if the trespassers were police officers? (Compare the behaviour in *Marsh v Arscott* (1982) 75 Cr App R 211, [1982] Crim LR 827 (QBD).) To what extent is the abuse commonly hurled at those who cross picket lines, eg shouts of "scab" or "blackleg", reasonable?

In *Lewis v DPP*, 1995, unreported, the Divisional Court also analysed the defence of reasonableness. In this case, discussed above, page 111, the defendant stood outside an abortion clinic holding a placard depicting a baby in a pool of blood. It was argued on his behalf that while the test of reasonableness of conduct can be answered only by reference to an objective standard of reasonableness in accordance with the decision in *DPP v Clarke* (see again page 111), in a s 5 case, the test should be applied to the facts as the particular defendant knew them. An analogy was drawn on behalf of the defendant with the notion of honest belief as a defence to a rape charge. This was rejected by the Divisional Court:

"The analogy is not sound . . . In this case the appellant's belief as to what was happening in the clinic accords with the actual state of affairs . . . he is not entitled to have his conduct judged only on the basis of his own moral stance or beliefs." (*per* Pill LJ)

The court went on to review whether the particular defendant had acted reasonably:

"In considering whether the defendant had established that he had acted reasonably, the Court was entitled to take into account that he persisted in his conduct after being asked to desist . . . the appellant, unlike the women who were not prosecuted, persisted in displaying the placard." (*per* Pill LJ)

The court went on with its review of reasonableness:

"It cannot be right that a trial court should have to adopt the same approach in judging the issue of reasonable conduct and view the matter entirely through the eyes of the defendant . . . That would lead to situations where the more extreme were the opinions of a defendant, the more readily would his conduct be regarded as reasonable." (*per* Keene J)

The case of *DPP v Lewis* therefore follows *DPP v Clarke*, highlighting problems which may arise if defendants attempt to find an alternative approach to the s 5 defence of reasonableness.

Prevention of Crime

A common defence to an allegation under s 5 is that the defendant was doing what he regarded as necessary to prevent offending behaviour by some other person. In *R v Ball* (1990) 90 Cr App R 378, [1989] Crim LR 579 (CA), B grabbed a police officer from behind to prevent his brother being arrested for a s 5 offence. B claimed that he was acting in reasonable defence of his brother and that the officer was acting unlawfully, there being no reasonable grounds for suspecting him of having committed an offence. The court did not agree that the arrest was unlawful and reviewed issues relating to honest belief. It was held that:

"honest belief on reasonable grounds in the unlawfulness of an arrest was not a defence to assault (*R v Fennell* [1971] QB 428, [1970] 3 WLR 513, [1970] 3 All ER 215) and it was logical that a similar belief in excessive force by the police in executing a lawful arrest would also not afford a defence."

Section 3 Criminal Law Act 1967 entitles a person to do that which is reasonable in the prevention of crime. Some public order cases, including s 5 cases, require the court to establish, as a question of fact, whether the defendant was engaged in lawful conduct to prevent crime. This defence cannot be used as a means of justifying action where the alleged crime being prevented is in fact a lawful activity to which the particular defendant takes exception. The abortion clinic cases of *Clarke v DPP* and *Lewis v DPP* are not the only examples of judicial analysis of protest against lawful activity. Protestors against live animal exports may regard the treatment of the animals during transportation as a crime. In reality that is a moral judgement and the export is both legal and lawful. Action to prevent it cannot therefore be protected by the notion of preventing crime. *Morrow v DPP* [1994] Crim LR 58 (DC) again related to protests over abortion clinics. In that case the appellants had entered an abortion clinic and created difficulties inside. They had been charged with s 5 offences and relied on the statutory defence that their conduct was reasonable, arguing that their conduct was lawful under s 3(1) of the Criminal Law Act 1967. The court held that the defence under s 3 was not apt to the situation in this case, where an aggressive demonstration was being held. The appellants were described by the court as participating in preventing people from exercising their lawful rights and therefore it was difficult to see the relevance of the s 3 defence. The court made the point that the s 3 defence was not created to protect people who plan a demonstration involving aggressive behaviour when on the premises of others and disrupting the perfectly proper conduct of others. This case should be seen alongside the decision in relation to the attempt by public authorities to prevent trade in live animals through their ports. Where protest and lawful activity meet, the courts see the protection of lawful activity as a matter of fundamental importance. In *R v Coventry City Council ex p Phoenix Aviation* [1995] 3 All ER 37, [1995] COD 300, (1995) NLJ 559 (QBD) it was said that (*per* Simon Brown LJ):

> "English law is unsurprisingly replete with examples of ringing *dicta* vindicating the rule of law . . . One thread runs consistently throughout all the case law: the recognition that public authorities must beware of surrendering to the dictates of unlawful pressure groups."

4.7   The Interface Between Sections 4 and 5

Section 4 is specifically designed to deal with activities which are likely to lead to fear of or provocation to violence. Section 5 is specifically designed to deal with activities which lead to a serious degree of discomfort. This is not to say that in appropriate instances conduct which falls squarely within s 4 may not be dealt with under s 5. Rather, conduct which does not fall within a "lesser" category should not be made to fit into a more serious category (see page 91 on the use of s 5 and Chapter 1).

4.8   Arrest

A constable, in uniform or not, may arrest without warrant in the circumstances set out in s 5(4) and (5). The first reference in s 5(4) to "he engages" may be read as meaning "is engaged in" and not "is or has been engaged in". The nature of the offence it such that it is unusual for a constable to witness the actual conduct and to issue a warning while it is continuing. If this interpretation is correct, then the power of arrest will be exercised on few occasions. The power of arrest under s 25 of the Police and Criminal Evidence Act is, of course, available if any of the general arrest conditions in that Act are satisfied.

The meaning of "shortly or immediately" is a question of fact for each case. "Immediately" would appear to be superfluous since any activity which occurs immediately can be said to have occurred shortly.

4.9   Avoidance of Duplicity

Section 7 precludes the risk of duplicity by providing that the section creates only one offence.

4.10 Sentence
The offence carries a maximum penalty of a fine up to level 3.

5   Racially Aggravated Offences

Checklist
- racially aggravated public order offences are either way offences;
- the maximum sentence is two years, the Court of Appeal emphasising the need for long sentences (see *R v Miller* [1999] CLR 590);
- "racially aggravated" is defined very widely;
- "racial group" is defined widely;
- associates and families of racial groups are protected by the provisions;
- additional motives do not preclude racial aggravation;
- in summary cases, non-racially aggravated offences must be charged as alternatives to avoid the risk of no conviction at all;
- the guideline penalty for a racially aggravated s 5 offence is a community penalty;
- the guideline for a racially aggravated s 4A offence is committal to Crown Court for sentence;
- the guideline penalty for a racially aggravated s 4 offence is custody.

5.1   Racial Aggravation
The incorporation of express provisions to counter racially aggravated offences was a Labour Party commitment which was implemented in the face of opposition founded on the notion that the courts could sentence more severely in such cases and that there was no need for new provisions. Section 4A POA 1986 had been expected to be used in cases of racial harassment notwithstanding the fact that it contained no express reference to race. The Government view was that the ethnic minority groups in the UK were entitled to particularised protection in statutory form, and that that protection should include greater penalties for offences with a racial component. The Crime and Disorder Act 1988 therefore introduced into the offences under ss 4, 4A and 5 of the POA 1986 the concept of racial aggravation.

The meaning of "racially aggravated" is set out in s 28 Crime and Disorder Act 1998. An offence is racially aggravated if, at the time it is committed, or immediately before or after it is committed, the offender demonstrates towards the victim hostility based on the victim's membership or presumed membership of a particular racial group; or if the offence is motivated wholly or in part by hostility towards members of a racial group based on their membership of that group. In *DPP v Weeks*, 14 June 2000, unreported (QBD) the defendant called the complainant a "black bastard" when they met by chance following a disputed business transaction. He was charged with a racially aggravated offence under s 4A POA. At first instance the case was dismissed on the basis that the court was not sure either that the respondent intended harassment alarm or distress to be suffered, or that he was aware his words might have been threatening, abusive or insulting. The prosecution appealed on the basis that the words "black bastard" were universally recognised as racial abuse. The appeal was refused because there might be situations in which the expression was not intended to cause harassment, alarm or distress. It was a question for the fact-finding tribunal and in the particular case it had been open to the court of first instance to make that finding.

The statutory definition of "racially aggravated" is extremely wide and enables the court to analyse behaviour before, during and after the alleged incident to determine the state of mind of the defendant. As with all criminal cases, drawing inferences from the evidence is important in determining the position of the defendant. The fact that the person abused does not belong to the racial group that the defendant had in mind when committing the offence will afford no protection to the offender.

"Membership" includes association with a particular racial group and "presumed" means presumed by the defendant. The fact that the hostility is based on membership of a religious group or any other factor is irrelevant once the above criteria are made out.

One of the most common targets of racists are the associates of a racial group who do not belong to that racial group. Spouses who do not share their partner's racial origin, or children of mixed race relationships, are often abused in this way. The Crime and Disorder Act affords protection to them whether they are abused in their homes, at work, when using public transport or in any other circumstance falling within the statutory framework.

"Racial group" means a group defined by reference to race, colour, nationality (including citizenship) or ethnic or national origins. Racial abuse may be based on skin colour, but the abuse of a Scot because he is Scottish can likewise amount to a racially aggravated public order offence. In *R v White (Anthony Delroy)*, 14 February 2001, unreported (CA), the court decided that it was not tied to dictionary definitions in assessing "racial group" and/or "race". In that case the defendant referred to a bus conductress from Sierra Leone as "a stupid African bitch". His claim was that he did not refer to a "racial group", and that as he belonged to the same racial group, there was no offence. Lord Justice Pill applied a broad non-technical meaning. He said "African" did describe a racial group. He also said it is possible to show hostility to a person of the same racial group. The defendant was sentenced to nine months imprisonment for a racially aggravated offence under s 4 POA.

5.2 Racially Aggravated Public Order Offences

An offence is a racially aggravated public order offence if it is an offence under s 4, 4A or s 5 of the Public Order Act 1986 and it is racially aggravated as defined above (see s 31, Crime and Disorder Act 1998).

Arrest

A constable may arrest without warrant a person he reasonably suspects to be committing a racially aggravated offence contrary to s 4 or s 4A Public Order Act 1986.

He may arrest without a warrant in respect of a racially aggravated s 5 offence only if the person engages in conduct the constable reasonably suspects to constitute a racially aggravated s 5 offence. If the person is warned by the constable to stop and then engages in further such conduct immediately or shortly afterwards, the constable may arrest him. The second conduct need not be of the same nature as the original conduct.

Sentence

Racially aggravated s 4 and s 4A offences are either way offences with a maximum sentence in the summary court of six months imprisonment or a fine up to the statutory maximum. In the Crown Court the maximum is two years imprisonment or a fine or both. The maximum penalty for a racially aggravated s 5 offence is a level 4 fine.

It is arguable, on the basis of current decisions, that most cases should find their way to the Crown Court for sentence (*R v Miller* [1999] CLR 590). Thus far there has been no guidance to determine how the less serious cases should be dealt with. There is anecdotal evidence of sentences of discharge through to imprisonment, with courts facing difficulty in determining the approach to racial insults uttered by defendants affected by alcohol. Given the comments in *R v Miller,* the tendency will be for increasing use of custody at all levels.

Alternative Verdict in the Crown Court

In the Crown Court the jury is permitted to return an alternative verdict of guilty of the non-racially aggravated offence where a racially aggravated offence was originally charged,

The Victim

In a racially aggravated s 5 offence, the person "likely" to be caused harassment etc is the victim of the offence for the purposes of s 28 of the Crime and Disorder Act.

6   Malicious Communications

The Malicious Communications Act 1988 was the product of the review by the Law Commission of the law relating to criminal libel. The Law Commission was aware that:

> "The absence of any offence at present which penalises the sender of a poison-pen letter is a gap in the law which is capable of causing appreciable social harm which requires the creation of a new criminal

offence."

Sections 4, 4A and 5 of the 1986 Act are ill-equipped to deal with this problem since they do not apply to behaviour which occurs in a dwelling; see *Chappell v DPP* (1989) 89 Cr App R 82, [1989] COD 259 (DC). Although the Law Commission was for the time being content to leave its proposal short of extending to telephone or electronic communication, this gap has been plugged by the amendments introduced by the Criminal Justice and Police Act 2001, s 43. The 1988 Act may be useful where the conduct of the defendant does not amount to a course of conduct within the Protection from Harassment Act 1997, eg because it is done only once, or where letters are sent to different people.

The Act, as amended by the Criminal Justice and Police Act s 43, provides that:

(1) Any person who sends to another person –

    (a) a letter, electronic communication or article of any description which conveys–

        (i) a message which is indecent or grossly offensive;

        (ii) a threat; or

        (iii) information which is false and known or believed to be false by the sender; or

    (b) any article or electronic communication which is, in whole or part, of an indecent or grossly offensive nature,

is guilty of an offence if his purpose, or one of his purposes, in sending it is that it should, so far as falling within paragraph (a) or (b) above, cause distress or anxiety to the recipient or to any other person to whom he intends that it or its contents or nature should be communicated.

(2) A person is not guilty of an offence by virtue of subsection (1)(a)(ii) above if he shows –

    (a) that the threat was used to reinforce a demand made by him on reasonable grounds, and

    (b) that he believed, and had reasonable grounds for believing, that the use of the threat was a proper means of reinforcing the demand.

(2A) In this section 'electronic communication' includes–

    (a) any oral or other communication by means of a telecommunication system (within the meaning of the Telecommunications Act 1984); and

    (b) any communication (however sent) that is in electronic form.

(3) In this section references to sending include references to delivering or transmitting and to causing to be sent, delivered or transmitted and 'sender' shall be construed accordingly.

(4) A person guilty of an offence under this section shall be liable on summary conviction to imprisonment for a term not exceeding six

months or to a fine not exceeding level 5 on the standard scale, or to both."

7 Harassment

Checklist (s 2, Protection from Harassment Act 1997)
- has there been a course of conduct?
- does the conduct amount to harassment (including alarm or distress)?
- did the defendant know or ought he to have known the conduct amounted to harassment?
- was the conduct reasonable or do other defences apply?

Checklist (s 4, Protection from Harassment Act 1997)
- has there been a course of conduct?
- did the course of conduct cause a person to fear violence would be used against him on at least two occasions?
- did the defendant know or ought he to have known the conduct would cause the other to fear violence?
- was the conduct reasonable or do other defences apply?

7.1 Introduction

Harassment has been tackled in a piecemeal fashion, protection having been afforded to specific groups such as residential occupiers (Protection from Eviction Act 1977); certain occupiers of caravans (Caravan Sites Act 1968); and debtors (Administration of Justice Act 1970). The protection offered by s 5 of the POA 1986 applies only in respect of threatening, abusive or insulting behaviour, and is further restricted by the requirement for *mens rea* in s 6. In *R v Johnson* [1997] 1 WLR 367, [1996] 2 Cr App R 434, [1996] Crim LR 828 (CA), a defendant who made hundreds of obscene telephone calls to at least thirteen women was convicted of the common law offence of public nuisance in the light of the widespread incidence of this behaviour (compare the law relating to bomb hoaxes, page 253, or obstruction of the highway, page 206). Only rarely does the offence under s 5 have a single person as the victim, although this may be so where there are special facts, as in *R v Millward* (1986) 8 Cr App R (S) 109 (CA).

The Protection from Harassment Act 1997 creates a specific civil remedy (s 3), with a specific criminal offence (triable either way) for breach of an injunction prohibiting behaviour contrary to the Act. This civil aspect is outside the scope of this book, although it may be referred to in the discussion of the cases. In addition, the Companies Act 1985 has been amended by the Criminal Justice and Police Act 2001 to permit confidentiality orders to be made in respect of the residential addresses of directors, secretaries or permanent representatives of companies where there is a serious risk of violence or intimidation.

The 1997 Act creates two criminal offences. The first is the summary offence under s 2, of conduct which amounts to harassment of another. The second offence, under s 4, is triable either way and consists of causing a person to fear that violence will be used against him. The mechanisms under the 1997 Act do not replicate the overlaps between the offences in ss 4, 4A and 5 of the 1986 Act, and provide a more effective scheme of protection. In serious cases or where a course of conduct cannot be proved, the offences under the 1986 Act or the Malicious Communications Act 1988 may be charged, and the other statutory assaults may also have a role to play; see *R v Ireland and Burstow* [1997] QB 114, [1996] 3 WLR 650, [1997] 1 All ER 112 (CA).

A court sentencing a person under s 2 or s 4 of the Protection from Harassment Act 1997 may impose a restraining order, breach of which is an offence (s 5).

Closely linked to the offences and restraining orders are the provisions in s 42 of the Criminal Justice and Police Act 2001, on directions to stop harassment outside a dwelling. Intimidation of vulnerable groups at home is tackled by this section; see page 137.

The 1997 Act has been applied to a far wider range of circumstances than the "stalking" context with which it was closely (but not exclusively) associated during its passage through the legislative process. The government foresaw its giving rise to only an extra 200 cases each year, but it is now commonly invoked in neighbour or domestic disputes, with the usual problems associated with prosecutions in connection with such disputes. It may also be used against protestors. There has been an early report on the application of the Act: Home Office Research Study 203, *An Evaluation of the Use and Effectiveness of the Protection from Harassment Act 1997* (2000). Stalking was considered in Home Office Research Study 210, *The Extent and Nature of Stalking: Findings from the 1998 British Crime Survey*. None of the reported cases concerns harassment in the workplace, but the Act – either its criminal or civil provisions – may have a role in that connection.

7.2   The Offences

The Summary Offence
Sections 1 and 2 of the Protection from Harassment Act 1997 provide that:
   "1 – (1) A person must not pursue a course of conduct–
      (a)   which amounts to harassment of another, and
      (b)   which he knows or ought to know amounts to harassment of the other.
   (2)   For the purposes of this section, the person whose course of conduct is in question ought to know that it amounts to harassment of another if a reasonable person in possession of the same information would think the course of conduct amounted to harassment of

the other.
>   2 – (1) A person who pursues a course of conduct in breach of section 1
>   is guilty of an offence."

Although this offence carries with it possible imprisonment for a term not exceeding six months, or a fine not exceeding level 5 on the standard scale, or both, it is an arrestable offence for the purposes of PACE 1984 (see s 2(3)). Where a jury acquits a defendant under s 4, it may as an alternative convict of an offence under s 2 (see s 4(5)).

The Either Way Offence

Section 4 of the Protection from Harassment Act 1997 provides that:

>   "(1) A person whose course of conduct causes another to fear, on at least two occasions, that violence will be used against him is guilty of an offence if he knows or ought to know that his course of conduct will cause the other so to fear on each of those occasions.
>
>   (2) For the purposes of this section, the person whose course of conduct is in question ought to know that it will cause another to fear that violence will be used against him on any occasion if a reasonable person in possession of the same information would think the course of conduct would cause the other so to fear on that occasion."

The offence is punishable on conviction on indictment by imprisonment for a term not exceeding five years, or a fine, or both. On summary conviction, it is punishable by imprisonment for a term not exceeding six months, or a fine not exceeding the statutory maximum, or both. The offence is thus an arrestable offence by virtue of s 24(1) PACE 1984. If a jury finds a defendant not guilty of the offence under s 4, it may find him guilty of the offence under s 2, and the Crown Court will have available to it the same sentencing powers as a magistrates' court (s 4(6)).

7.3 Course of Conduct

"A 'course of conduct' must involve conduct on at least two occasions". "Conduct" includes speech (s 7).

The particular utility of the 1997 Act is that, on conviction, a restraining order may be made, and in an appropriate case damages may be sought by way of civil action. But, if it is not possible to establish a course of conduct, it would be better for the prosecution to seek to establish relevant and distinct offences.

The requirement that there should be a course of conduct is common to both offences and is central to the operation of the Act. It is unusual to find such a provision in the criminal law and police and prosecutors may well find it useful to proceed by way of prosecution for a substantive offence in respect of one or more of the earlier elements of a course of conduct, and then rely on the conviction, linked to later events, to prove a course of conduct.

The statutory definition of a "course of conduct" has been the subject of adverse criticism by commentators. The requirement that there must be conduct on at least two occasions has served more to confuse than to clarify. It has, perhaps, encouraged prosecutions where there have been two events only, and where they have been separated by a considerable period of time. This has led to suggestions that the Act is being misused.

There must be at least two distinguishable occasions which, taken together, are capable of being described as a course of conduct. The events which occur may be similar or dissimilar, but it is the impact on the victim, together with the mental element required by both ss 2 and 4, which are crucial.

Whether or not there is a course of conduct is essentially a matter of fact. A course of conduct consists of a sequence of events over a shorter or longer period. Where events occur on the same day, it may be possible for the arbiters of fact to conclude that there is only one occasion. In *DPP* v *Ramsdale*, 12 February 2001, unreported (QBD), a magistrate was held to have been entitled to conclude that three visits paid to the victim's house on one day, including one where the defendant broke into the house, amounted to a single occasion.

Where there is a wide gap between occasions, it may be difficult, but not impossible, to establish a course of conduct. Randomly distributed events might also properly be held to constitute a course of conduct, but there has to be material before the court which establishes a course of conduct: "the fewer the occasions and the wider they are spread the less likely it would be that a finding of harassment can reasonably be made" (*Lau v DPP* [2000] 1 FLR 799, *The Times* 29 March 2000). In *R v Hills* [2001] FLR 580, the Court of Appeal, relying of the approach in *DPP v Lau*, described the need for evidence of "cogent linkage" between the two specific events relied on. Words such as "connection" or "nexus" are helpful in focusing the mind on the right questions to ask, but it is suggested that a better approach is simply to ask whether or not, looked at as a whole, what happened can be described as a course of conduct. In *Pratt v DPP*, 21 June 2001, unreported, the Divisional Court approved of the comments in *Lau v DPP* and *R v Hills,* and said:

> "The issue for the court is whether or not the incidents, however many they may be, can properly be said to be so connected in type and in context as to justify the conclusion that they can amount to a course of conduct."

The court in *Pratt v DPP* felt that:

> ". . . prosecuting authorities should be hesitant about using this particular offence in circumstances such as this where there are only a small number of incidents. They should ensure that what they are seeking the court to adjudicate upon can properly fall within this category of behaviour

which is behaviour causing harassment of the other, not merely that there have been two or more incidents. The mischief which the Act is intended to meet is that persons should not be put in a state of alarm or distress by repetitious behaviour."

Particular problems arise where the events relied on to establish a course of conduct are separated by intervening neutral or even friendly acts (such as a couple living together where the events relied on are separated by a period of reconciliation). This problem is distinct from that where the victim of a campaign of harassment and the defendant have a normal relationship on one level (eg at work) but, unknown to the victim, the defendant is in fact the perpetrator of the acts of harassment.

Commonly, the prosecution specifies the dates between which the events alleged to be a course of conduct are said to have been committed, as well as the specific dates on which the events are alleged to have occurred. The courts have not yet stated that there is a general duty always to do so (see *R v Sheffield Crown Court & Sheffield Stipendiary Magistrate ex p DPP* (1994) 158 JP 334, (1994) 158 JPN 274), but it may not always be appropriate for a court to permit amendments to an information (*R v Sheffield Stipendiary Magistrate ex p DPP*, and *Bishop v Uxbridge Magistrates' Court*, 2 February 2001, unreported (QBD)). The offence is made out on the happening of the second (or final) event relied on (*Baron v Crown Prosecution Service*, 13 June 2000, unreported (QBD)), and, for the purposes of the Magistrates' Courts Act 1986, time will begin to run from that date. Evidence may be admissible of events which fall outside the dates specified in the information where these tend to demonstrate that the defendant either was aware of the impact of his actions, or ought to have been so aware (*Bishop v Uxbridge Magistrates' Court*).

Type of Conduct

There seems to be no restriction on the types of conduct which fall within the scope of the Act. Common types of conduct include repeated verbal or physical abuse, threats, persistent following or photographing, letters, gifts, telephone calls, e-mails or faxes. They take on an offensive character because of their inherent nature (such as verbal abuse, offensive *per se*); because things sent are unwanted; or by reason of factors such as the identity of the sender, the nature of the item sent, or repetition. Unobjectionable conduct may become objectionable because of excess. For example, in *King v DPP*, 20 June 2000, unreported (QBD, CO 759/2000), the court examined a range of conduct, some of which it said could not amount to harassment on the facts:

"Whilst I accept that the repeated offers of unwelcome gifts or the repeated sending of letters could well amount to harassment, nevertheless the single offer of a gift of modest value and the sending of one innocuous letter in the circumstances of this case cannot amount to harassment within the meaning of the 1997 Act."

Of course, conduct has always to be examined against all the circumstances. Thus, perfectly lawful behaviour may become offensive if pursued in a particular fashion. If the prosecution is able to establish a course of conduct amounting to harassment, then at this stage the defence of reasonableness often falls to be considered.

It was suggested in *Tuppen v Microsoft, The Times* 15 November 2000 (a civil case), that the defendants had harassed the claimants by conduct including (it was alleged) conducting oppressive litigation. The Queen's Bench Division held that this fell outside the scope of the Act, although the precise reasoning is not apparent from the report and the case may simply be one where the proceedings were conducted perfectly properly. In *Baron v CPS* (above) it was suggested, *obiter*, that:

> "Persons will or may feel harassed as a result of the lawful conduct of forcefully conducted litigation. On the other hand, if proceedings are being used for an ulterior purpose, namely not to air legitimate grievances but to cause distress to those involved in the process, then the line may be crossed and the acts may become unlawful under the . . . Act."

In *Thomas v Newsgroup Newspapers Ltd,* 18 July 2001 (unreported, CA) – a civil case – it was held that newspaper reporting might fall within the meaning of harassment; whether or not it did would be a question of fact, bearing in mind the importance of freedom of expression under the European Convention on Human Rights.

Collective Conduct

A particular problem has been that a campaign of harassment may involve several persons, the individual conduct of each of whom does not amount to a "course of conduct". This is relevant in the context of, for example, protest groups such as animal rights groups aiming their conduct at particular targets. Section 7 of the 1997 Act has been amended by the Criminal Justice and Police Act 2001 with a view to making the 1997 Act more effective; a new subsection (3A) has been added to s 7:

> "A person's conduct on any occasion shall be taken, if aided, abetted, counselled or procured by another–
>
> (a) to be conduct on that occasion of the other (as well as conduct of the person whose conduct it is); and
>
> (b) to be conduct in relation to which the other's knowledge and purpose, and what he ought to have known, are the same as they were in relation to what was contemplated or reasonably foreseeable at the time of the aiding, abetting, counselling or procuring."

By this mechanism, both the planners and the individual executors of separate elements of the course of conduct fall within the scope of the Act.

7.4   The Mental Element

Both s 2 and s 4 of the 1997 Act require either actual or objective knowledge of the offensive nature of the behaviour. In the light of the likely mental state of many stalkers, the Act adopts the objective test as an alternative and the processes of the Act are thereby rendered more useful than many other substantive provisions. This point was reinforced by the Court of Appeal in *R v Colohan (Sean Peter)*, 17 May 2001, unreported, where it was held that a paranoid schizophrenic was not entitled to claim that the reasonable man should be endowed with the particular mental characteristics of the defendant for the purposes of the test in s 1(2)(b). The question of the mental state of the defendant was relevant to the knowledge which the defendant actually possessed and which would then be vested in the objective reasonable person.

7.5   The Summary Offence

In s 1, the singular includes the plural and a charge that the defendant harassed two or more named complainants is not necessarily duplicitous: *DPP v Williams (Michael)*, 27 July 1998, unreported (QBD) *(obiter)*; *Mills v DPP*, 17 December 1998, unreported (QBD) *(obiter)* and *DPP v Dunn (Robert John)* [2001] 1 Cr App R 352, *The Times* 1 November 2000. In the latter case, Bell J remarked:

> "I can see no unfairness in principle to a defendant, provided that his acts amount to pursuing a single course of conduct which amounts to harassment of a number of closely connected victims in a close knit definable group . . ."

In that case there were two named complainants (husband and wife); it was held not to be necessary that both should have been present on each occasion forming the course of conduct. It had to be shown that there was a course of conduct aimed at the named individuals as a whole. In *Mills v DPP* the two named complainants were neighbours and their complaints were unrelated; they were not members of a close knit definable group and there was no other "nexus" between them. Examples of a close knit definable group given by the court were sisters living in the same house, or a family subjected to racial abuse.

In the case of a large number of named complainants failure to establish harassment by all the named complainants may cause the information to fail; see *DPP v Dunn* where the court preferred not to deal with the point specifically.

Section 7 provides that "References to harassing a person include alarming the person or causing the person distress." This echoes s 4A and s 5 of the 1986 Act, and these are ordinary words which should be given their ordinary meanings. They should be read disjunctively not conjunctively: *DPP v Ramsdale*, 12 February 2001, unreported (QBD).

Under the 1997 Act there must be actual distress or alarm or harassment. In seeking to establish this, the best approach is simply to ask whether the complainant was harassed, alarmed or distressed by the conduct, and then to ask whether the defendant knew or ought to have known that the conduct amounted to harassment. There is some suggestion that the Divisional Court is intimating an objective test of whether or not there was harassment, ie whether or not, having regard to that particular victim and all the circumstances, what occurred can be described as harassment.

Can behaviour of the defendant which is aimed at something or someone else be taken into account as supporting its harassing impact on the complainant? This point has been answered affirmatively in the context of s 4 and it is suggested that the same would follow in the context of s 2. Behaviour aimed at a complainant's family, friends, workmates, property etc is quite capable of amounting to harassment of the complainant. But it becomes such only when the complainant is made aware of the conduct; see *Kellett v DPP*, 12 February 2001, unreported (QBD):

"The offence was only complete when the complainant was told of the telephone calls made by the appellant in that it was the knowledge of his conduct that caused her distress. But the fact that she had been informed of the course of conduct by a third party rather than by the appellant himself did not mean that there was no offence committed once she had been so informed, even in circumstances where the appellant had asked that she should not be so informed, so long as there was evidence on the basis of which the court could properly conclude . . . that the appellant was pursuing a course of conduct which he knew or ought to have known amounted to harassment of the complainant."

A case which might be taken to contradict this is *King v DPP*, 20 June 2000, unreported (QBD, CO 759/2000), where the the defendant secretly video-recorded the complainant and the police told the complainant about the video-recording. The Divisional Court suggested that the justices had been entitled to find that repeatedly making video films amounted to harassment. Later, the court referred to incidents when the defendant rummaged through the complainant's bin bags; the complainant became aware of this and was caused alarm and distress. The decision must be correct, but on the basis that the offence was complete when the complainant became aware of the video recording.

7.6 Fear of Violence

To constitute either of the two offences, there must be a course of conduct (which requires conduct on two occasions), and the course of conduct must cause the victim to fear, on at least two occasions, that violence will be used (s 4). Despite the temptation to read the section as requiring the course of conduct to comprise at least four occasions, it is submitted that this is beyond what Parliament can have intended; see *R v DPP, The Times* 20 February 2001. Properly read, s 4 simply requires proof of a course of conduct, and that on two occasions the complainant was put in fear. The course of conduct may or may not include other occasions where fear was caused.

The distinction between the offences under the 1997 Act and those under s 4 of the 1986 Act is that under the 1986 Act the violence must be shown to be both immediate and unlawful. For the purpose of s 4 of the 1997 Act it is sufficient to show that the victim is caused to fear violence, irrespective of whether it is immediate and unlawful (as is usually the case) or at some future, even if undetermined, time ("I'll get you later"). In any event, a threat of some future violence may well be sufficient to cause a person to fear that violence will be used at once; this is a question of fact.

The requirement that the complainant be shown to have feared violence (rather than unlawful violence) places a burden on the defendant to establish the lawfulness of his behaviour. This may be contrasted with s 4 of the 1986 Act where it is for the prosecution to demonstrate the unlawfulness of the violence threatened.

There is nothing to suggest that the reasoning underpinning the 1986 Act should not apply in respect of a person who is alarmed or distressed by something being done or threatened etc to a third party; see *Lodge v Andrews, The Times* 26 October 1988 and *DPP v Orum* [1989] 1 WLR 88, [1988] 3 All ER 449, (1989) 88 Cr App R 261 (QBD). Here, the behaviour which potentially falls within the Act is much broader than at first sight. A person may be caused to fear violence will be used against him even though the threat is made against someone or something else. In *R v DPP* (above) threats made to the complainant by the defendant that he would blow her dog's brains out were held capable of giving rise to a fear on her part of violence against her within the section; such questions are matters of fact in all the circumstances. A similar conclusion, but *obiter*, was reached in *R v Henley (Clifford James)*, 11 February 2000, unreported, where the Court of Appeal observed that:

> "There could certainly be a case in which conduct ostensibly directed against the family of a complainant may cause that complainant to fear that violence will be used against him or her."

In all these instances, what must be shown is that there was the requisite awareness on the part of the defendant. In the case of conduct directed to another person or thing, it may be more difficult to prove that the defendant must have been aware that his course of conduct would have the impact required to make out the offence, or objectively that he ought to have been so aware (s 4(1) and (2)). The Court of Appeal has recommended that a jury ought routinely to be directed on the meaning of s 4(2) (*R v Henley*). The judge should direct the jury on the actual words used, rather than substituting words such as "seriously frighten her as to what might happen" (*R v Henley*).

7.7   *Defences*

The defences must be seen in the context of *R v Lambert* (see page 91). Section 2(3) of the Protection from Harassment Act 1997 provides that:

"Subsection (1) does not apply to a course of conduct if the person who pursued it shows–

(a) that it was pursued for the purpose of preventing or detecting crime,

(b) that it was pursued under any enactment or rule of law or to comply with any condition or requirement imposed by any person under any enactment, or

(c) that in the particular circumstances the pursuit of the course of conduct was reasonable."

Section 4(3) of the 1997 Act provides that:

"It is a defence for a person charged with an offence under this section to show that –

(a) his course of conduct was pursued for the purpose of preventing or detecting crime,

(b) his course of conduct was pursued under any enactment or rule of law or to comply with any condition or requirement imposed by any person under any enactment, or

(c) the pursuit of his course of conduct was reasonable for the protection of himself or another or for the protection of his or another's property."

Although the defences in s 2(3)(a) and (b) are identical with those in s 4(3)(a) and (b), the defence in s 4(3)(c) is drawn in narrower terms than that in s 2(3)(c). In either instance, threats issued in connection with asserting lawful rights, eg in connection with a boundary dispute, may well contravene the Act.

The defence of reasonableness in s 2(3)(c) is fraught with uncertainty. There is a fear that it may not adequately protect investigative reporters or those who seek to inform appropriate authorities of matters within their responsibility. For example, in *Kellett v DPP*, 12 February 2001, unreported (QBD), an informant went beyond merely reporting his suspicions that a DSS civil servant was at home when she should have been at work, and added references to fraud and an extortionate salary. This was unreasonable. In *Baron v Crown Prosecution Service*, 13 June 2000, unreported, similar comments were made in the context of grossly offensive letters written by an unsuccessful appellant for state benefits as part of a long running dispute with the Benefits Agency. Morison J, in the Queen's Bench Division, was keen to draw a distinction between the:

"legitimate expression of disgust at the way a public agency has behaved and conduct amounting to harassment. The right to free speech requires a broad degree of tolerance in relation to communications. It is a legitimate exercise of that right to say things which are unpleasant or possibly hurtful to the recipient. Persons in the public service . . . are used to rudeness, aggression and unpleasantness of every form and the courts are likely in my judgment to expect of them a degree of robustness and fortitude beyond what other members of the public may be expected to show."

The activities of protestors or journalists may be alleged to fall foul of the Act. If so, it may be appropriate to consider the impact of the Human Rights Act and the extent to which the terms of the 1997 Act may be disproportionate and not necessary in a democratic society. In *R v DPP ex p Moseley*, 9 June 1999, unreported (QBD), a course of conduct amounting to harassment in breach of an injunction – the injunction not naming the defendants, or the defendants being unaware of the terms – was held to be unreasonable. It was not permissible to go beyond the injunction and to seek to balance the rights of protestors and the rights of the complainants. Conduct in breach of the terms of an injunction, the defendants being unaware of those terms, would not of itself be unreasonable, and the court would have to carry out a balancing process disregarding the injunction.

The defendant's mental state or mental disability is not a matter to be taken into account in assessing the reasonableness of the defendant's behaviour (*R v Colohan*) (*Sean Peter*), 17 May 2001, unreported (CA).

7.8 Restraining Orders

Section 5 of the Protection from Harassment Act 1997 provides that:

"(1)   A court sentencing or otherwise dealing with a person ('the defendant') convicted of an offence under section 2 or 4 may (as well as sentencing him or dealing with him in any other way) make an order under this section.

(2)   The order may, for the purpose of protecting the victim of the offence, or any other person mentioned in the order, from further conduct which–

(a)   amounts to harassment, or

(b)   will cause a fear of violence,

prohibit the defendant from doing anything described in the order.

(3)   The order may have effect for a specified period or until further order.

(4)   The prosecutor, the defendant or any other person mentioned in the order may apply to the court which made the order for it to be varied or discharged by a further order.

(5)   If without reasonable excuse the defendant does anything which he is prohibited from doing by an order under this section, he is guilty of an offence.

(6)   A person guilty of an offence under this section is liable–

(a)   on conviction on indictment, to imprisonment for a term not exceeding five years, or a fine, or both, or

(b)   on summary conviction, to imprisonment for a term not exceeding six months, or a fine not exceeding the statutory maximum, or both."

The Terms of the Order

Restraining orders are regarded as the teeth of the Act. Yet the Act does not create a scheme for ensuring that complainants are provided with copies of restraining orders, or of ensuring that orders are recorded in such a way as to enable speedy resolution of complaints that an order has been breached. Good practice requires that the complainant, and anyone else named in the order, should receive a copy.

Courts, prosecutors and defendants' representatives need to be meticulous in ensuring that the terms of an order are unambiguous. Usually this means the parties should prepare a draft for the court to consider. In the magistrates' court a guilty plea leading to the making of a restraining order might appear in a very heavy list, where the risk of ambiguity is greater. Should the passage of time demonstrate a problem of interpretation, the prosecutor, defendant or anyone named in the order may apply to the court for variation or discharge (s 5(4)).

The circumstances of complainants should be thoroughly investigated, probably by the police during the initial stages, so that the terms of the order are consistent with the proper protection of complainants. For example, an order protecting a complainant at a named place of work or at home may not be appropriate if the work involves visiting different locations. The restraining order may only prohibit the defendant from doing something which amounts to harassment or threat of violence; it cannot be in substance mandatory but expressed in negative terms. For example, an order prohibiting someone from absenting himself from work is in substance a positive requirement not a negative one, and falls outside s 5. An order restraining someone from shopping at a particular shop or from walking down a particular street is a negative requirement and properly falls within s 5.

Restraining orders must identify the complainant and anyone else they are intended to protect: *R v Mann (Andrew)*, 21 February 2000, unreported (CA). In most instances the identity of those who need protection is readily available and does not commonly extend beyond the complainant and close family. But, in some instances, there may be a need for a more general description of the others who are intended to receive protection, eg the supporters of a hunt, or the customers or workforce of an employer. Whether an order drawn in such wide terms would be acceptable remains in some doubt after *R v Mann,* where the court declined to give any further guidance.

Courts have to consider the duration of restraining orders. Sometimes it may be appropriate to impose an indefinite order and to leave to the defendant the burden of returning to court to have the order varied or discharged. In other instances it may be possible to specify a definite period. If there is an allegation of breach of a time-limited restraining order, the court, on finding the breach, may choose to extend the order (s 5(4)).

Restraining orders are capable of being applied in a draconian way, sometimes inadvertently. In *R v Crown Court at Southwark ex p Howard*, 12

April 2000, unreported (QBD), on appeal against conviction and a sentence of imprisonment for a serious instance of the summary offence, a restraining order was imposed. The defendant was required not to come within 50 yards of the block of flats where the complainant lived and where the defendant had lived for 25 years. The judge had expected that the defendant or complainant would be rehoused, but instead the local authority began possession proceedings, which were successful (see *London Borough of Lambeth v Howard*, 30 November 2000, unreported (CA)). The Queen's Bench Division felt unable to interfere with the Crown Court's decision but did point out that the defendant could apply to the Crown Court for a variation of the order. The Crown Court refused to vary the order in the light of the potential impact on the complainant. In *London Borough of Lambeth v Howard*, the Court of Appeal hearing the possession proceedings referred to the balancing of rights under the Human Rights Act 1998; arguably this ought to be an important factor for the court when considering the imposition of the order.

Breach

Breach of a prohibition is punishable on conviction on indictment by five years imprisonment or a fine; or, on summary conviction, by imprisonment for up to six months or a fine up to the statutory maximum (s 5(5) and (6)). Breach of an order is thus an arrestable offence for the purposes of the statutory powers of arrest, entry, search and seizure under the Police and Criminal Evidence Act 1984.

During breach proceedings the court is aware of the conviction leading to the restraining order, although not necessarily of the penalty imposed. This is contrary to the established position that a defendant's character is not admitted except in carefully prescribed circumstances which, with care, can usually be avoided. An allegation of breach is inevitably more compelling when set in the context of the previous finding of conduct (usually) of a similar type. This tends to demonstrate that the evidence of prosecution witnesses has been preferred to that of the defendant, whose account, if he pleaded not guilty, must have been rejected. This can be a particular problem when dealing with neighbour dispute cases.

7.9 Directions Stopping Harassment of a Person at Home

Section 42 of the Criminal Justice and Police Act 2001 has created a new power for the police to give directions to stop the harassment of a person in his home. The provision came into force on Royal Assent (11 May 2001). Breach of the direction is an offence triable summarily only and is punishable by imprisonment for up to three months or a fine up to level 4 or both. A constable may arrest without warrant anyone he reasonably suspects is committing an offence.

". . . a constable . . . at the scene may give a direction to any person if:
(a) that person is present outside or in the vicinity of any premises that

are used by any individual ('the resident') as his dwelling;

(b) the constable believes, on reasonable grounds, that the person is present there for the purpose (by his presence or otherwise) of representing to the resident or any other individual (whether or not one who uses the premises as his dwelling) or of persuading the resident or such another individual–

    (i) that he should not do something he is entitled or required to do; or

    (ii) that he should do something he is not under any obligation to do

and

(c) that constable also believes, on reasonable grounds, that the presence of that person (either alone or together with that of any other persons who are also present)–

    (i) amounts to, or is likely to result in, the harassment of the resident; or

    (ii) is likely to cause alarm or distress to the resident."

The power is available only to the senior officer present at the scene (s 42(6)(a)). Where a direction has previously given under the section, a constable may give a direction varying or withdrawing it, providing there is not a more senior officer present at the scene.

The direction requires the person to whom it is directed to do all such things as the constable may specify as the things he considers necessary to prevent the harassment of the resident or the alarm or distress of the resident.

The direction may be oral and may be given individually or all together to a group of persons who are outside or in vicinity of the premises (s 42(3)). "The vicinity" may give rise to problems of interpretation, but it is essentially a matter of fact.

The direction may require those to whom it is directed to leave the vicinity immediately or after a specified time (s 42(4)).

The direction may make exceptions to the requirements and may impose conditions on those exceptions, including conditions as to the distance from the residence or location of those permitted to remain in the vicinity, or as to the number or identity of those permitted to remain in the vicinity.

Anyone knowingly contravening a direction is guilty of an offence. This is summary only and is punishable by imprisonment for up to three months or a fine up to level 4. A constable in uniform may arrest any person he reasonably suspects is committing an offence.

8   Racial Hatred

Checklist
- "behaviour" includes gestures;
- "display" does not have a restricted meaning;
- conduct in a dwelling is not caught unless seen from outside;
- private meetings outside dwellings are caught;

- there must be an intention to stir up, or the likelihood of stirring up, racial hatred;
- offences of publishing/distributing are now arrestable offences;
- the Race Relations Act 1976 protects any racial group in Great Britain.

The common law provided little protection against incitement to racial hatred. Such incitement may have been sedition, and the gravity of incitement to racial hatred as an offence is shown by the decided cases. In *R v Edwards* (1983) Crim App R(S) 145 a comic strip designed to prejudice children against Jews and Asians led to a sentence of twelve months. But in *R v Relf* (1979) 1 Cr App R(S) 111 (CA), a sentence for distributing leaflets which were derogatory to West Indians was reduced from fifteen to nine months. The creation of the new s 4A of the POA 1986, expressly for cases of serious racial harassment, further reinforced that offences with a racial element are penalised with particular seriousness. The new racially aggravated public order offences, discussed above, take this further. Historically, the custodial sentences mentioned above were upheld on the basis that each ethnic or religious group was entitled to protection from such incitement under the Queen's peace. Section 5 of the 1936 Act could be used in appropriate circumstances, although its reliance on breach of the peace restricted its usefulness and it was ineffective against more insidious forms of incitement, or incitements which occurred privately. Section 6 of the Race Relations Act 1965 was the first statutory provision to attempt to deal with the mischief, but that too suffered from restrictive provisions, eg the need to prove both an intention to incite racial hatred and a likelihood that racial hatred would be stirred up. Section 70 of the Race Relations Act 1976 introduced s 5A into the 1936 Act. This was substantially the same as s 6 of the Race Relations Act, although the need to prove intent was removed and the likelihood of racial hatred being stirred up became the sole test. The section remained limited in its application. It did not contain a power of arrest. "Publication" and "distribution" were defined restrictively, not dealing with the distribution of material to members of a club or organisation. There were provisions in other Acts dealing with incitements to racial hatred. The Cable and Broadcasting Act 1984 and the Theatres Act 1968, together with s 5A of the Public Order Act 1936, were repealed by Sch 3 to the POA 1986 and six new offences were created in ss 18–23.

The European Court of Human Rights has determined that it is not a breach of art 10 of the European Convention on Human Rights to restrict the expression of racist views to protect others, given that the freedom under art 10 is defined in para 2 as carrying duties which may be subject to restrictions if prescribed by law, proportionate and necessary in a democratic society (*Glimmovern and Hagenbeck v Netherlands* (1979) 18 DR 187; *Kohnen v Germany* (1988) 56 DR 205; and *Jersild v Denmark* (1994) 19 EHRR 1, *The Times* 20 October 1994).

8.1   The Racial Element

To constitute an offence under POA 1986, the hatred stirred up must be "against a racial group in Great Britain". The definition of "racial group" (s 17) was adapted from the Race Relations Act 1976. It is wide enough to cover Jews (*Seide v Gillette Industries* [1980] IRLR 427 (EAT)) and Sikhs (*Mandla v Dowell Lee* [1983] 2 AC 548, [1983] 2 WLR 620, [1983] 1 All ER 1062, (HL)), as well as many other groups such as gypsies. The meaning of "ethnic origins" was considered in *Mandla v Dowell Lee* where the House of Lords provided guidelines as to the criteria for deciding whether a group might be classed as having ethnic origins. See also *Commission for Racial Equality v Dutton* [1989] QB 783, [1989] 2 WLR 17, [1989] 1 All ER 306 (CA).

8.2   Words, Behaviour and Display

It is an offence under s 18 POA 1986, (a) to use threatening, abusive or insulting words or behaviour, or (b) to display threatening, abusive or insulting written material, either where the defendant intends racial hatred to be stirred up by such use, or where, having regard to all the circumstances, racial hatred is likely to be stirred up by such use. The word "gestures" is not used in the section; they fall within "behaviour". In certain circumstances, a Nazi-style salute falls within the section, as might a clenched fist salute. Certain words or behaviour are not included (see s 18(6) and s 22(1)). "Written material" is defined in s 29. "Display" is not restricted to display to the public or a section of it.

8.3   Venue

The Act prohibits the specified conduct generally in public and private places. Where the offending words or behaviour are used in a private place, eg at a private meeting, an offence may still be made out. The only restriction is that there is no offence where the prohibited conduct occurs in a dwelling (which is defined in s 29) and is observed only by people inside that or any other house. If it is observed outside a dwelling house then it is a defence for the defendant to show, on the balance of probabilities, that he was inside a dwelling house and had no reason to believe that the conduct would be observed by a person outside that house and not in another dwelling (s 18(4)). Where the conduct occurs in any other place, eg a factory, club or private meeting, the defence does not apply.

8.4   "Threatening, abusive or insulting"

These words are interpreted as under ss 4 and 5 (see pages 93, 113). While blatant propaganda can be brought within the scope of these words relatively easily, it may be difficult to prove that more sophisticated propaganda meets the test. Some propaganda may obfuscate the issues to the extent that the "ordinary person" does not perceive its true nature, eg if the material purports to have an "educational" flavour. Brownlie observes that the formula is not very helpful, "at least superfluous" and "likely to have a restrictive effect" (*Brownlie's Law of Public Order and National Security*, 2nd edn, Butterworths, 1981). Where spoken words or behaviour are used a prosecution under s 18 may be sustained, but where the audience is mixed (ie not composed of like-minded people) offences contrary to s 4 or 5 may be easier to establish. Where a person is not shown to have intended to stir up racial hatred (ie where the prosecution is based on likelihood), the prosecution must establish that the person did intend his words or behaviour to be threatening, abusive and insulting or was reckless as to that (s 18(5)).

8.5   Intention or Likelihood

All the offences now adopt the alternative of either intent to stir up racial hatred, or the likelihood of racial hatred being stirred up. Section 5A of the 1936 Act relied on likelihood alone. The material may indicate the intention of the defendant. If not, it is necessary to demonstrate the likelihood of racial hatred being stirred up. The words "in all the circumstances" indicate that regard should be had to the facts surrounding each event. Words or gestures which are threatening, abusive or insulting and which might be likely to stir up racial hatred in some circumstances might not be likely to do so in other circumstances. There is the world of difference between threatening, abusive or insulting material displayed during a respectable seminar discussing problems of racial harassment, and such a display at a meeting to promote the views of a particular organisation.

8.6   Arrest

A constable, in uniform or not, may arrest without warrant a person he reasonably suspects is committing an offence (s 18(3)). Where this is not applicable, eg because the conduct has stopped, then recourse may be had to s 25 of the Police and Criminal Evidence Act 1984. See pages 9 and 10 for some of the dilemmas facing police officers.

8.7   Publication or Distribution of Racially Inflammatory Matter

It is an offence to publish or distribute threatening, abusive or insulting written material either with intent to stir up racial hatred or whereby it is likely that racial hatred will be stirred up (s 19(1)(a), (b), POA 1986). Where a person is not shown to have intended to stir up racial hatred but the prosecution is able to prove likelihood, it is a defence for the defendant to prove that he was not aware of the content of the material and did not suspect or have reason to suspect that it was threatening (s 19(2)). "Written material" is defined in s 29 as including any sign or other visible representation. "Writing" includes typing, printing and photography but does not extend to videos or films; but see in this respect ss 21 and 22.

   "Publishes" and "distributes" are restricted by s 19(3) to distribution or publication to the public or a section of the public; "publish or distribute" is not otherwise defined.

Distribution or publication to the members of an association to which the defendant belonged was not an offence under the amended 1936 Act. Since the 1986 Act, it is an offence. Thus the private circulation of material within an association is an offence provided (a) it can be said to be publication or distribution to "the public or a section of it"; and (b) there is the necessary intention or likelihood.

The meaning of "section of the public" is not entirely clear. While Parliament obviously intended to include members of an association, it is not clear whether members of a club are also within the scope of the Act. Although it dealt with an earlier Act, *Charter v Race Relations Board* [1973] AC 868, [1973] 2 WLR 299, [1973] 1 All ER 512 (HL) appears to be persuasive of the point that a genuine club exercising strict membership restrictions would not be "a section of the public" for the purposes of the Act. However, since that case concerned the supply of goods or services, the same result may not follow for the purposes of the offences under the Act.

For an example of the judicial approach to the meaning of "distribution or publication" see *R v Britton* [1967] 2 QB 51, [1967] 2 WLR 537, [1967] 1 All ER 486 (CA), where the court took a pragmatic view. Leaving pamphlets in the front porch of an MP's house was capable of being a distribution. Had the pamphlets been visible from the road, there might also have been a publication. However, in that case the distribution had not been to a "section of the public". Posting a bill on a wall or daubing a slogan might be said to be both publication and display for the purposes of s 4.

8.8   Arrest

Section 155 of the Criminal Justice and Public Order Act 1994 amended s 24(2) of the Police and Criminal Evidence Act 1984 to make offences contrary to s 19 of the POA 1986 arrestable offences. Publishing material intended to or likely to stir up racial hatred is now an arrestable offence.

8.9   Possession of Racially Inflammatory Matter

Section 23(1) of the POA 1986 provides that:

"A person commits an offence if:
  (a) he has in his possession threatening, abusive or insulting written material or a recording of visual images or sounds,
  (b) with a view to the purposes specified in s 23(1)(a) and (b) provided,
  (c) he intends racial hatred to be stirred up or if it is likely to be stirred up."

"Written material" and other terms in s 23 are explained in s 29. Section 23 does not extend to possession for certain purposes outlined in s 23(4). The "purposes" in s 23(1)(a) and (b) include publication, distribution, showing or playing, and these must be to the public or a section of the public (see ss 29,

19(3) and 21(2)). "Display" is also included but is not so restricted. It must be a display for the purposes of s 18.

Possession of a video recording or film is within s 23. It is complementary to s 21 which prohibits the distribution, showing or playing of, *inter alia*, video recordings. A person who receives a video recording or film for editing purposes or as part of a chain of distribution is in possession of the recording even though the actual distribution may be by another person. In so far as written material is concerned, s 23 is complementary to ss 18 (display) and 19 (distribution or publication). Both the physical element of possession and the required mental element are dealt with in the reported cases on matters such as the unlawful possession of drugs (see *DPP v Brookes* [1974] AC 862, [1974] 2 WLR 899, [1974] 2 All ER 840 (PC); *Warner v Metropolitan Police Commissioner* [1969] 2 AC 256, [1968] 2 WLR 1303, [1968] 2 All ER 356 (HL); *R v Wright* [1962] Crim LR 783 (CCA); *R v Ashton-Rickhardt* (1965) Cr App R 67; *R v Lewis* (1987) Cr App R 270). The offence is not "knowingly possess"; the defendant need only know that he has some written matter or recording. Accordingly, there is a defence of innocent possession in s 23(3), which may be of assistance to a defendant not shown to have intended to stir up racial hatred. This may apply to a firm which delivers to a printer, in an envelope, proofs of an offending piece of art, or delivers a bundle of leaflets to an address of a political party (provided this can be said to be possession within the Act).

The defence must prove the relevant matters upon the balance of probabilities, but see page 91 on the transferred burden of proof.

A journalist who has collected racially inflammatory material for research purposes does not "possess" it for the purposes of s 23 if he intends only to use it as background material. If he intends that it should be published in whole or in part, and if he has an intention that racial hatred should be stirred up, he may be convicted. If this is not his intention, regard should be had to the circumstances of the proposed publication etc in deciding whether or not racial hatred is likely to be stirred up, eg publication in a respectable social science journal or as part of a genuine educational programme (s 23(2)).

There is no power of arrest attached to s 23. The power of arrest under s 25 of the Police and Criminal Evidence Act 1984 is available in appropriate circumstances.

There is power for a justice of the peace to issue a search warrant to search for material falling within ss 23 and 24. For procedures in connection with search warrants and their execution, see Police and Criminal Evidence Act 1984 and the Code of Practice.

8.10 Plays, Recordings, Broadcasts and Cable Programmes
It is an offence to present or direct a public performance of a play which includes threatening, abusive or insulting words or behaviour with the inten-

tion thereby to stir up racial hatred or whereby in all the circumstances racial hatred is likely to be stirred up (s 20). These provisions replace those in the Theatres Act 1968 which dealt with incitement to racial hatred.

It is an offence for a person to distribute, show or play a recording of visual images or sounds which are threatening, abusive or insulting if he intends thereby to stir up racial hatred or whereby racial hatred is likely to be stirred up (s 21). This offence is intended to deal with video or other recordings used to promote racially inflammatory propaganda. There is evidence of the growth of video recordings for this purpose. The offence is not restricted to particular venues and may be committed in both public and private places, including private meetings. The distribution must be to the public or a section of the public (ss 29 and 21(2)). In some instances there may be doubt as to what is a "section of the public" for this purpose (see *Charter v Race Relations Board,* above).

Certain persons identified in s 22(2) may be guilty of an offence if a programme containing threatening, abusive or insulting visual images or sounds is broadcast or included in a cable programme service. There must be the usual intent or likelihood of racial hatred. The offences do not extend to certain broadcasts or cable programmes (s 22(7)). Section 29 explains the terms used in s 23. Certain minor changes are made to the Cable and Broadcasting Act 1984; the amendments are clearly set out in Sch 2, para 5.

There are no powers of arrest attached to any of these offences, and the provisions of s 25 of the Police and Criminal Evidence Act 1984 apply.

8.11 Miscellaneous Matters

Section 26 protects certain court reports and parliamentary proceedings. A court must order forfeiture upon conviction for an offence contrary to s 18 (relating to written material), or s 19, 21 or 23. The court must order forfeiture of all written materials or recordings produced to it and shown to be materials or recordings relating to the offences.

Section 28 provides that, where offences are committed by bodies corporate, certain other people, eg directors, may also be prosecuted if it can be shown that they connived at or consented to the offence.

The consent of the Attorney-General is required to all prosecutions, or he must himself bring the action (s 27(1)). The offences are triable summarily or on indictment (s 27(2)). They are punishable by two years' imprisonment, a fine or both on conviction on indictment; or by imprisonment for six months, a fine or both on summary conviction. For cases on sentencing see *R v Edwards* (1983) 5 Crim App R(S) 145, [1983] Crim LR 539 (CA); *R v Pearce* (1981) 72 Cr App R 295, [1981] Crim LR 639 (CA); *R v Relf* (1979) 1 Cr App R (S) 111 (CA).

8.12 Avoidance of Duplicity

Each of ss 18 to 23 creates a single offence (s 27(3)).

Chapter 5

Processions and Assemblies

1 Processions

Checklist

- statutory powers cover processions in any public place;
- the procession must be moving – not necessarily on foot;
- whether procession or not is a question of fact;
- written notice required unless not reasonably practicable;
- spontaneous processions do not, by their nature, require advance notice;
- no notice required for customary or common processions and funerals;
- organisers and participants may commit offences;
- conditions may be imposed before or during processions;
- "serious disruption to life of community" difficult to define;
- power to prohibit to prevent serious public disorder.

There are important statutory preventive powers relating to public processions in ss 11–13 of the Public Order Act 1986, which were not modified by the Criminal Justice and Public Order Act 1994. The object of these powers is to provide a means of identifying public processions with a view, where appropriate, to imposing conditions to avoid consequences specified in the Act, or seeking to prohibit public processions to avoid the risk of serious public disorder. The law relating to processions does not incorporate an express right to protest or to march subject to the proviso that the highway is dedicated for passage and repassage. To that extent, processions are *prima facie* lawful. These rights, in so far as they exist at all, are inextricably enmeshed with the rights of the individual and are more fully developed in Chapter 1. In *Duncan v Jones* [1936] 1 KB 218, [1935] All ER 710, (1935) 52 TLR 26, Lord Hewitt said "The right of assembly . . . is nothing more than a view taken by the court of the individual liberty of the subject".

Essentially, the individual may do anything which is not proscribed by statute or common law. Groups of individuals are entitled to process as a matter of UK law, subject to the statutory provisions. The legislation has taken account of the European Convention on Human Rights and Fundamental Freedoms. In the White Paper (*Review of Public Order Law*, Cmnd 9510) which led to the 1986 Act, the right to peaceful protest and the right to march were acknowledged. Article 11 of the Convention confirms the right to freedom of peaceful assembly and to freedom of association with others.

These rights cannot be restricted:

> "unless the restrictions are prescribed by law and are necessary in a democratic society in the interests of national security or public safety, for the prevention of disorder or crime, for the protection of health or morals, or for the protection of the rights and freedoms of others".

Thus far there is little case law on the impact of the Convention on the restrictive components of the Public Order Act dealing with processions and assemblies, but see *DPP v Jones* [1999] 2 AC 240, [1999] 2 All ER 257, [1999] 2 Cr App R 348 (HL) and *Broadwith v Chief Constable of Thames Valley Police*, 22 February 2000, unreported (QBD), below, page 161. Article 11 is obviously relevant to many assemblies and processions and to the police control of such events. It is difficult to envisage the courts establishing a precise set of guidelines, but the public authorities must justify interference with the fundamental right by reference to the provisos in the second part of art 11.

Justification for interference is usually by reference to the expression "necessary in a democratic society", and may well depend on the particular circumstances of specific cases. Courts will find themselves analysing the proportionality of the restrictions proposed by public authorities. One of the practical problems found in procession, assembly and other public order cases is that people appear to be aware that they have a "right" of protest, but they regard it as an unfettered right which can be exercised in any way they choose. They make themselves the arbiters of legitimate protest. There is much to be said for a programme of civic education on the complex of ways in which protest is constrained, the reasons for those constraints and the ways in which they have been challenged and can be challenged in the future.

In *Rassemblement Jurassien etc v Switzerland* (1979) 17 DR 93 it was determined that the obligation to notify the police and the requirement for permission for a march or assembly were not necessarily infringements of art 10 or art 11 of the Convention.

1.1 Definition of "Public Procession"

Section 16 of the Public Order Act ("POA") 1986 defines a "public procession" as a procession which takes place in a public place. A "public place" is defined as:

"(a) any highway, or in Scotland any road within the meaning of the Roads (Scotland) Act 1984, and

(b) any place to which at the material time the public or any section of the public has access, on payment or otherwise, as of right or by virtue of express or implied permission."

The *Oxford English Dictionary* defines "procession" as the "action of a body of persons going or marching along in orderly succession in a formal or ceremonial way . . . a body of persons marching in this way".

In *Flockhart v Robinson* [1950] 2 KB 498, [1950] 1 All ER 1091 (DC), "procession" is defined as "not a mere body of persons; it is a body of persons moving along a route". In that case the problem arose when a lawful procession in the City of London broke up to disperse. A group of people had moved into an area where processions were prohibited. They were in a loose formation and not in ranks, and in the form of a rabble not a compact body. It was held that at some stage the group had spontaneously become a procession by adopting an orderly formation, even though there was no prior plan to do so.

Lord Denning observed in *Kent v Metropolitan Police Commissioner*, *The Times* 15 May 1981 (CA):

"A public procession is the act of a body of persons marching along in orderly succession – see the *Oxford English Dictionary*. All kinds of processions take place every day up and down the country – carnivals, weddings, funerals, processions to the Houses of Parliament, marches to Trafalgar Square and so forth".

Whether or not a particular group is a procession is a question of fact on each occasion. A group of rugby supporters leaving a coach on the way to a match may not be a procession despite their numbers, because their progress may be disorganised. If they are marshalled carefully they may take on the nature of a procession, as may a crocodile of school children organised by their teachers, although they are not caught by the statutory provisions.

The procession need not be people on foot. The dictionary definition incorporates the word "going" in addition to the word "marching". A procession comprising only driven vehicles would be caught. Thus a lord mayor's parade or a student rag parade would fall within the definition, as would a procession of cyclists making their protest against traffic pollution.

An individual walking a given route, whether in a formal or ceremonial way, would not be a procession. The element of a "body" of people would be missing. In certain instances an individual doing that could create public disorder if rival groups gather to encourage him or to prevent his passage. Other provisions to prevent disorder might need to be invoked. An example of such a disruptive walk by an individual was the walk by Martin Webster, a member of a far right political party, along the route of a proscribed procession through Manchester. His walk, albeit not a procession, attracted both supporters and counter-demonstrators and the police were obliged to keep the groups apart.

An individual temporarily moved away from a procession and on his own at the time of any alleged contravention would be caught by the definition. Although there is no case on the point directly, the principle is set out in the assembly case, *Broadwith v Chief Constable of Thames Valley Police* (see page 161).

Given that the definition in s 16 extends to any place to which the public has access, public processions are not restricted to the highway and include parades preceding rallies held in arenas, even if they are as innocuous as a boy scout or girl guide rally. They also include an Easter parade around the grounds of a church, although many such parades are excluded from statutory control as common or customary processions (s 11(2)).

1.2 Advance Notice

Section 11 of the POA 1986 is intended to obviate the difficulties that might arise if the police are unaware of public processions; it requires that in certain contexts advance written notice of a procession must be given to the police. Failure to give notice does not vitiate the validity or legality of the procession itself.

Section 11(1) provides that:

"Written notice shall be given in accordance with this section of any proposal to hold a public procession intended–

(a) to demonstrate support for or opposition to the views or actions of any person or body of persons,

(b) to publicise a cause or campaign, or

(c) to mark or commemorate an event,

unless it is not reasonably practicable to give any advance notice of the procession."

Inevitably, many processions fall into more than one of these categories. In particular, processions relating to terms of employment might fall into the category of opposing a body's view, and the category of being intended to publicise a cause. Political processions invariably require advance notice under the section, as are processions designed to express grief for a person who has died in a context which has caused public anxiety, except where it is a funeral procession within s 11(2).

A difficulty arises in relation to a procession organised at very short notice. The statutory mechanism for written notice assumes at least six days' notice (s 11(5) and (6)), or, if that is not reasonably practicable, notice must be given as soon as is reasonably practicable (s 11(6)). If the notice requirement is not met, an offence is committed (s 11(7)). Section 11(1) envisages a circumstance where it is not practicable to give any advance notice, by using the formula "unless it is not reasonably practicable to give any advance notice". Occasionally a procession is incapable of notice, being entirely spontaneous. Examples are where a factory closure announcement is made and the employees stop work to march to the company headquarters; or where a group of neighbours responds to the death or injury of a child in a road accident by marching immediately on the local council to protest about the unsafe nature of a road; or where, in the course of an election campaign, supporters spontaneously decide to march in solidarity with their chosen candidate. In these cases it is possible that, as a question of fact, the organisers could be held not to be required to give advance notice because it is not reasonably practicable to do so. Given that the reference to "any advance notice" at the end of s 11(1) does not include the word "written", it might be thought that there is a category of case where oral notice would suffice, but this cannot be so. "Any advance notice" must relate back to the last use of the word "notice", which is "written notice" used in the first words of s 11(1); there is therefore no provision for oral notice. In the event of prosecution, a defendant may be assisted in proving, on a balance of probabilities, that it was not reasonably practicable to give the statutory written notice if he did, in any event, give oral notice to the police. This would apply to a procession taking place as a spontaneous reaction to an immediate and unforeseeable matter, such as waste spills or unexpected visits by political leaders. That it was not reasonably practicable to give notice would be a matter for the defendant to prove. There can be very few cases where a delay of a few hours would render a procession meaningless. A delayed procession following a sporting success might become meaningless (in practice such processions are generally planned in advance on a contingency basis). Such a delay would, however, enable the police to be notified so that they may take appropriate precautions and reduce the risk to the organiser of prosecution and conviction.

Certain processions are excluded from the requirements for advance notice. Section 11(2) provides that notice is not required "where the procession is one which is commonly or customarily held in the police area (or areas) in which it is proposed to be held or is a funeral procession organised by a funeral director acting in the normal course of his business".

If there is doubt whether a particular procession is common or customary, it may be wise to give the notice, to avoid the risk of prosecution. Many cases are straightforward. Remembrance Day parades, university rag parades, Easter parades and other religious parades may be clear to all concerned, but notice of even these may be required if the procession is to move from area to area and that movement is not protected by custom or common practice. Sometimes issues of custom and common usage raise wider constitutional issues relevant to processions. Parades in Northern Ireland are a case in point, where custom comes into conflict with current public order requirements.

Form of Notice

The advance notice to the police must comply with the following:
- it must be in writing (s 11(1));
- it must be delivered to any police station in the police force area where the procession is intended to start; or in the case of a procession which will start in Scotland and cross into England, notice should be given to a police station in the first police area in England on the proposed route (s 11(4)(a), (b));
- it must be delivered either by hand not less than six days before the date of the procession or by recorded delivery post provided actual delivery

takes place not less than six clear days before the procession's intended date (s 11(5)); there is no presumption of service;
- if six days' notice cannot be given, then notice must be given in writing by hand as soon as delivery is reasonably practicable (s 11(6));
- the notice must specify the intended start time, route and the name and address of at least one of the organisers (s 11(3)).

This is subject to the proviso in respect of cases where no notice is possible. Usually the police have prescribed forms of notice incorporating provision for much more information than this. This is to enable them to police the event adequately from the points of view of both public safety and traffic management, and to determine whether they need to impose conditions under s 12 of the POA 1986 (see page 151).

Offences Relating to Notice
There are two statutory offences in relation to notice of public processions. They can be committed only by an organiser, who is liable whether or not he takes part in the procession. The offences are:
- failure to satisfy the notice requirements (s 11(7)(a));
- non-adherence to the date, time or route specified in the notice (s 11(7)(b).

Two statutory defences are available to an organiser, who may prove, on the balance of probabilities, that (s 11(9)):
- he did not know of and did not suspect or have reason to suspect the failure to give notice;
- the failure arose from something beyond his control and from the agreement or direction of a police officer.

These offences are triable only summarily and are punishable by fines up to level 3 (s 11(10)). Given the wording of the provision, anyone who organises a procession without due diligence is unlikely to be able to prove the defence. On the transferred burden of proof, see page 91.

1.3   The Organiser
The word "organiser" is central to the provisions on public processions, but it is not defined in the statute. It should therefore be accorded its ordinary meaning. The case of *Flockhart v Robinson* [1950] 2 KB 498, [1950] 1 All ER 1091 (DC) sets out two points of view – the first in the majority decision, the second in the dissenting judgment. In the majority judgment, it was said:

> "'Organised' is not a term of art. When a person organises a procession, what does he do? A procession is not a mere body of persons: it is a body of persons moving along a route. Therefore the person who organises the route is the person who organises the procession . . .". (*per* Goddard CJ)

This assessment of the position appears to be too all-embracing. To give the word "organise" its ordinary meaning implies an element of preparation prior to the event that would not apply to mere stewards. This statutory provision envisages an organiser as a person who gives the advance notice and is therefore involved from before the start of the procession. Given that this was a case on the POA 1936, perhaps the words of Goddard CJ are not definitive; an analysis nearer to today's position is set out in the dissenting judgment, where Finnemore J said:

> "The mere fact that a person takes part in a procession would not of itself be enough. I do not think that the fact the defendant was the leading person in the procession would by itself be enough, although it might be some evidence to be considered . . . I think organising a procession means something in the nature of arranging or planning a procession . . ."

In *DPP v Baillie* [1995] Crim LR 426, the Divisional Court looked at a more modern aspect of the definition of "organiser" in the context of assembly, but it is also applicable to the provisions on processions. The respondent distributed news sheets with free festival information; he operated an in-coming telephone calls and answering machine service. Believing that a particular festival was to take place, the police served a notice of conditions (relating to assembly) on the respondent, whom they treated as an organiser. The relevant notice began "Re proposed festival on 12 June *et sequentes*", and referred to "this event or any similar event". The court commented adversely on the vagueness of the notice. There were three questions to resolve:

(1) was the person served by the police "an organiser" merely by disseminating information?

(2) had the police had regard to the time or place of the event, given that they did not have any details of it?

(3) could an offence be committed if the person was arrested before the event and still had time to comply with the conditions?

The Divisional Court did not deal with the third question, but decided that the police were not operating within the terms of s 14(1) because they did not know the time or place of the festival. In other words, they could not have made their decisions taking into account the time or place because they did not know either. Such information would likewise be necessary for a procession prosecution under s 12 (see below). The court did not give a comprehensive definition of "organiser", but felt that there was just sufficient evidence to support the magistrates' decision that the defendant was an "organiser". What weighed with the court was the absence of a public announcement relating to the event, thus elevating the defendant's role as a purveyor of information. This exemplifies the difficulties facing the police in relation to processions and/or assemblies organised as informally as possible, via web sites and e-mails.

1.4 The Imposition of Conditions

The power to impose conditions on processions is contained in s 12 of the POA 1986; it does not circumscribe either the preventive powers of the police (Chapter 2) or their other common law and statutory powers and duties in connection with public order. The power to impose conditions does not restrict the civil liabilities of the organisers of or the participants in the procession. The mere fact that notice has been served and conditions imposed by the police does not prevent an interested party from seeking an injunctive remedy to prevent a given procession. Section 12 applies to any public procession of any character, even if it is a procession outside the terms of s 11 as to notice.

Conditions may be imposed on the organisers or the participants; they are imposed by way of directions containing conditions (s 12(1)). Conditions may be imposed either before or during a procession, by "the senior police officer". During the period before the procession, the "senior police officer" is the chief police officer for the relevant area (s 12(2)(b)), subject to the power to delegate (s 15). The exercise of the power to delegate may occasionally repay investigation. Usually delegation is dealt with in a structured way but there is potential for the process to be overlooked. The conditions imposed must be in writing (s 12(3)). For the duration of the procession or while participants are assembling for an intended procession, the senior police officer is the most senior ranking officer at the scene (s 12(2)(a)). Conditions imposed during the procession or the assembly period need not be in writing.

The criteria for imposing conditions are set out in s 12(1) of the POA 1986. The senior officer must have regard to:

(a) the intended or actual time or place of the procession . . .; and
(b) the circumstances in which it will be held; and
(c) its route.

The officer may impose conditions if he reasonably believes (ie actually believes on objective grounds) "that the procession . . . may result in serious public disorder, serious damage to property or serious disruption to the life of the community" (s 12(1)(a)); or that the purpose of the organisers is to intimidate others (s 12(1)(b)). The reasonableness of the belief is to be ascertained objectively, as is any other reasonable belief or suspicion, by reference to the normal principles.

"Serious"

There is a view that the word "serious" in s 12(1)(a) does not further qualify the terms "public disorder" or "damage". That is a curious approach both to statutory interpretation and to the clear fact that public disorder is graded in the POA 1986 by reference to particular aspects and level of seriousness. The requirement is that the senior police officer present has to carry out an assessment of the procession, taking account of the available information. If that leads to the belief that there may be disorder, but falling short of *serious* public disorder, then conditions cannot be imposed. If conditions are imposed, then quite apart from the fact that any prosecution would fail (notionally, in the case of a procession in course; and actually in the case of an intended procession), the organisers or any interested party might seek judicial review of the decision to impose conditions. Whether the courts would be able to make the distinction between "serious" and other public disorder, and whether a court would substitute its view for that of a senior officer on the ground, are open to doubt, but each exercise of power may be reviewed to ensure its compliance with the requirements of art 11 of the European Convention on Human Rights (and see *Mohammed-Holgate v Duke* [1984] AC 437, [1984] 2 WLR 660, [1984] 1 All ER 1054 (CA)).

"Serious disruption"
"Serious disruption to the life of the community" is undefined in the Act. By their nature, processions might be said to disrupt the community, if only to the extent of slowing the progress of traffic through towns and cities. This might lead to conditions being imposed to reduce the impact of the procession on the community, even though some would maintain that processing is not disruptive to normal life, but a part of normal life. It is arguable that such conditions are imposed for reasons not included in the Act. Reducing the speed of traffic might not be regarded as a serious disruption to the life of the community. It is difficult to envisage a procession seriously disrupting local life in the same way that an assembly might. Large gatherings of people in pickets have an impact on the local community which a procession could not be expected to match. Perhaps a 24-hour procession circulating in a limited area might mean that shops could not function, and to that extent it would be a serious disruption. Generally, however, "serious disruption" would arise from serious public disorder and the inclusion of the expression in s 12(1)(a) does not develop the impact of the provision.

"Community" is not defined and so has its ordinary meaning. In many locations "community" has more than one meaning. In a busy shopping street in London, there is the community of shopkeepers, the community of local residents and the wider community of London as a whole. The "serious disruption" could be to any of those communities. When London taxi drivers block the streets of London by driving extremely slowly to demonstrate a particular viewpoint, it could be argued that they are part of the wider London community, but not part of the community where the demonstration takes place. They are clearly capable of causing disruption to the community. It is a question of fact whether they cause serious disruption to the life of the community.

Intention to Intimidate
Whether the intention to intimidate contemplated by s 12(1)(b) is present is a question of fact in each case. The notion that interference with the lawful activities of other members of the community should be prevented by the criminal law is central to parts of both the POA 1986 and the CJPOA 1994 (see, for example, s 68 on aggravated trespass, page 181). The provision in s 12(1)(b) is based on s 7 Conspiracy and Protection of Property Act 1875,

which is referred to in Sch 2 POA 1986 with the addition of a power of arrest (without warrant) by a constable on reasonable suspicion that an offence is being committed under s 7. In the White Paper which preceded the 1986 Act, the provision was described as "a libertarian safeguard designed to prevent demonstrations whose overt purpose is to persuade people from being used as a cloak by those whose real purpose is to intimidate or coerce".

Given that processions are commonly designed to persuade – politicians, workers or the authorities generally – the risk that persuasion may be misconstrued as coercion requires a delicacy of touch on the part of those enforcing the provision. The police are always vulnerable to allegations of an inappropriately heavy-handed approach to conditions for processions. They are accused of interfering with the liberty of the subject and his right to protest and process. They are also vulnerable to claims of disproportionate action under the terms of art 11 of the European Convention on Human Rights.

Intimidation was defined to a degree in *R v Jones* (1974) 59 Cr App R 120, pursuant to the Conspiracy and Protection of Property Act 1875:

"'intimidate' in this section includes putting persons in fear by the exhibition of force or violence or the threat of force or violence; and there is no limitation restricting the meaning to cases of violence or threats of violence to the person."

A procession precedent to an industrial picket could fall within the definition in s 12 and be subjected to conditions by directions from the senior officer. One of the many difficulties facing the police in relation to processions is the foundation for the "reasonable belief" as to the purpose of the procession. It is not uncommon for there to be more than one purpose. While it may be obvious in the context of mass picketing that the purpose is intimidatory (although mass picketing is a species of assembly rather than a procession), there are cases where the purpose is not clear. In *Thomas v NUM* [1986] Ch 20, [1985] 2 WLR 1081, [1985] 2 All ER 1 (Ch D), Scott J said:

". . . counsel for the . . . defendants submitted that mass picketing (by which I understand to be meant picketing so as by sheer weight of numbers to block the entrance to premises or to prevent the entry thereto of vehicles or people) was not *per se* tortious or criminal. In my judgement, mass picketing is clearly both common law nuisance and an offence under s 7 of the 1875 Act."

In non-industrial cases the question of purpose is more of a problem. Persuading a firm to discontinue animal experiments may not be obviously intimidatory. An implied threat to embargo the company's goods would not be intimidatory. Threats of violence towards customers or employees would be. In the context of assembly, blocking the premises' entrance in numbers would fall foul of the judgment in *Thomas v NUM*.

In *DPP v Fidler* [1992] 1 WLR 91, (1992) 94 Cr App R 286, [1992] Crim LR 62 (DC), two separate groups, one in favour of abortion, the other opposed to abortion, were stationed outside an abortion clinic. Opponents of abortion were charged with watching and besetting, contrary to s 7 of the Conspiracy and Protection of Property Act. It was held that although their intention was to prevent abortions from being carried out, their chosen method was to dissuade by means of graphic photographs, models and verbal persuasion. The court held that to establish the offence under s 7, it would be necessary to prove that the purpose of the defendants was to compel relevant parties to cease performing abortions. It was not sufficient to constitute the offence merely to seek to dissuade. This case contrasts with other cases involving abortion clinics where the allegation has been of conduct contrary to s 4 or s 5 of the POA 1986.

Relevance of Conditions

The conditions must be such as appear, to the relevant police officer, necessary to prevent the apprehended disorder, damage, disruption or intimidation. Despite the absence of the word "reasonably" from the relevant part of s 12 ("such conditions as appear to him necessary"), there must be a correlation between the anticipated problem and the conditions imposed. (Some of the dilemmas facing police officers are set out at pages 9 and 10.) The conditions specifically referred to in the section relate to the re-routing of a procession and preventing a procession from going to specified public places – "no go" areas. Inevitably the police use their experience to prevent political extremists from entering areas where opposing views are held in circumstances which might lead to disorder. Racially sensitive areas will be vetoed in appropriate cases. A dilemma for the police is that the very existence of a procession by one group may lead to an apparently impromptu gathering to demonstrate against the processors. The best example of this is processions which can be excluded from racially sensitive areas; their opponents, however, may gather to protest at the procession wherever it may be.

Notwithstanding the areas of conflict, most conditions are consensual and obvious. Conditions routinely cover:
- place and time of assembly prior to start;
- time of departure, route and duration;
- carrying of flags, banners and emblems;
- loudhailers;
- stewarding;
- use of vehicles;
- numbers in line abreast on the route;
- provision of medical services.

A developing area of controversy concerns the wearing of masks, balaclavas and even face paint. On the premise that masks etc are commonly interpreted as intimidating, it seems likely that conditions precluding such items would be supported by courts. From Home Office Research Paper RS 190 it appears that in the context of aggravated trespass some police forces regard the wearing of masks by hunt saboteurs as intimidatory (see also page 225, on s 60 CJPOA). The converse view is that routinely photographing people at processions and assemblies is intimidation by the state, and that it is therefore legitimate for a person to hide his identity.

1.5 Offences

It is an offence for an organiser knowingly to fail to comply with a condition imposed under s 12. The condition must be properly imposed. Whether a person is an organiser is a question of fact (*Flockhart v Robinson* [1950] 2 KB 498, [1950] 1 All ER 1091 (DC)). "Knowingly" requires *mens rea*, and includes deliberately closing one's mind or deliberately not making enquiries.

It is a defence for an organiser to show, on a balance of probabilities, that the failure arose from circumstances beyond his control. Thus if a participant uses a loudhailer in contravention of a condition, this does not amount to an offence by the organiser if the organiser knew nothing of it and had taken steps to make the condition known.

A non-organiser participant offends if he knowingly fails to comply with a condition, unless he can show that the failure arose from circumstances beyond his control. The participant with the proscribed loudhailer has a defence if he used it because he had seen no warnings, but if he continues to use it in the face of advice he commits an offence. A processor who is swept by a crowd into a proscribed area by weight of numbers may well have a defence.

A police officer in uniform may arrest without warrant anyone he reasonably suspects of committing an offence (s 12(7)). If the offence has already occurred, he may use the power in s 25 of the PACE Act 1984. Incitement to commit an offence is an offence (s 14(6)).

1.6 The Prohibition of Public Processions

The power to prohibit public processions is set out in s 13 of the POA 1986 and was not amended by the CJPOA 1994. The Act distinguishes between the roles of, on the one hand, the Commissioner of Police for the City of London and the Commissioner of Police for the Metropolis, and, on the other hand, chief officers of police. In the two London areas, the chief officer may, with consent from the Secretary of State, prohibit by order the holding of all public processions, or any specified class of public procession, in the whole or part of his area (s 13(4)).

Outside London, a different procedure applies. In those areas, in the qualifying circumstances, the chief officer must apply to the district council for an order prohibiting all public processions or a specified class of public procession in the district as a whole or in part of the district (s 13(1)). Section 13(1) is mandatory on the chief officer – he must make the application if the circumstances arise, although the council's decision in response to the application is discretionary. In London, by contrast, it is the chief officer's decision that is discretionary, local authorities playing no part. In both areas the order may relate to part only of the relevant area.

Criterion for Prohibition

The only criterion for imposing the prohibition or requesting it from the council is the chief officer's reasonable belief that serious public disorder cannot be prevented by the exercise of the condition-making power in s 12. Disruption to the community and intimidation are not included as grounds for the prohibition or application, although there is no doubt a view that both of those are capable of giving rise to the anticipation of serious public disorder. The chief officer's belief must be reasonable and based on his assessment of the prevailing circumstances. A reasonable belief that serious public disorder might occur may be based on the fact that a counter-rally is to be held; that the area concerned is small and the procession risks swamping it; that there have been recent disturbances; or the existence of high local tension.

Whether it is legitimate to prohibit a procession is subject to the tests in art 11 of the European Convention on Human Rights. Is the decision necessary in a democratic society? Is it proportionate? In cases of challenge, it is for the court to carry out a factual analysis of the risks described by the deciding officer, and then rule on whether his decision is consistent with art 11. The response of a district council acting with the consent of the Secretary of State is discretionary and may therefore be reviewed in the court in the same way. In *Kent v Metropolitan Police Commissioner, The Times* 15 May 1981 (CA), an application for judicial review was made in respect of the chief officer's decision to impose a blanket prohibition. It was claimed that he had not directed his mind properly to the matters to be considered, and in particular to the fact that the ban would affect a large number of processions over a large area. The Court of Appeal's view was that there was:

"a climate of activity . . . hooligans and others were attacking the police, who were simply doing their duty . . . they might attack the peaceful procession itself . . . This is a matter for the judgement of the Commissioner himself . . . 'There is such a risk of public disorder – even from the most peaceful demonstration being attacked by hooligans – that a ban must be imposed'."

In this case the evidence of the Commissioner was described as "meagre", but even with the changed regime under the Human Rights Act it seems clear that in the absence of evidence of bad faith the courts will find it difficult to overturn the senior police officer's professional assessment of risk.

In relation to blanket bans, it was said:

". . . a class or group of classes of processions can be as well identified by expressly excluding certain classes as it can by listing all the classes which are not excluded."

Duration of Prohibition

The permitted duration of a prohibition order is up to three months, but it may be as short as 24 hours. The evidence of banning orders made in the 1980s is that periods beyond 30 days are the exception, and generally the preferred ban has been the blanket ban for a given area. A blanket ban is a ban on all processions, subject to exceptions, within certain classes. Such bans may be revoked or varied by a subsequent prohibition (s 13(5)). In 1961 the following was prohibited: "[a]ny public procession organised by the body of persons known as the Committee of 100 or any such public procession organised by any person or persons acting on behalf of the said committee". In 1974, "any public procession in connection with the death of James McDade", one of the IRA hunger strikers, was prohibited.

Offences

The organiser of, participant in, or person who incites participation in or organisation of, a prohibited procession commits an offence (s 13(7), (8) and (9)) if he acts knowingly. The penalty varies according to the particular offence. An organiser is liable to a fine up to level 4 or imprisonment for up to three months. A participant is liable to a fine up to level 3, and the inciter is liable to imprisonment for up to three months or a fine up to level 4 (s 13(11), (12) and (13)).

A person may be arrested without warrant by a constable in uniform on reasonable suspicion that the person is committing the offence (s 13(10)). A person who organises a prohibited procession which in the end does not occur commits an offence. This is not the same as the offence committed by an organiser who breaches a condition – where the offence arises only if the procession takes place.

2   Assemblies

Checklist
- an assembly is made up of twenty or more persons;
- an assembly includes pickets, vigils and queues;
- conditions may be imposed before or during an assembly;
- conditions may relate only to place, duration and numbers.

Until the Public Order Act 1986 there were no general statutory provisions to control assemblies. The innovation made in the 1986 Act has been developed further by ss 70 and 71 of the Criminal Justice and Public Order Act 1994, dealing with trespassory assemblies and their prohibition, and the power to stop people en route to a prohibited assembly. The 1994 developments had their genesis in anxiety about assemblies at places such as Stonehenge and the risk of damage to such historic monuments. Wider powers to control assemblies by advance notice requirements were not actually sought by the police or recommended by the House of Commons Home Affairs

Committee Report.

2.1 Definition

Section 16 of the POA 1986 defines "public assembly" as "an assembly of 20 or more persons in a public place which is wholly or partly open to the air". The *Oxford English Dictionary* describes an "assembly" as a "gathering together, meeting, the state of being collected or gathered. The coming together of persons or things. A gathering of persons, a number of people met together". While it is clear from both the statutory and the dictionary definitions that a procession would generally be an assembly as well, subject to numbers, it is clearly the intention that there should be different provisions dealing with the relatively static assembly on the one hand, and the moving procession on the other.

"Assembly" is a broad description embracing pickets, lobbying groups, vigils, festivals, some queues, groups drinking in pub gardens and football crowds. The statutory definition is sufficiently wide to require the application of the ordinary meaning of the words used. The higher courts regard the issue of whether or not an assembly was constituted as a question of fact for the fact-finding tribunal, and do not generally interfere in the absence of a bizarre analysis.

"Public place" is analysed above (page 146). The expression is sufficiently wide to include the factory entrance where a picket line might be stationed. The concept of "partly open to the air" means that a closed building with its door open is not caught, but a Dutch barn or football stadium is caught.

Prior to 1986 the definition of "public place" had been reviewed in *Cawley v Frost* [1976] 1 WLR 1207, [1976] 3 All ER 743, [1976] Crim LR 747 (DC), in which "open to the air" was also considered. Lord Widgery said:

"where you have an establishment which is set up to provide for the public, such as Halifax Town football club or Wembley Stadium, one ought to approach it on the basis that is a public place in its entirety . . . *Prima facie* you look at the whole of the establishment and you are not . . . deterred from doing that merely by finding that certain portions of the establishment have been denied to the public for one reason or another."

"Open to the air" is an expression reminiscent of the definition in the 1936 Act before its amendment by the Criminal Justice Act 1972. This created a category of open space which did not include, for example, a railway platform since that was integral to a building (*Cooper v Shield* [1971] 2 QB 334, [1971] 2 WLR 1385, [1971] 2 All ER 917 (DC)). "Open to the air" must not be *de minimis*. A roof with no walls or walls with no roof would be open to the air, but a building with wide open doors would not.

A practical problem in relation to "public places" is the extent of the relevant place. It may be that conduct beyond the boundary of a relevant place will not be caught and so the definition will be crucial. In respect of an assembly in a marquee in the grounds of a school, it may be necessary to determine whether the "place" is the marquee or the school grounds, even if the marquee is partly in the open air. Again this is a question of fact to be analysed in accordance with the approach in *Cawley v Frost*, above.

2.2 Conditions on Assemblies

The powers to impose conditions on assemblies essentially reflect those to impose conditions on processions, and are found in s 14 of the POA 1986, although the conditions which may be imposed are more limited. In the case of an assembly involving harassment, then the powers in s 42 Criminal Justice and Police Act 2001 may be appropriate (see page 137). Under s 14 POA 1986 conditions may be imposed by the senior police officer either before the assembly or during its course (s 14(2) and (3)).

Conditions may be imposed on organisers or on those taking part, and the police officer must have regard to the intended or actual time or place of the assembly, and the circumstances in which it will be held. He may impose conditions if he reasonably believes that the assembly may result in serious public disorder, serious damage to property or serious disruption to the life of the community, or if the purpose of the organisers is to intimidate others.

The various expressions used are analysed on page 151 *et seq*; what is said there applies equally to assemblies. The conditions the officer may impose must be such as appear necessary to prevent the apprehended disorder, damage or disruption or intimidation.

Conditions in respect of assemblies may relate only to the place at which the assembly may, or may continue to, be held, its maximum duration and the maximum number of persons who may participate. The existence of conditions does not prevent the police from using their other powers, including those in relation to obstruction. A negative condition as to place, eg not within 200 yards of a particular location, is permissible. By the same token, if part of an assembly remains after the time limit, it is a question of fact whether the assembly is then in breach of the condition. Simply changing the personnel of the assembly will not enable organisers or participants to avoid breach. It may suffice to reduce the number of participants below twenty, but moving location may well leave the assembly in breach of the location condition, depending on its terms.

In *DPP v Baillie* [1995] Crim LR 426 (DC), the following conditions had been imposed:

"(1) Any event must be licensed in accordance with the Local Government (Miscellaneous) Provisions Act 1982 in respect of public entertainment and environmental health.

(2) The place will be subject to advance agreement with the police to ensure the life of the community is not disrupted by noise nuisance from whatever source associated with the event.

(3) The maximum duration will be subject to advance agreement with the police to ensure there is no public disorder or disruption to the life of the community caused by noise or unsociable hours.

(4) The maximum number of persons who constitute the assembly will be subject to advance agreement with the police to ensure:

    (a) there is no public disorder caused by overcrowding and/or inadequate lighting;

    (b) there is no damage caused to roadside verges and neighbouring property resulting from inadequate arrangements for offstreet parking;

    (c) there is no damage or disruption to the life of the community resulting from inadequate sanitary arrangements;

    (d) there is no disruption to the life of the community resulting from too great a volume of traffic for the access and egress routes to and from the assembly."

Although the matter was not contested before the court, it is arguable that the second, third and fourth conditions are too vague, and amount not to conditions but a requirement for advance notice of an assembly. No doubt the conditions were drawn thus because of the secrecy of the event and the problems the police had in knowing when or where the event would be held, or whether it would be held in a public place. Absence of reliable information does not justify the imposition of such a direction in advance.

It is also possible that the first condition was invalid. Section 14 refers to the imposition of a condition "as to the place at which the assembly may be (or continue to be) held". The licensing requirement clearly relates to the *use* to which the place is put, and as such can be said to relate to the place, but that is not what was intended by the POA. It is arguable that s 14 should be narrowly construed so as to permit the police to decide only *where* the assembly may be held. As drawn, the condition is an attempt to enforce a different Act.

In the case of *Broadwith v Chief Constable of Thames Valley Police*, 22 February 2000, unreported (QBD), a young man had attended an assembly to protest against the breeding of cats for scientific research. Restrictions as to times and locations had been imposed. The appellant went to the demonstration with friends in a minibus but then attempted to walk along a road to which access was denied until a time set out in the conditions. He persisted and was arrested both for breach of condition and for obstructing a police officer in the execution of his duty.

The appellant said that because he was alone when arrested he was not part of the assembly. The High Court's view was that, having attended for the purpose of the assembly with others, and wearing a mask, it was correct to define him as a member of the assembly. It was also correct to convict him of non-compliance with the condition because he was told of the road restriction, which was set out in the conditions, and he sought to use the road in contravention of it. It followed that he was in breach of the condition. Whether this case is consistent with the House of Lords' decision in *DPP v Jones* [1999] 2 AC 240, [1999] 2 All ER 257, [1999] 2 Cr App R 348 (HL) (see below, page 166) is open to question. In *Broadwith,* a person sought to walk down a proscribed road on his own and this was an offence. In *Jones,* a group of over twenty was permitted to use a restricted route so long as their activity was reasonable.

Directions containing conditions in relation to assemblies which are intended but not yet under way must be given in writing. Once the assembly is under way, there is no requirement for the directions imposing conditions to be in writing (s 13(3)).

The penalties for offences in relation to conditions imposed on assemblies are the same as for processions. The right to seek judicial review of such conditions is also the same.

3 Trespassory Assembly

Checklist
The following are the preconditions for prohibiting a trespassory assembly:
- application may be made in respect of intended assemblies only;
- existing assemblies are excluded;
- serious disruption or significant damage must be anticipated;
- there may be no prohibition if the occupier permits the assembly;
- knowingly organising, participating or inciting are offences;
- the police have power to stop those en route, within a five mile radius, but see *DPP v Jones.*

In response to the perceived need both to protect public monuments from the ravages of large assemblies purportedly exercising historic rights, and to protect ordinary members of the community from the consequences of trespassory assembly, a new s 14A of the Public Order Act 1986 was inserted by the Criminal Justice and Public Order Act 1994. The provision goes beyond the powers contained in the 1986 Act and reflects a view different from that expressed in the *Review of Public Order Law* (Cmnd 9510), which was to the effect that a power to ban such assemblies might be too great an infringement of the rights of free speech and assembly. The logical relationship between that position and the power to ban processions remains unclear.

Section 14A goes further than the common law power to prevent a reasonably anticipated breach of the peace, although the common law power remains and can be applied to prevent a meeting and therefore an assembly (*Duncan v Jones* [1936] 1 KB 218, [1935] All ER 710, (1935) 52 TLR 26). The provision again distinguishes between the Metropolitan and City areas of London and the rest of England and Wales and Scotland, in that the prohibition mechanism in London permits the chief officer of police to make the order with the consent of the Secretary of State (POA 1986, s 14A(4)). In the district council areas the chief officer may apply to the relevant district council. In England and Wales the district council may, with the consent of the Secretary of State, grant the prohibition applied for, or grant it subject to modifications approved by the Secretary of State.

3.1 Grounds for Prohibition

The problem of trespassory assembly is demonstrated by *R v Historic Buildings and Ancient Monuments Commission for England ("English Heritage") ex p Firsoff*, 1991, unreported (CA). The case related to processions and the exercise of discretion by *English Heritage* in response to a request from the chief constable to support his ban on processions under s 13 of the 1986 Act in relation to Stonehenge because of certain difficulties which had occurred there. The issue was whether it was a proper exercise of discretion to close Stonehenge at the summer solstice so as to prevent a peaceable and lawful person from exercising his right to have free access to the site in accordance with the terms of the gift of Stonehenge to the nation. As a result of serious disturbances on previous occasions, English Heritage had felt it was necessary to close Stonehenge during the solstice period. The court analysed the position carefully on the basis that decisions of English Heritage are capable of being judicially reviewed, and looking at Mr Firsoff's arguments that, because his conduct would be proper in every sense, barring him with everybody else could not be a proper exercise of the discretion. The court found:

> "It is satisfactory to the court to know that English Heritage recognises its continuing duty to keep the matter under review. It may be that, although several alternative methods of coping with the problem have been tried in the past, some combination of an all ticket event and an order under s 13 is the sort of arrangement to which it would be worthwhile giving further consideration." (*per* Nourse LJ).

The *Firsoff* case remains helpful, but since the Human Rights Act, the test to be applied is no longer the "reasonableness" test. Now, the question is whether a public authority making a relevant decision acts in compliance with the European Convention on Human Rights. Is the restriction "proportionate", or is it more than is "necessary in a democratic society"? It appears that, in response to the implementation of the Human Rights Act, English Heritage has changed its approach to the problem of Stonehenge, permitting some access, but seeking still to avoid damage.

The chief officer may apply at any time for an order prohibiting, for a specified period, all trespassory assemblies in the district or part of it. He may apply only if he reasonably believes that an assembly is intended to be held on land to which the public has no right of access or only a limited right of access and that the assembly:

"(a) is likely to be held without the permission of the occupier of the land or to conduct itself in such a way as to exceed the limits of any permission of his or the limits of the public's right of access, and

(b) may result–
  (i) in serious disruption to the life of the community, or
  (ii) where the land or a building or monument on it is of historical, architectural, archaeological or scientific importance, in significant damage to the land, building or monument.
  (POA 1986, s 14A(1) inserted by CJPOA 1994)

In *R v Tunbridge Wells Borough Council and Another ex p The Gypsy Council for Education, Culture, Welfare and Civil Rights and Another*, 7 September 2000, unreported (QBD), the court had to deal at short notice with some of the issues relating to trespassory assembly. In that case the local parish council had cancelled the local horse fair. As a result, the chief constable applied to the borough council for an order preventing the trespassory assembly which was expected to occur when many travellers and Romanies attended the location even though the fair had been cancelled. He anticipated large numbers and serious disruption, based on experience in previous years. His application was considered and in due course passed to the Home Secretary for approval – which was given. Initially there was no reaction, but late in the day application was made to the court disputing the validity of the order. It was contended that irrelevant considerations had been taken into account and that relevant ones had not. It was argued that there had been no enquiry into whether there was a prescriptive right to hold the fair, nor any enquiry into the reality of the risk of serious disruption. There were also particular issues with regard to Romany rights under the Convention for the Protection of National Minorities and under the European Convention on Human Rights, arts 8, 11 and 14. It was argued that the impact of the order would be disproportionate upon the Romany community. In the event the court found that the Secretary of State had expressly considered the Convention issues and that, in regard to arts 8 and 11, recognised "that a balance must be struck between the interests of the individual and the interests of society generally". Having analysed the decision-making processes of the various authorities involved, the court was satisfied that the order was proportionate in its response to the risk of serious disruption and that it should not be overturned.

The police officer's application is in respect of an *intended* assembly. In the event of an assembly in progress, there is no right to seek a prohibition and the officer is dependent on his common law powers to prevent a breach of the peace. Not all trespassory assemblies give rise to a risk of breach of the peace and to that extent the police officer's power may be limited. The difficulties this may create for the police are demonstrated by *DPP v Baillie* (see page 160). The police rely on advance knowledge of what is planned. This may be well known in the case of the summer solstice at Stonehenge, but less well known in other cases, particularly where relatively covert tactics are adopted by organisers using websites and e-mail to disseminate information.

Before seeking a prohibition, the police officer must have a "reasonable belief" that the assembly is intended, and this may be tested on normal principles.

Trespassory assembly is not restricted to a public assembly. The statutory provisions focus on the right to apply for prohibition. To fall within the provisions, the anticipated assembly must be on land in the open air. There must be no public right of access, or a limited public right of access. Even then the prohibition is available only if the assembly is without permission or exceeds any limited permission which may have been given. In addition, there is a requirement that serious disruption is anticipated, or, in the case of land with an important building or monument on it, significant damage is anticipated. The police officer need only have reasonable belief that serious disruption or serious damage may result. This is a lower requirement of "belief" than that required in the case of the trespass, which is not expressed in the conditional.

"Serious disruption" is discussed at page 153. It could include the creation of traffic difficulties; the consequences of large numbers not having toilet facilities; noise pollution; thefts on a large scale from the local community; or damage in the sense of local woodland being used for firewood, ie an assault on local amenity. All must be serious and disruptive for the Act to come into play. The Act does not define "serious disruption" and it is a matter for the judgement of the police officer whether to make application.

"Significant damage" is not defined by the section and is a change from the "serious damage" formula used in ss 13 and 14. It may be that "significant" means something different from "serious", and in the context of monuments may be expected to fall short of "serious", given its ordinary meaning. The Act does not help as to what is of historical, architectural, archaeological or scientific importance. It is a question of fact in each case, but the fact that a building is listed or a monument scheduled is inevitably conclusive. Difficulties might arise in relation to property of lesser significance.

While s 14A has the potential to cover lawful trade union picketing in the form of peaceful persuasion of workers not to work (s 220, Trade Union and Labour Relations (Consolidation) Act 1992), the reality is that such conduct will not be caught. There is generally no basis for reasonably believing that either serious disruption or significant damage may be the result of such an assembly of people.

An assembly may be prohibited only if it is to take place without the permission of the occupier of the land on which it is to be held, or so as to exceed the limits of any permission to be there or the limits of any public right of access. "Limited" is defined at s 14A(9) and means restricted to a particular purpose or restricted in some other way.

In the first place, a permitted gathering cannot be prohibited, so long as the permission is given by the occupier. The focus is *trespassory* assembly.

The disruptive consequences of a meeting held with permission are not targeted by these provisions.

Whether the average citizen understands the restrictions on his right to use land may be open to question, even taking into account the most recent developments in *DPP v Jones* (see below). In *Harrison v Duke of Rutland* [1893] 1 QB 142 it was established that, in relation to a right of way, if a person does something other than walk along the right of way, or something incidental to passage, then he is a trespasser. In that case he waved his umbrella as a deliberate act to interfere with a pheasant shoot. He was a trespasser because he had exceeded his right in relation to the right of way and had done more than merely pass and repass. In *Hickman v Maisey* [1900] 1 QB 752, the limitations on a person's rights in relation to the highway were even more starkly illustrated. In that case a racing tout used the highway to spy on horses in training. It was held that his use of the highway was beyond passing and repassing and therefore he trespassed. Each of these examples shows the ease with which a person may "exceed the limits of any permission of his or the public's right of access", and therefore the ease with which the basis for reasonable belief could be made out. The House of Lords reassessed the position in *DPP v Jones* [1999] 2 AC 240, [1999] 2 All ER 257, [1999] 2 Cr App R 348. It ruled that a public highway is a public place which the public may enjoy for any reasonable purpose. So long as users of the highway for purposes other than passage or repassage avoid public or private nuisance, then their user is unlikely to exceed the public's primary right of passage or repassage. It is for the trial court to decide whether a particular use was in fact unreasonable and therefore a trespass. It would be interesting to see how a 21st century court would define user of the highway in the circumstances of *Harrison v Duke of Rutland* and *Hickman v Maisey*.

In *DPP v Jones*, the House of Lords left open the question whether an assembly with a view to trespassing on adjacent land would be a trespass on the highway. The use of a right of way across a historic monument with a view to assembly ought not to be a trespass unless, on its facts, the particular use is found to be unreasonable. Such a finding might be expected, but it is not automatic.

Section 14A refers to an assembly, and not a "public assembly". Section 14A(9) defines an "assembly" as twenty or more persons. It also defines "on land" as meaning in the open air. There are restrictions on the prohibition that may be imposed. It cannot last for more than four days and cannot specify an area greater than a five mile radius of a specific centre. The prohibition is therefore always centred on a specific monument, building or place.

The police officer must apply for an order banning all trespassory assemblies within the area defined. He cannot elect to ban one or a class of such assemblies. Whether this limitation has any practical significance is difficult to assess, given that its focus is trespassory assemblies, which by their nature ought not to be happening.

3.2 Offences

The offences arising from trespassory assemblies are set out at s 14B of the POA 1986 (CJPOA, s 70). They reflect the offences arising from the provisions on public assembly. It is an offence knowingly to organise a prohibited assembly, knowingly to participate in a prohibited assembly or to incite the commission of either of those offences in England or Wales (s 14B(1), (2) and (3)). The offences require *mens rea*, yet there are no specific requirements for notice of the decision to be served on organisers or participants. The maximum penalties are imprisonment or a fine on level 4 for the organising offence; a fine on level 3 for the participation offence; and imprisonment for up to three months or a fine on level 4 for the incitement offence (s 14B(5), (6) and (7)). Special provision is made in relation to incitement in Scotland (s 14B(8)).

A constable in uniform may arrest on reasonable suspicion that an offence is being committed.

If a proscribed assembly becomes non-trespassory by virtue of the occupier's giving permission, it is no longer a proscribed assembly (s 14A(5)).

The difficulties of defining an "organiser" were considered in *DPP v Baillie* (see page 151).

3.3 Police Powers to Stop

Section 14C POA 1986 (s 71 CJPOA) gives the police the power to stop people en route to an unlawful trespassory assembly and direct them not to proceed to the assembly. It provides that if a constable in uniform reasonably believes that a person is on his way to a proscribed assembly in an area to which an order under s 14A relates, he may stop the person and direct him not to proceed in the direction of the assembly (s 14C(l)(a) and (b)). This power may be exercised only within the area to which the order applies, ie within five miles of the specified location.

Non-compliance with a direction which a person knows has been given is an offence and a constable in uniform may arrest without warrant, on reasonable suspicion that a person is committing the offence (s 14C(2), (3) and (4)). This offence carries a penalty of a fine up to level 3 (s 14C(5)).

This is an important power to control a situation before a crowd reaches the proposed site of the assembly. It has also been seen as an assault on fundamental rights, although, conversely, it has also been seen as a proper means of protecting communities, ancient monuments and historic buildings. It reflects the tension between the right to assemble and the right to have life protected from disruption. At the time the provision was created television scenes of confrontations at Stonehenge indicated a need to intervene before participants reach their target. The Government was clear about its objectives:

> "1,000 lager louts may decide to pile into a little village . . . It is up to the chief officer of police . . . to consider the law . . . There could be

hundreds of different cases, and thousands of hypothetical ones and it is up to the chief officers and the council to decide what they think will happen." (HC SCB, 10/2/94, cols 643, 645).

The intention was to protect the lawful occupation and use of land, with or without monuments or buildings, and to preserve the rights of lawful land users from interference by those without rights. The Act provided an ample demonstration of the risk that public order legislation is perceived as an attack on fundamental and historic rights, even though earlier judgements had emphasised the need to protect the lawful occupation of land. This is another example of the need for civic education on the ways in which rights are definable, restricted and amenable to analysis by the courts to determine whether or not restrictions are proportionate.

In *DPP v Jones* (above), an order under s 14A had been made. There was a peaceful assembly of more than twenty people on the public highway, within the area and time covered by the order. The particular assembly did not obstruct the public's rights to pass and repass on the highway. It was claimed that to prevent the assembly amounted to a breach of the rights of the individual members of the assembly under art 11 of the European Convention on Human Rights.

The House of Lords found that such an assembly could not constitute a trespassory assembly, thus preventing the use of s 14C to exclude groups from being on the highway. Provided that activity on the public highway is reasonable, does not involve the commission of public or private nuisance and is not an obstruction of the highway, then such activities should not amount to a trespass. To that extent there exists a public right of peaceful assembly on the highway, and in consequence of the House of Lords' finding, the operational effectiveness of s 14C has been diminished. But assemblies and the offences allegedly committed during them still give rise to a significant number of trials. Parties argue over the appropriateness of actions taken, the need for conditions, the extent of conditions, the methods of enforcement on the day and the myriad ways in which public authorities and groups of protesters can interpret their own rights and the rights of others.

Chapter 6

Trespass, Raves and Squatters

1   Introduction

The relationship between trespass, protest and public disorder has been long recognised. Television pictures of the removal of new age travellers and pro-testors against road schemes, alongside documented policing difficulties arising from large-scale unlicensed open air gatherings, have led to various statutory interventions. In general terms these have conferred powers to di-rect trespassers to leave and created offences for non-compliance with such directions. Section 39 of the Public Order Act 1986, which dealt with mass trespass, was repealed by the Criminal Justice and Public Order Act ("CJPOA") 1994 (Sch 11).

Aspects of offending related to trespass were redefined in Part V of the CJPOA 1994, which introduced provisions on the unlawful use of land. The Act created powers to remove trespassers from land; to divert people pro-ceeding to particular sites; and in respect of those organising or attending raves. The offence of aggravated trespass was created to deal with the behav-iour of individuals such as hunt saboteurs. In relation to squatters, interim or-ders for the recovery of possession of premises were provided for, with pen-alties for false statements made in support of applications for such orders. The obligation, formerly contained in Part 2 of the Caravan Sites Act 1968, on local authorities to provide sites for gypsies was removed, and local authorities were given the power to remove persons and vehicles unlawfully on land.

These provisions have not been modified by the Labour Government which came to power in 1997. Alleged trespassers may need to consider whether any step taken by the public authority is proportionate. If not, it may be an interference with one of the rights protected by the Human Rights Act.

The Home Office undertook research (Research Study 190) into the use and impact of the provisions under the CJPOA 1994, interviewing four-teen police forces and 64 officers experienced in this category of policing. The study was published in 1998 under the title *Trespass and Protest: Polic-ing under the CJPOA*. The research found:

"Overall, the introduction of the CJPOA did not appear to have led to a significant change in officers' approach to disorder or an expansion of the types of situation they attended. However, the use of the CJPOA pro-visions rather than pre-existing powers resulted in officers being placed in a stronger legal position when dealing with cases of disorder."

2   Trespass

Checklist
- two or more people trespassing on land may be directed to leave;
- senior police officer must reasonably believe they have a common purpose to reside;
- steps must have been taken by or for the occupier to ask the trespassers to leave;
- removal is permitted if one person has caused damage or there are more than six vehicles.

Before the 1994 Act, despite various statutory interventions, the courts had been unable to provide a speedy and effective remedy for local communities affected by large groups of travellers taking up residence in a particular area or trespassing on farmland, common land or other sites. Identifying these problems had taken time. Section 39 of the POA 1986 had been implemented to deal with specific problems during the early 1980s, particularly mass trespass by hippies or hell's angels. The modifications made by ss 61 and 62 of the CJPOA were intended to provide more effective measures than those in the previous s 39. Sections 61 and 62 CJPOA may be applicable to certain trespasses by gypsies, assuming that chief constables are prepared to contemplate using these powers against them, but research suggests unwillingness (RS 190, above). Reservations about the 1994 Act concern the dangers that its provisions could affect other groups to a degree inappropriate in a liberal democracy. In practice, there have been instances when the police have apparently not had the resources to enforce the powers contained in the Act. They have been prepared to exercise a monitoring and/or persuasive role, with some adverse reaction from local residents who had expected more.

The view of the government of the day was that the provisions of the 1994 Act would not be capable of misapplication because of the limitations to which they were subject and the discretion of the police in implementation. The objective was to provide a quick and fair remedy to remove disruptive trespassers or significant groups of trespassers.

There was concern that the provisions would conflict with fundamental human rights of movement and assembly, and the rights set out in the European Convention on Human Rights and the International Covenant of Civil and Political Rights. During the passage of the Bill through Parliament, it was stated that "None of the clauses in this part of the Bill aims to criminalise trespass. We want to deal with specific problems involving aggravated trespass, whether with intimidation or mass invasion with vehicles, with which clause 45 deals." (Mr Maclean, HC SCB,812194, col 531)

In Home Office Research Study 190 (above), it was found that police were less willing to use the provisions of the 1994 Act to direct gypsies to leave land than in relation to new age travellers. They also found one force that did not use the powers under the CJPOA at all, and left it to landowners to take legal action. Seizure of vehicles was unpopular because of the organisation required and the cost. Police were also anxious about the risk of simply displacing the problem to another illegal site.

2.1   Direction to Leave

Under s 61(1), CJPOA 1994, the senior police officer present may direct all members, or any member, of a group to leave land and remove vehicles or other property if he reasonably believes that:

- there are two or more people;
- they are trespassing on land;
- they have a common purpose to reside there for any period;
- reasonable steps have been taken by or on behalf of the occupier to ask them to leave; and
- either one or more person(s) has damaged land or property on the land or used threatening, abusive or insulting words or behaviour towards the occupier, a member of his family or his employee or agent; or that they have six or more vehicles on the land.

"Direct to leave" is not defined by the Act. It is therefore accorded its ordinary meaning. The direction may be given to persons who, while not originally trespassers, have become trespassers (see page 172). The direction must be capable of being heard by the recipient and its form therefore depends to a degree upon the size of the gathering. Section 61(3) provides for a constable other than the directing constable to communicate the direction to the person directed. Loudhailers and even helicopter loudhailers may sometimes be the only way to give the direction. Unlike under s 63(4) (raves, see page 176), "reasonable steps . . . to bring [the direction] to their attention" is not sufficient to make a direction valid for the purposes of s 61(3).

The Act does not allow for conditions, for example, as to the route to be taken, or the sequence of departures, to be added to the direction. It might well be that conditions could be imposed to avoid the risk of breach of the peace or threat to the safety of the public (see page 34), so that failure to comply with a route or sequence condition might be wilful obstruction of a constable acting in the execution of his duty (Police Act 1964, s 51).

The details of the giving of the direction may be important. In case of challenge, an advocate may seek to prove that the direction in question was not in fact given. If no definitive record has been maintained, this might be exploited by a defendant. If the directing officer has not kept a detailed record of the precise direction he gave, the court may find that no definable direction had been given and therefore that no offence was committed by not moving on. If the communication of the direction differs from the actual direction in detail, the court has to determine whether it should have been communicated *verbatim* or in substance only.

Reasonable Belief

The powers in s 61 depend on the existence of reasonable belief. The validity of the direction is unaffected by the fact that the reasonable belief may transpire to be mistaken. On the other hand, it would be a defence to an allegation of non-compliance with a direction that there was no trespass.

Persons Present

Where the persons present are there with the occupier's consent, s 61 has no application, whatever the implications of their presence for local people. Trespass takes place only as against the occupier of the land, and the police officer must reasonably believe that such a trespass exists. The initial entry on to the land need not have been trespassory, nor need the trespassers have arrived at the same time, so long as the occupation is trespassory or reasonably believed to be so by the directing constable at the time he gives the direction. The possibility of esoteric argument as to the precise status of a particular notional trespasser may be dissuasive as far as constables are concerned, effectively confining the provision to the large-scale trespasses against which the sections were directed.

Land

"Land" does not include buildings apart from agricultural buildings and scheduled ancient monuments. The occupation of factories, universities or a house would not be covered by this provision.

The geographical extent of land is not defined in the Act. Thus a constable could issue a direction to leave a very substantial area so long as it was in the same occupation. Generally the land is circumscribed by reference to adjacent fields or possibly a particular farm. A direction would be meaningless if it could not be understood by the recipients.

The definition of land has now to be seen in the context of the Countryside and Rights of Way Act 2000, which gives any person the right to enter and remain on any "access land" for the purposes of open air recreation, subject to certain provisos. "Access land" has a wide definition, including open country and registered common land. There may be arguments seeking to set the CJPOA in the context of the Countryside and Rights of Way Act. Such arguments are unlikely to succeed because, although the CJPOA is not referred to in Sch 2 to the Countryside and Rights of Way Act (restrictions on entering onto access land), trespass in contravention of s 61 is not protected by the 2000 Act because the trespassers are not on the land for open air recreation. The CJPOA requires a finding of "common purpose to reside" which is clearly different from "open air recreation".

Common Purpose to Reside

"Reside" has its ordinary meaning and therefore implies living regularly at a particular location. It does not necessarily mean sleeping there each and every night. The persons concerned may have a multiplicity of reasons for trespass, but it is sufficient for the purposes of s 61 that the constable reasonably believes that one of those reasons is the common purpose to reside. It may be a purpose formulated after the initial decision to stop, but it must be common to the persons in question. If only one has the intention to reside, then this element is missing. The section is aimed at persons who might ordinarily be expected to have mobile homes or other accommodation with them. There is a risk of argument over the purpose to reside, particularly if the direction is being given very quickly after the trespass commences.

A person may have a "purpose to reside" even though he has a home elsewhere. The fact that a child is accompanying an adult enables the common purpose to be made out in that there are two people together and if they intend to stay they have a common purpose to reside.

Request to Leave

The constable must also reasonably believe that reasonable steps have been taken by or on behalf of the occupier to ask the trespasser to leave. The constable should note the basis of his belief about the steps taken. Whether those steps are reasonable depends on the circumstances of the case. Posting notices, shouting from a parked car, visiting and speaking to persons may all be appropriate, but the steps are reasonable only if there was a real prospect that the request would come to the attention of the persons addressed.

Damage or Threats

Criminal damage is not a prerequisite to a direction to leave. Any damage, however small and however caused, suffices. "Damage" is not defined by the section, save to the extent that it is expressed to include the deposit of any substance capable of polluting the land (s 61(9)). On "damage to property" see *Morphitis v Salmon* (1990) 154 JP 365, (1990) 154 JPN 186, [1990] Crim LR 48 (DC). If it suffers temporary or permanent physical harm or impairment of use or value, then property is damaged. It is arguable therefore that chopping firewood, causing grass to be crushed and causing ruts would be damage. It does not matter that the damage is caused by only one person in the group, or that the abusive words are said by only one person. The provision is triggered in respect of the group as a whole. Nor do the threats, abuse or insults require a specific intent. It is sufficient that such words are used.

"Vehicle"

The definition of a "vehicle" is set out at s 61(9). A car and a caravan constitute two vehicles, not one. The vehicles need not actually have been brought on to the land by the trespassers so long as they have control of them. This precludes the trespasser from using the fact that a particular vehicle belongs to somebody else to exclude the operation of the section.

Person not Originally a Trespasser

Where persons were not originally trespassers but have become such, the same power under s 61 arises so long as the qualifying criteria are met after they became trespassers and not before (s 61(2)).

2.2 Offences

It is an offence if a person knows that a direction as above applies to him and he fails to leave the land as soon as reasonably practicable, or returns to the land as a trespasser within three months of the date on which the direction was given.

The offence is summary and the maximum penalty is three months' imprisonment or a fine on level 4 or both (s 61(4)).

Power of Arrest

A constable in uniform may arrest without warrant on reasonable suspicion that an offence is being committed (s 61(5)). The general arrest provisions also apply (PACE, s 25).

Police officers may find it difficult to decide whether or when to use the power under s 61, even assuming that they view it differently from s 39 of the POA 1986. The role of the police was discussed in Parliament:

> "A landowner may want the police to chuck people off his land, but if the police reasonably conclude that those people do not have 'the common purpose of residing there for a period' or that they are not causing damage, have not been abusive or do not have six vehicles, the police will use their discretion . . . the police know the situations for which they need the power." (Mr Maclean, HC SCB, col 539).

As is commonly the case with public order provisions, the powers appear draconian and an assault on individual freedoms by the state. In reality, the effect of the provision depends on the police, the courts and the impact of the Human Rights Act in determining the respective rights of landowners and trespassers.

"As soon as reasonably practicable"

"As soon as reasonably practicable" does not mean as quickly as a reasonable police officer requires, but rather, what is practicable for the trespasser: *Krumpa v DPP* [1989] Crim LR 295 (DC):

> "It will be up to the police to determine that in each circumstance. If it is true that there are no spark plugs – not that they have been deliberately removed – or if the trespassers need parts from a garage and it is Christmas day, I understand that it will be difficult to leave within minutes . . .
> The norm will be that when the direction is given, people will have to leave sooner rather than later and, in the vast majority of cases, much earlier than 24 hours." (Mr Maclean, HC SCB, col 550).

In practice this has meant that applications to courts have led to negotiations behind the scenes to set realistic timetables to reflect the realities of broken down vehicles etc.

Trespassers have become aware of the powers under s 61 and have been prepared to challenge their use. Police officers anticipate using them when making preliminary inspections of trespass sites. This has precluded instant action in many cases.

Direction or Arrest

It is a matter for the police officer present to decide whether to arrest a person under the POA 1986 or the Criminal Damage Act 1971, or to give a direction under the 1994 Act (assuming he is the senior officer present), if he attends the scene and himself sees conduct described by both Acts. If he arrests under the POA 1986 or Criminal Damage Act 1971, then the directive powers may well have to be used at the same time as the arrest. That is a problem if the arresting officer is not the senior officer present.

Reasonable Steps by the Occupier

Reasonable belief that reasonable steps have been taken by the occupier to ask trespassers to leave will be made out if the officer is told the position by a person apparently telling the truth (see page 173). There should therefore be no delay in formulating the basis of the direction, although, of course, the power to direct arises only once the apparent trespass exists. If the occupier wishes to prevent an anticipated trespass, he must avail himself of his civil injunctive remedies, assuming he can identify defendants adequately. If the police wish to prevent an anticipated trespass, it is a question of choosing between their preventive powers and seeking a prohibition on a trespassory assembly.

Defences

There is a statutory defence (s 61(6)) where the accused can show either:

(a) he was not trespassing; or

(b) he had a reasonable excuse for failing to leave the land as soon as reasonably practicable or for re-entering the land.

A common explanation for non-departure is the broken down vehicle mentioned above; the problem can be resolved by allowing time for repair.

2.3 Seizure

Section 62(1) of the CJPOA states that:

> "If a direction has been given under section 61 and a constable reasonably suspects that any person to whom the direction applies has, without reasonable excuse—
>
> (a) failed to remove any vehicle which appears to the officer to belong to him or to be in his possession or under his control; or
>
> (b) entered the land as a trespasser within the period of three months beginning with the day on which the direction was given,
>
> the constable may seize and remove that vehicle."

This provision relates only to vehicles, not other property. The objective is to end the trespass and the inconvenience caused by the vehicle.

3   Loud Open Air Music at Night ("Raves")

The powers in relation to "raves" are set out in ss 63–67 of the CJPOA.

Checklist
- only a superintendent or above may give a direction to leave;
- the event must be for 100 or more;
- "amplified music at night" includes repetitive beats;
- "open air" includes a venue partly open to the air;
- the occupier cannot commit an offence;
- there is power to stop people en route to a rave;
- there is a power to order forfeiture of goods.

The provisions in the 1994 Act enable the police to give a direction to leave if a rave is taking place or being prepared (s 63). The provisions create the offence of failing to comply with such a direction (s 63(6)); and confer powers to seize property (s 64) and to stop people making their way to raves (s 65). There is a power for the court to order the forfeiture of sound equipment (s 66) and for charges to be made for storing seized property (s 67).

These provisions are aimed at loud music played at high volume through modern sound systems at gatherings lasting many hours and sometimes many days, to the considerable annoyance of neighbours and the community at large:

> ". . . a case where people in 11 vehicles formed a bridgehead and in a few days 4,000 to 5,000 people had turned up. That is a typical example of the rave we are trying to get at." (Mr Maclean, HC SCB, col 591)

In the period leading up to the 1994 Act, there was much publicity focused on large-scale outdoor raves involving several thousand participants descending by car on the venue. Noise levels were enormous and the noise went on all night without remission. The gatherings were highly profitable to the organisers and there was a perceived link to the unlawful use of drugs.

More recently, there has been a number of well-publicised failures by the police to act effectively on behalf of local communities against the proponents of the rave culture, raves often now being organised via e-mail and the internet, and the police being under-resourced. In such cases the police have had to stand between the two communities and attempt to influence the rave organisers to reduce noise and limit hours.

Other commercially organised events which last all night cause serious inconvenience to neighbours. Indoor events require a licence if they are commercial, and should be dealt with under the law on entertainments licensing. It may be difficult to demonstrate that a party in a flat or series of flats is not truly private, but the narrow focus persists and such events are generally treated as private. It is for local authorities to serve notices under the Control of Pollution Act 1974 to deal with noisy indoor parties. The police can be called on to assist if such a notice is breached. Only unlicensed events in the open air are caught by ss 63 to 67 of the CJPOA.

Home Office Research Study 190 (above, page 155) reported that the power to seize equipment (below, page 179) was rarely used because persuasion was often successful. Police found that there was a high level of compliance with directions to leave or not attend and therefore there were few court proceedings. Only seven persons had been prosecuted for failing to leave a rave, and none for ignoring a direction not to proceed.

3.1   Directions to Leave and/or Remove Vehicles or Property

Under s 63(2), a police officer of at least the rank of superintendent may direct people to leave land and remove vehicles or other property from that land if he reasonably believes that:
(a) two or more people are on the land in the open air preparing for a gathering of 100 or more persons;
(b) ten or more are waiting for such a gathering to start; or attending such a gathering in progress;
(c) ten or more persons are attending such a gathering.

There are problems with the specified numbers. While it may be possible to say that two people are preparing for a gathering of 100 (s 63(2)(a)) or that ten are waiting for such an event (s 63(2)(b)), it is simply impossible to say that ten people are attending a gathering of 100 (s 63(2)(c)), unless the intention is to catch the ten people left at what was previously a gathering of 100. Even if that is the intention the drafting is at fault; the gathering is either a gathering of ten or of 100 at the moment the police officer formulates his belief. It cannot be both.

"A Gathering"

For the provisions to apply, there must be:
(a)   100 or more people on land in the open air;
(b)   amplified music played during the night with or without intermission;
(c)   music likely to cause serious distress to the inhabitants of the locality because of its loudness, duration and the time at which it is played.

The target of these powers is narrow. Section 63 does not itself refer to a "rave", although that word appears in the heading to ss 63–66.

Open Air

The open air rave is the specific focus, but s 63(10) sets out that that includes "a place partly open to the air". Anything taking place in an aircraft hangar, for example, will escape, as will anything taking place in a closed building. A Dutch barn may be caught; an ordinary barn will not:

> "A tent or a marquee can be in the open air. A Dutch barn is not enclosed and is therefore in the open air. An aircraft hangar without doors is in the open air. The interpretation must be left to the officers at the scene." (Mr Maclean, HC SCB, col 592)

The police discretion as to interpretation may well be circumscribed in due course by the judiciary.

Numbers of Persons
The choice of the number 100 as the trigger is clearly to keep the focus on the bigger events, but the threshold for the organisers – ten people on land setting up the event – might delay police intervention if the organisers seek to circumvent the provisions; all they need to do is deploy nine people instead of ten.

Night
The amplified music must occur during the night to constitute the offending gathering (s 63(1)). It does not have to be continuous and the absence of music during the daytime does not prevent the gathering falling within the Act. It is for the courts to define "night" in due course. It may mean the hours of darkness by reference to dawn and dusk, or between specific hours. The reality is that it probably does not matter. Raves goes on all night and are not restricted by twilight and sunrise. The section focuses on "all nighters", designed to make money for the organisers.

Intermissions
The gathering is deemed to continue during intermissions. When it lasts several days, it is only the night time element which qualifies. "Music" includes repetitive beats (s 63(1)(b)). "Gathering" does not include a licensed gathering (s 63(9)(a)).

Communicating the Direction
The direction to leave or remove property must be communicated to the people concerned; it may be the constable at the scene who tells them (s 63(3)); and the direction is deemed given if reasonable steps have been taken to let those people know of it (s 63(4)). This contrasts with the basis of communication in s 61(3) where there is no reference to "reasonable steps". "Reasonable steps" in the context of a rave might include using the public address system to make an announcement. It might be sufficient to switch off the public address system and reduce the lighting, especially strobe lighting. That done, the crowd should be aware that the event is over.

3.2 Offences
It is an offence for a person to fail without reasonable excuse to leave as soon as reasonably practicable or, having left, to return within seven days without reasonable excuse. The offence carries imprisonment of up to three months or a fine up to level 4 or both. On reasonable belief that the offence is being committed, a constable may arrest without a warrant. (s 63(6)–(8))

3.3 Exemption
The occupier, his family, his employee or agent, or any person whose home

is situated on the land in question, is exempted from direction (s 63(5) and (10)).

3.4 Powers of Seizure

If a superintendent reasonably believes that a direction would be justified, he may authorise a constable (who need not be in uniform) to enter land without warrant to:

(a) ascertain if the direction would be justified;

(b) exercise any powers in s 63; or

(c) if the direction has been given, seize and remove vehicles or sound equipment on the land, belonging to or under the control of the person given the direction.

Although there is no express provision on the use of force, the act of seizure itself is permitted. Anybody seeking to prevent that might be liable to arrest for wilfully obstructing a police officer in the execution of his duty.

The power to seize applies only if the directed person has:

(a) failed to leave;

(b) been arrested; or

(c) failed to remove property or vehicles in accordance with the direction.

The property of exempted people cannot be seized (s 64(5)).

3.5 Stopping People en Route

Once a direction has been given, a constable in uniform has various powers. Within five miles of the boundary of the land in respect of which the direction was given, he can stop any person he reasonably believes is en route to the gathering and direct the person not to proceed in the direction of the gathering. He cannot give such a direction to those in the exempted class (s 65). There may be problems about the interpretation of the five mile radius in the case of barns in large fields. Is the measurement taken from the barn or the boundary of the field? The police officer giving the direction in the first place should make such matters clear. In the event of non-compliance with such a direction, he may arrest a person he believes is committing the offence of failing to comply with a direction not to proceed in the direction of the gathering (s 65(5)). In an appropriate case, s 25 of PACE applies.

In *DPP v Jones* [1999] 2 AC 240, [1999] 2 All ER 257, [1999] 2 Cr App R 348, the House of Lords upheld the individual's right to use the highway so long as he does not unreasonably impede other individuals' rights to pass and repass. The House of Lords emphasised that each prospective interference with an individual's right to use the highway was a question of fact for the court of first instance. It is reasonable to expect that the courts will find that interference with rave-goers' rights on the highway is proportionate and necessary in a democratic society, taking into account the competing rights of local residents.

3.6   Forfeiture

A person convicted of non-compliance with a direction under s 63 may be ordered to forfeit goods seized from him, provided they were in his possession or under his control at the time (s 64(4)). Before making an order, the court is obliged to take into account the value of the items, and the effect on the offender of forfeiture (s 66(3)). A person who is not the person from whom the items were seized, seeking to reclaim the property seized, must apply within six months under the Police (Property) Act 1897. He will have to show that he had not consented to the offender's having the item or had not known, and had no reason to suspect, that the equipment was likely to be used at a gathering, as defined (s 67(7)).

Vehicles and sound equipment seized may be retained until the end of the case against the person from whom they were seized. There are powers to charge for storage and to retain the property pending payment of the storage charges (s 67).

3.7   Organisers

Rave organisers have moved away from the type of event targeted by the 1994 Act because of the potential for substantial losses consequent on the seizure provisions. The provisions on the volume and time of noise are ill-defined and have been left to the courts to resolve. "Serious distress" may well be a higher requirement than the government intended. The "serious distress" may arise from daytime music rather than the music during the night. Therefore, even if the organisers turn the music down at night, they will be caught by the provision. The borderline between distress and serious distress is difficult to determine, but "serious distress" is to be defined in accordance with the principles in *Brutus v Cozens* [1973] AC 854, [1972] 3 WLR 521, [1972] 2 All ER 1297 (HL). No offence is created in respect of non-compliance with a direction to remove vehicles or other property, although non-compliance may lead to seizure or to a charge of obstruction.

The method adopted in the 1994 Act is to target the expensive equipment required for raves. The impact may be dented if organisers choose to hire the equipment under a contract which excludes its use for events defined by s 63, since such contractual provision would protect the hirer from loss generally and he would recover the equipment. But this would be a substantial risk, because s 65(5) requires the owner of the equipment to apply to the magistrates for the return of the equipment. The magistrates may order its return, but are not *required* to do so. There is therefore a risk to the owner that they would not make the order. Organisers may nevertheless consider whether an event is viable even allowing for equipment to be held pending a court decision. The web of statutory provisions has curtailed huge unlicensed outdoor gatherings, but smaller gatherings publicised via the internet continue to occur.

As noted above, the police may not, under these provisions, seize property from exempted persons, including the land occupier's agent. In certain cases this exemption may extend to those setting up the gathering and to the equipment if the organiser is operating in part as the agent of the occupier of the land.

Although the court must consider the consequences of forfeiting items seized, it will do so in the context of weighing the loss to the offender against the benefits generally of depriving an offender of the means of committing the offence.

4   Aggravated Trespass

The offence of aggravated trespass and police powers to remove offenders are set out in ss 68 and 69 of the CJPOA.

Checklist
- difficulty of defining "adjoining land";
- trespass in open air required;
- any act with intent to intimidate, obstruct or disrupt required;
- only the senior policeman present may direct persons to leave;
- direction can be expressed as a question even if it masks an imperative.

Section 68(1) of the 1994 Act makes it an offence for a trespasser on land in the open air, in relation to any lawful activity engaged in by persons on that or adjoining land in the open air, to do anything with the intention of intimidating any of those persons or deterring any of them from that activity; or obstructing or disrupting the activity. The police may give a direction to leave the land (s 69).

The provisions on aggravated trespass are designed to deal with trespassers who disrupt lawful activity on land. The most obvious example is hunt saboteurs. In *Winder and Ors v DPP* (1996) 160 JP 713, (1996) 160 JPN 786, *The Times* 14 August 1996 (QBD), hunt saboteurs argued that in running across fields towards the hunt, they were mere trespassers and did not have the required intent to disrupt. The court found they were trespassers. It was a question of fact whether they intended to disrupt, and in this case they did. Their movement towards the hunt was, for the purposes of the Act, an act going beyond mere trespass.

Sections 68 and 69 have been criticised because of their potential application to situations never envisaged by the government when it passed the legislation. As noted elsewhere in this book, this is a common problem in public order law and gives rise to the risk of greater state intervention in individual rights than the community will tolerate, thereby jeopardising public order rather than protecting it. As always, much depends on how the provisions are applied in practice. A demonstration on the town hall steps might be caught because the demonstrators might be trespassing, and their intention might well be to disrupt; however well behaved they were, the circumstances might be caught by the "open air" element of the provision. The government view was that the discretion would be sparingly exercised. If not, it is disproportionate and breaches the Human Rights Act by going beyond what is necessary in a democratic society. Either or both arts 10 and 11 would be breached, laying the public authority, here the police, open to claims in damages, declarations and failed prosecutions.

Home Office Research Study 190 (above, page 155) reported, in relation to fox hunting, that police forces were using the provisions of the CJPOA 1994 in relation to "intelligence led" and "proactive" approaches to the issue. They were also using the provisions in relation to "agreement led" approaches, under which the police would agree not to use their powers in return for the protestors' agreement to refrain from certain things. The research also showed that police officers interpret the wearing of masks and balaclavas as among the activities capable of being aggravated trespass. On a practical level, failures in court and the discontinuance of cases were seen as an indicator of the difficulties of finding the evidence to achieve a conviction.

The same research revealed the greatest use of the provisions in connection with protests about environmental issues. The Newbury Bypass protest alone led to 356 arrests for aggravated trespass, resulting in 59 cautions and 258 prosecutions. During 1996, 359 people were prosecuted for aggravated trespass compared with 111 in 1995. Just over half were convicted.

4.1 Constituents of the Offence

Aggravated trespass is committed if (s 68(1)):

> "A person . . . trespasses on land in the open air and, in relation to any lawful activity which persons are engaging in or are about to engage in on that or adjoining land in the open air does there anything which is intended by him to have the effect–
> (a) of intimidating those persons or any of them so as to deter them or any of them from engaging in that activity,
> (b) of obstructing that activity, or
> (c) of disrupting the activity."

Trespass may occur where there is no licence (express or implied) to be on the land in question; after a time limited licence has expired; or where a person lawfully on the land engages in conduct going beyond his permission. Trespassers often plead necessity as a defence in cases where the "necessity" is to achieve some greater good. "Necessity" has been strictly limited by the courts in the operation of the civil law, and in *London Borough of Southwark v Williams* [1971] Ch 734, [1971] 2 WLR 467, [1971] 2 All ER 175, the Court of Appeal effectively rejected necessity as a defence to a claim save in the narrowest circumstances involving immediate and obvious danger. This proposition was applied in the context of protest in *Monsanto v Tilly* [1999] EGCS 143, (1999) 149 NLJ 1833, *The Times* 30 November 1999 (CA), where the appellant company sought an injunction to prevent mass trespass by individuals protesting about the growing of genetically modified crops. The public interest that the defendants were trying to promote had been effectively delimited by Parliament and was not a matter which could be left to the defence of necessity. In the criminal law context the same law applies, but there is greater scope for departure from the strictness of the principle, especially in jury trials. In one Crown Court case the jury acquitted when the defendants claimed that they had to do what they did to protect the community at large, a species of "prevention of crime" defence.

Aggravated trespass under s 68 occurs only in the open air. Partly open buildings, such as Dutch barns, fall outside the section, although conduct en route to a Dutch barn might well be caught.

"Engaging in or about to engage in lawful activity"

Activity is lawful if it can be undertaken without committing an offence (s 68(2)). The lawful activity must be "being engaged in" or "about to be engaged in". There may be difficulty with the meaning of "about to". How proximate must it be? If hunt saboteurs go to a field and prepare to disrupt a hunt that in fact will not visit that field, are they attempting to commit an offence contrary to the section? Additionally, the lawful activity must be on the land in question or on adjoining land, and in the open air.

In *Nelder v DPP, The Times* 11 June 1998 (DC), the court was asked to review the position when the members of the hunt, although engaged in a lawful activity for part of the time, were themselves trespassers in that they went on to railway land without permission and possibly in breach of railway bye laws. The argument for the hunt saboteurs was that they should not be convicted because they had not disrupted a *lawful* activity. In the event the court found that:

> "by the time the trespass had ended, the hunt activity had become lawful so that, by thereafter maintaining their protest for an appreciable time over an appreciable distance, the appellants had committed the *actus reus* . . . with the intention of obstructing or disrupting that lawful activity . . ."

Thus it appears that if the main hunting activity is unlawful then the offence is not made out against protestors. If the protestors confine their trespass to the time when the hunt is itself acting unlawfully, the protestors do not commit the offence.

In *Hibberd v DPP*, 27 November 1996, unreported (QBD), the court had to consider "lawful activity". The case concerned the Newbury Bypass protest; the appellant had been refusing to come down from a tree. It was argued that the tree fellers were not engaged in lawful activity because they were not complying with the Health and Safety Etc at Work Act 1974 in that they were not wearing protective gloves. The court had no difficulty in rejecting that argument on the basis that the lawful activity was the tree felling. Staughton LJ stated that: "one should define the activity as the task to be carried out and not the way it is to be done".

The word "adjoining" may cause difficulty. If, in the context of this section, "land" means land in single ownership, then "adjoining land" means neighbour's land lying next to the land in question. This may be as difficult for protestors to resolve as it is for the police. If "land" means an identifiable parcel of land, the adjoining land may be a separate field in the same ownership but lying next to the one first trespassed on.

Finally, the meaning of "engaging in" may need examination. A farmer may be "engaged in" farming even though he is not in the field in question. A protestor who conducts himself in a way calculated to disrupt the farming operation, even though the farmer is not present, may be caught. One example may be a case of trespass with a view to strewing metal objects in a field to prevent harvest. This issue has not yet been resolved, although in one case a district judge determined, on the particular facts, that the combination of "engaging in" and "lawful activity" require that there must be somebody actually doing something, rather than simply a field with crops growing in it. This proposition is to some extent supported by the background of *Lucy and Ors v DPP* (1997) 73 P&CR D25 (QBD), where the police suggested that the quarry should have staff working to avoid the risk that the aggravated trespass provision might not be triggered (see page 185).

Intention

The intention has to be that the conduct will intimidate, obstruct or disrupt. If the intention is not one of these, no offence is committed. It is for the court to determine, on the facts, the person's intention. In most cases it is obvious, but engaging in the peaceful persuasion of hunt members might not fall within the section. In *DPP v Barnard and Ors* (1999) 96(42) LSG 40, (1999) 143 SJLB 256, *The Times* 9 November 1999 (QBD) the court found that the occupation of land could constitute an act intended to intimidate, obstruct or disrupt, but only if it was overt and distinct from a mere act of trespass. This decision reflected the decision in *Winder* (above), when the court decided that running towards the hunt demonstrated the requisite intention, going beyond mere trespass.

"Land"

"Land" for these purposes does not include land forming part of the highway unless the highway is a bridleway, footpath or byway. Thus protest on the highway is not precluded by s 68, although such protest often raises the problem of defining the relationship between tolerated protest in the community and wilful obstruction of the highway contrary to s 137 of the Highways Act 1980. Protest on a footpath, bridleway or byway may well constitute an offence under this section, assuming the other elements are present.

"Does there anything"

Although it may be argued that this part of the section requires positive action to constitute the offence, that is not necessarily so. A person or group doing nothing other than standing in a particular place may be doing something within the terms of the Act if they, as trespassers, stand and thereby obstruct the lawful activity of the other persons (see *Winder*, above, page 181). Generally, it is more positive conduct which is caught, but not always. In *Fagan v Metropolitan Police Commissioner* [1969] 1 QB 439, [1968] 3 WLR 1120, [1968] 3 All ER 442 (DC), the court was divided 2:1 on whether declining to remove a car from a police officer's foot constituted assault.

In *Lucy and Ors v DPP* (above) the court was called upon to analyse the conduct of quarry protestors who entered a quarry in the belief that no quarrying was intended on that day. Had that been all, then they would not have had the required intent to disrupt etc. But once in the quarry, the protestors discovered that quarry staff were in fact working. The protestors continued with their protest and the quarry personnel were not able to load lorries because of the danger to the protestors standing on high piles of material. The court found that because they stayed after they became aware that the quarry staff were in fact working, they fell within the section in the sense that they developed the intention to disrupt. They also met the test in "does there anything" because they elected to stand on the piles of material waiting to be loaded. It was not therefore mere trespass; the protestors were standing on the piles with a particular purpose. (See also the *Winder* and *Bernard* cases, above).

4.2 Direction to Leave

The senior police officer present may direct a person or people to leave land if he reasonably believes that the person(s) is committing, will commit or has committed the offence of aggravated trespass; or that two or more are trespassing with the common purpose of intimidating people so as to deter them from engaging in a lawful activity, or of obstructing or disrupting the lawful activity (s 69(1)).

It had been anticipated that there could be difficulty, in cases which came to court concerning s 69, of proving that a direction to leave had been given, if details of the exact terms and the time it was given were not available. In most cases, however, a police officer simply says to the trespasser, "get out of this field now", and courts should have little problem with that.

Capon, Gill and Schofield v DPP, The Independent 23 March 1998, concerned a prosecution for failure to comply with a direction under s 69(1). Hunt protestors followed the hunt to a location where a fox had gone to ground and where hunt members were planning to use their terriers. The protestors' intention was to video record the events. A police sergeant, having spoken to a hunt member, said ". . . and that, as far as I'm concerned is interfering with the hunt. You either leave the land or you're arrested". He went on to ask "Are you leaving the land?" The hunt protestors said they had not understood they were being given a direction and regarded themselves as having been arrested for aggravated trespass, not for non-compliance with a direction. The court found that the only prerequisite for a direction under s 69 was that the police officer had reasonable grounds for believing that the protestors were committing aggravated trespass, whether or not they in fact were. The court found that the officer did have reasonable grounds because he had spoken to a hunt representative who had given him information. The court also found that, despite the unspecific formula, his question did amount to a direction and the protestors heard it and understood it as such. The arrest for non-compliance was therefore lawful. "An imperative may masquerade as a question without ceasing to be an imperative". The difficulty with this case is that the offence of non-compliance with a direction to leave land requires the person to know that the direction has been given. To permit a direction which "masquerades" as a question puts at risk the requirement for knowledge of the direction. It is a matter of fact in every case. The situation would be clearer if police were obliged to tell the recipient that the direction was a s 69 direction founded on reasonable grounds. The defendants in *Capon, Gill and Schofield* did not take the point that the officer might not have been the senior police officer present. Whether their ignorance of the nature of the direction, despite the court's finding, could have supported an argument of breach of art 6(3)(a) of the European Convention on Human Rights, "to be informed promptly, in a language which he understands and in detail, of the nature and cause of the accusation against him" was not resolved. A case on the same issues following the Human Rights Act would certainly require an analysis of that proposition.

4.3 The Offence

Having been given a direction and knowing it has been given, it is an offence for a person to fail to leave the land as soon as practicable or to return to the land within seven days once he has left it. The penalty is up to three months' imprisonment or a fine up to level 4 or both. Arrest may be without warrant (s 69(5)).

It is a defence for the accused to show that at the time of arrest for breach of the direction he was not trespassing, or that he had a reasonable excuse for not leaving or for returning (s 69(4)).

4.4 Comment

The provisions discussed above protect lawful activity on land from interference by trespassers intent on intimidating, obstructing or disrupting it. Hunting remains lawful and the government's view is that people should be able to go about their lawful activities even if they are distasteful to other members of the community. This view has also been developed in the abortion clinic cases, and in the cases relating to the export of live animals for slaughter where the right of the exporter to be protected in his lawful trade has been protected by the courts (the *Phoenix Aviation* case; see page 7). Any person who is trespassing and, while doing so, blows a horn or shouts or lays false trails on adjacent land will fall foul of ss 68 and 69 of the 1994 Act. So will a person who chases the hunt, or stands on quarry works while work is in progress, or chains himself in a tree to prevent the lawful felling of the tree. He is liable to a direction to leave, or to arrest, or to both. The only steps that appear to remain permitted to a hunt saboteur are to operate from places where he is not *prima facie* a trespasser, ie footpaths, bridleways and highways, or to wait and see if the hunt acts unlawfully. He must stop once the hunt action becomes lawful again. This is unlikely to enable saboteurs to function as they have in the past. The risk is that the increasing restriction on their activities may lead some to take the law into their own hands and move towards more extreme action. Some part of this risk might be reduced by sensitive policing, but protest does not necessarily stop because particular facets of it are illegal.

On a practical basis, some hunt saboteur incidents occur on footpaths and it may not be immediately apparent whether or not the saboteur is trespassing. If he is not, he commits no offence. Further, as the hunt saboteur makes his way quietly from one place to another by trespassing across land, doing nothing intimidating, obstructive or disruptive, he commits no offence. If he then makes his protest from a footpath, he may well become a trespasser and render himself liable under the section. In *Harrison v Duke of Rutland* [1893] 1 QB 142, the protestor waved his umbrella from the perceived security of a public footpath to disrupt a pheasant shoot on the Duke's land. The question was whether he was protected by being on the footpath, or whether he was in fact a trespasser as against the Duke who owned the land over which the footpath ran. The court decided that because he used the footpath for a purpose other than the passing and repassing for which a footpath existed, he was a trespasser. Thus a protestor on a footpath might, according to the *Harrison* test, easily be a trespasser in relation to the footpath.

In *DPP v Jones* [1999] 2 AC 240, [1999] 2 All ER 257, [1999] 2 Cr App R 348 the House of Lords tried to deal with the conflict of rights in relation to the public highway. It determined that the public may enjoy a public highway for any reasonable purpose so long as there is neither a private or a public nuisance. It determined that a peaceful and non-obstructive assembly did not necessarily exceed the public right of access. Each case depended on its own facts and it was for the court of first instance to decide whether the user was unreasonable and therefore a trespass.

It might have been thought that the Labour Government would view these matters differently from its predecessor. In reality the increasingly violent nature of some animal rights activists appears to have created a climate where more, rather than less, restrictive legislation is likely. Detective work undertaken by some protestors, leading to assaults on individuals and attacks on their personal property, and protestors' ability to target banks financing organisations they oppose, also give rise to the possibility of legislation to curb their activities.

5 Unauthorised Occupation of Premises

Sections 72–76 of the CJPOA tackle the issue of squatting.

The 1994 Act deals with the consequences of not complying with an interim possession order made in summary proceedings, and the offences of obtaining such an order by false statements (ss 75–76). It also contains provisions to improve the position of displaced residential occupiers and intending occupiers (ss 72 and 74), and on residential squatting (s 73):

> "The existing remedy for removing squatters from property has clearly been inadequate for some time . . . it is much too expensive and too slow. It should not be solely the province of the exceptionally wealthy . . . . The law must be accessible to those of modest or little means who suddenly find their property occupied." (Mr Maclean, HC SCB, col 663)

The provisions are consistent with the then Government's developing policy of protecting all categories of lawful occupant of land. The exact extent of squatting was uncertain, but there was some measure of agreement in committee that some steps were necessary. The anxiety was that the measures addressing the problem could be abused by unscrupulous landlords to the disadvantage of vulnerable tenants. The government view was that the problems of squatting should, nevertheless, be addressed. In essence the squatter was the one acting unlawfully and that, as the law stood, he was overprotected:

> ". . . it will be for a civil court to decide whether to order the squatters to leave, as a form of interim relief. That power will be subject to the safeguard that, having left, the alleged squatters will be entitled to a full hearing of the case in the usual way and to recover costs and damages as well as reinstatement in the property, if it is found that they had lawful entitlement to possession." (Mr Maclean, HC SCB, 664)

5.1 Interim Possession Order

The procedure for obtaining an interim order for possession of premises occupied by trespassers is set out in the County Court Rules 1981, Ord 24, Part 2. This procedure is an alternative to that in Part 1 of Ord 24, and applies to premises as defined in s 12 of the Criminal Law Act 1977: a building or part of a building under separate occupation, any land ancillary to a building or buildings with any land ancillary thereto. The definition includes any immovable structure and any moveable structure designed or adapted for residential purposes. This includes caravans and houseboats. The order is not available against trespassers on land which is not ancillary to a building. The rules provide for notice of the proceedings to be served on the alleged squatters, and for a hearing *ex parte* on application, except in the case of residential premises where the occupier may file an affidavit if he believes he has a right to occupy. In certain instances this may lead to a hearing which he may attend. If the applicant satisfies the court, on a balance of probabilities, that he is entitled to occupation, then an interim possession order will be made, requiring the squatters to leave the premises within 24 hours. Generally the notice must be served within 48 hours and lodged with the local police station within 24 hours of service. In due course a final hearing takes place, at which the court considers making a final order of possession and deals with any applications from a squatter who claims a right of occupation.

The 1994 Act makes it an offence punishable by six months' imprisonment or a fine up to level 5 for a person either not to leave the premises within 24 hours of service of the order, or to return within a year of service of the order (s 76(2)). The section also applies to any trespasser who occupies the premises during the currency of the interim possession order. Thus a person who takes over from an original squatter falls within the provision. A constable in uniform may arrest without warrant on reasonable suspicion (s 76(7)).

To protect occupiers abusing the provision, it is an offence, triable either way, to make a statement to obtain an interim possession order, knowing it to be, or being reckless as to its being, false or misleading in a material particular (s 75). This offence is punishable, on conviction on indictment, by two years' imprisonment or a fine or both. Summarily, it is punishable by six months imprisonment or a fine not exceeding the statutory maximum. The maximum penalty is the same as that under the Protection from Eviction Act 1977 for the offence of unlawfully depriving a residential occupier of his premises: "There is a tremendous discrepancy between the penalty which squatters may suffer and that for owners who knowingly or recklessly seek an interim possession order" (Mr Maclean, HC SCB, col 672).

5.2 Displaced Residential Occupiers

Under s 7 of the Criminal Law Act 1977, it is an offence punishable by six months' imprisonment or a fine up to level 5 for a squatter to fail to leave premises when ordered to do so by a displaced residential occupier of the premises. The CJPOA Act 1994 added to the Criminal Law Act 1977 a new s 12A, which redefines "displaced residential occupier" under three categories:

(a) a person with a freehold interest or a leasehold interest with at least two years to run;

(b) a person with a tenancy or a licence to occupy granted by a person in the first category;

(c) a person with a tenancy granted by an "authority" as defined in the subsection;

excluded by a trespasser as defined, and holding a certificate signed by him and a JP or commissioner of oaths specifying his interest and the fact that he requires the premises as a residence for himself.

It is a defence to proceedings under s 7 of the 1977 Act to show that no certificate was produced at the time the squatter was required to leave (s 12A(9)). It is an offence punishable by six months' imprisonment or a fine up to level 5 or both (except in the case of the tenants of an "authority") to make a false or reckless statement (s 12A(8)).

The provisions of s 6 of the Criminal Law Act 1977 have been amended (by s 72 of the 1994 Act) by the addition of a new subs 6(1A), excluding displaced residential occupiers from liability for violent entry.

5.3   Reasons for Change

The provisions on interim possession orders were designed to make proceedings against squatters quicker, more effective and less expensive. The civil court decides whether the squatter goes, but once the decision is made, then if he stays, he commits an offence. To guard against the removal of non-squatters by the unscrupulous, the penalties for misinforming the court include imprisonment for matters falling short of perjury.

For displaced residential occupiers also, the law on squatters was changed by the 1994 Act. They are no longer criminals if they use force to gain entry to their property. It could be argued that this endangers public order by permitting force in these confrontations. The government view was that people should be able to use reasonable force to effect an entry to their own property.

By the relatively straightforward procedure of preparing a certificate containing the relevant information, signing it and having it signed by a magistrate or commissioner of oaths, the displaced residential occupier is entitled to the assistance of the police in regaining occupancy of his home. The squatter commits an offence if he does not vacate and is therefore liable to arrest. The procedure is to prepare the certificate and have it countersigned, and then attend the premises with a police officer who will, in effect, enforce the removal of the squatter (CLA 1977, s 12A).

6   Unauthorised Campers and Gypsy Sites

The powers to remove unauthorised campers are set out in ss 77–79 of the CJPOA 1994 and are discussed below.

Checklist

- The local authority must avoid breach of the Children Act 1989;
- DoE Circular 18/94 still requires councils to act in a humane and compassionate way;
- notice to leave may be given to those residing on the highway or unoccupied land generally;
- no specific names are required on a notice to leave;
- wide definition of "vehicle"; it includes a body without wheels;
- home elsewhere is no defence;

• provisions affect all nomadic people, whether gypsy or not.

6.1 Background

Sections 77 to 79 of the CJPOA 1994 were designed to deal with persons camping on land without authority. Although it does not criminalise trespass, it certainly criminalises non-compliance with a direction to move and has been seen as the *de facto* criminalisation of certain lifestyles. The provisions do not distinguish between different categories of traveller. They may conflict with international conventions (see page 195).

The obligation on local authorities under the Caravan Sites Act 1968 to provide gypsy sites was revoked by s 80 of the 1994 Act. They may provide such sites, but there is no government funding, and local opposition and the tightening of planning controls commonly militate against it. The definition of "gypsy" has been amended to include any person of a nomadic lifestyle. This new definition may be affected by the decision in *South Hams DC v Gibbs*, *The Times* 8 June 1994, which makes it clear that "nomadic habit of life" implies an identifiable connection between the nomadic life and the means of making a living. It excludes groups such as new age travellers whose nomadic life is not related to the generation of income.

Local authorities are empowered to require unauthorised campers to move on (s 77). It is an offence not to comply, and, on complaint, a magistrates' court may order vehicles or property to be removed if present in contravention of a direction (s 78), permitting the local authority to make the arrangements. Section 79 deals with the problem of service of the direction on unnamed persons.

In *R (on the application of Ward) v Hillingdon London Borough Council* [2001] All ER 176, the court reviewed the decision of a local council to issue a removal direction in respect of a person who had entered an official site without authority. A number of issues arose, including questions under art 8 of the European Convention on Human Rights. It had been decided that the particular site was overcrowded. The claimant moved onto a vacant plot without permission. The council carried out a review of his personal circumstances after which it served on him a removal direction under s 77(1) CJPOA. It also sought an order under s 78 CJPOA. The claimant's application for judicial review failed. The court held that the enquiries and decisions made by the local authority were not unreasonable given that he was a trespasser and others had a greater claim to the plot. He could not avail himself of art 8 because he was a trespasser and because the plot could not properly be described as his home. The local authority's response was proportionate to the legitimate aim pursued. It had balanced the competing interests in an appropriate way.

The decision in *R v Hillingdon London Borough Council* took account of *Chapman v UK* [2001] 10 BHRC 48, a case concerning travellers, where the applicant appealed against an adverse planning decision in respect of her own land, arguing that it was a contravention of her rights under art 8. The European Court of Human Rights stated:

"An interference will be considered 'necessary in a democratic society' for a legitimate aim if it answers a 'pressing social need' and, in particular, if it is 'proportionate to the legitimate aim pursued . . . When considering whether a requirement that the individual leave his or her home is proportionate to the legitimate aim pursued, it is highly relevant whether or not the home was established unlawfully."

During the early 1990s the government view was that the policy of requiring local authorities to provide sites for gypsies was not working, and that the more sites that were provided, the more people were attracted to the itinerant life:

"As more sites have been provided, more people have taken to the lifestyle. I believe that genuine gypsies have been disadvantaged as more and more people who could not be considered as genuine gypsies get on the bandwagon. Genuine gypsies are forced out of their traditional haunts . . . by others who do not deserve the same protection." (Mr Maclean, HC SCB, col 69s)

The provisions are comparable with other provisions on trespass in that they permit the control – in this case by local authorities – of unauthorised use of land for residence. Under the 1968 Act, a local authority designated as having provided sufficient sites, could move promptly to remove illegal campers from unofficial sites. The risk to caravan-dwelling children was highlighted by the opposition as one of the primary negative consequences of the provisions:

"With the repeal of the 1968 Act the proposal will be inefficient and ineffective, will undermine child care and education and will work to the detriment of local communities. Campers will arrive . . . and be moved around in the unproductive way of the past which was damaging to travellers, and, above all, to local communities" (Mr Michael, HC SCB, col 691)

This view was considered in *Wealden DC v Wales, The Times* 22 September 1995. It was argued that the council was required by DoE Circular 18/94 to act in a humane and compassionate way and to comply with the obligations in the Children Act 1989 with regard to the children among the travellers. DoE Circular 18/94 provides:

"Where gypsies are camped unlawfully on council land and are not causing a level of nuisance which cannot be effectively controlled, an immediate forced eviction might result in unauthorised camping in the area which could give rise to greater nuisance. Accordingly, authorities should consider tolerating gypsies' presence on the land for short periods and could examine ways of minimising the level of nuisance on such tolerated sites, for example, by providing basic services for gypsies . . ."

The Divisional Court ruled that the local authority "adopted the wrong approach to the case and omitted entirely to inform itself of potentially relevant matters both before giving a removal direction and before seeking a removal order". Sedley J made it clear that the local authority had a duty to think about those encamped and local residents and to balance their conflicting needs. These considerations had to be kept in mind both at the time of the decision to give the removal notice and before any complaint was made to the magistrates. It applied only to the people encamped. New arrivals would have to be considered anew and new notices prepared and served if appropriate.

From 26 July 2000, clauses 6 to 9 of Circular 18/94 have been modified to deal with the risk of misinterpretation and non-use of the powers. The powers are regarded as available in any case which constitutes a nuisance on the basis that nuisance is nuisance no matter who is involved. The powers should, however, always be exercised in a humane and compassionate way.

Although magistrates were restricted to consideration of the formalities, the local authority had an obligation to make itself aware of the circumstances of the people concerned *before* they issued the notice, not afterwards: *R v Wolverhampton Metropolitan District Council ex p Dunne* (1997) 29 HLR 745, [1997] COD 210 (QBD). Thus it appears that the magistrates have limited power and it is for the Divisional Court to determine matters on judicial review.

The government view relied on the gypsies' own capacity to provide sites for themselves so long as they were treated favourably from the point of view of planning control and assisted by local authorities. This view failed to take account of DoE Circular 1/94 which withdrew advice in favour of granting permission for caravan sites in green belt areas on a special case basis. The circular makes it less likely that gypsies will be given permission because the policy is no longer expressed positively. The purpose of the provisions in the 1994 Act was to provide a universal set of remedies for local authorities to deal with all unauthorised camping by whomsoever.

6.2 Direction to Leave

A local authority may give a direction to leave land and remove vehicles and any other property if it appears that persons are residing in a vehicle or vehicles on land forming part of the highway, any unoccupied land or any occupied land, without the permission of the occupier (s 77(1)).

Notice

A notice of the direction must be served. A notice which identifies the land and is addressed to the occupants of the vehicles on the land is sufficient. A specific name is required only where the direction is aimed at a single person (s 77(2)).

Offence

It is an offence carrying the penalty of a fine up to level 3 not to comply with such a notice (s 77(3)). The offence is committed if a person served fails to leave the land as soon as practicable (or fails to move the vehicle or property). It is also an offence to return to the land in a vehicle within three months from the day of the direction.

Defence
It is a defence if the non-departure, non-removal of property or re-entry was due to illness, mechanical breakdown or other immediate emergency (s 77(5)).

Vehicle
"Vehicle" is widely interpreted to include any vehicle, whether or not it is in a fit state for use on the roads, and includes any body, with or without wheels, appearing to have formed part of such a vehicle, and any load carried by, and anything attached to, such a vehicle; and a caravan as defined in s 29(1) of the Caravan Sites and Control of Development Act 1960.

Home Elsewhere
Having a home elsewhere is not a defence to an allegation of residence.

6.3 Magistrates' Order
If satisfied that there is a direction and continuing residence, the magistrates' court may, on complaint, make an order that vehicles, property and people residing in them be removed (s 77(6)(a)). The court order authorises the local authority to take reasonable steps to ensure the order is complied with, including entering on land and doing what is necessary to enter the vehicles and make them ready for removal. It is an offence to obstruct anyone doing so, and the penalty is a fine up to level 3.

The summons following the complaint may be served on the occupant of a particular vehicle or on all occupants of vehicles on specified land. There is no power to arrest for non-attendance at court. Good service is effected by attaching the document to a prominent place on all the vehicles concerned (s 79(2)). It must also be displayed prominently on the land and copied to the owner or occupier of the land unless, upon reasonable enquiry, the owner or occupier cannot be ascertained (s 79(4)).

6.4 Comment
The focus of the Act is not gypsy people but nomadic people of any sort. The provisions are not complicated and enable local authorities to require unauthorised campers to move on. Whether this power will, in the long term, prove more effective than the regime it replaced is difficult to assess. The decision was taken that it is essential to remove promptly all categories of trespasser, and nomadic people are frequently trespassers. The then government's view was that the 1994 Act did not discriminate because it used the expression "nomadic habit of life". It may prove difficult to relate that to the

provisions of the Human Rights Act. Respect for privacy and family life, home and correspondence are all guaranteed by art 8, and art 14 guarantees the enjoyment of such rights without discrimination on grounds of association with, among other things, a "national minority". The UN Convention on the Rights of the Child specifically acknowledges the right of gypsy children to enjoy their own culture and to preserve their own identity without interference. Their culture depends upon a nomadic habit of life. That lifestyle is unprotected by these provisions. UK law is possibly in conflict with international conventions and in particular, the European Convention on Human Rights.

Chapter 7

Obstruction and Public Nuisance

Many offences feature obstruction. The most common are the offences of assault on, or wilful obstruction of, a constable acting in the execution of his
duty, and wilful obstruction of the highway. The offences may be committed
in widely varying circumstances, many falling outside the scope of public
order, eg warning a driver of an imminent speed trap, or allowing a market
stall or supermarket trolley to encroach on the highway. Nonetheless, the
principles which emerge from the cases apply equally in the context of public order.

1   Assault or Wilful Obstruction of a Constable

Checklist
- has the constable committed a battery or assault?
- was the constable acting correctly under a power?
- was the constable a trespasser on private property?
- was the constable on private property pursuant to a power?
- where the charge is wilful obstruction, was the task of the constable
  made more difficult?
- where the charge is wilful obstruction, was the citizen acting intentionally and without lawful excuse?

1.1   The Offences
Section 89 of the Police Act 1996 deals with assault or wilful obstruction of
a constable in the execution of his duty. The section states:
"(1) Any person who assaults a constable in the execution of his duty, or a
     person assisting a constable in the execution of his duty, shall be guilty
     of an offence and liable on summary conviction to imprisonment for a
     term not exceeding six months or to a fine not exceeding level 5 on the
     standard scale or both.
(2) Section 17(2) of the Firearms Act 1968 (additional penalty for posses-
     sion of firearms when committing certain offences) shall apply to off-
     ences under subsection (1) of this section.
(3) Any person who resists or wilfully obstructs a constable in the execution
     of his duty, or a person assisting a constable in the execution of his duty,
     shall be guilty of an offence and liable on summary conviction to im-

prisonment for a term not exceeding one month or to a fine not exceeding level 3 on the standard scale or both."

1.2   Acting in Execution of Duty

To make out an offence under s 89 it must be shown that the police officer in question was acting "in the execution of his duty". "Duty" is not necessarily the same as "power", although many duties are complemented by appropriate powers. Thus, although the police have a general duty to detect crime, the common law does not furnish them with complete powers to achieve that end, nor does the common law accept that what they do is necessarily done lawfully.

The offences in s 89 are wider than assault or wilful obstruction in the execution of a power, and an offence may be committed even though the constable is not acting pursuant to a power conferred by law, or by refusing to cooperate with the police, although precisely when these offences arise is not always clear.

It is insufficient to meet the test in s 89 to establish that the police officer was "on duty" when the assault or obstruction occurred; nor is it a defence to show that the police officer was doing something he was not obliged by law to do. In *Coffin v Smith* (1980) 71 Cr App R 221 (DC), police officers attended a youth club where the youth club leader was ejecting youths; the officers were held to have been acting in the execution of their duty. The court preferred not to follow the decision in *R v Prebble* (1858) 1 F & F 325, where a police officer clearing licensed premises was held not to have been acting in the execution of his duty where there had been no actual or threatened breach of the peace. For further discussion see page 16.

Establishing that an officer was acting in the execution of his duty is based on two considerations. The first is whether or not the officer was doing anything which falls within the range of activities which might be said to be a police officer's duties. The second is whether or not the officer has committed any act which requires justification at law.

Good faith, or lack of it, on the part of the police officer is irrelevant, and a police officer acting in good faith may nevertheless be acting outside the execution of his duty.

General Police Duties

The courts have never sought to specify in detail the nature and scope of the duties of the police. Such a precise and inflexible approach would run counter to the general approach of the common law, even though the law, as it develops, almost inevitably gives rise to extensions of police powers, as in *Chief Constable of Kent v V* [1983] QB 34, [1982] 3 WLR 462, [1982] 3 All ER 36 (CA).

In *Johnson v Phillips* [1976] 1 WLR 65, [1975] 3 All ER 682, [1975] Crim LR 580 (DC), it was said of police duties that:

"The first function of a constable has for centuries been the preservation of the peace. His powers and obligations derive from the common law and from statute . . . The powers and obligations of a constable under the common law have never been exhaustively defined and no attempt to do so has ever been made . . ."

And in *R v Waterfield* [1964] 1 QB 164, [1963] 3 WLR 946, [1963] 3 All ER 659 (CCA), Ashworth J observed that: ". . . it would be difficult . . . to reduce within specific limits the general terms in which the duties of police constables have been expressed."

If a court finds that there was a police duty, then disobedience by a citizen to orders given in pursuance of that duty may in some instances be an offence; in other instances it may not. See *Johnson v Phillips* (above) where a motorist refused to obey a constable's instruction to reverse down a one-way street in contravention of road traffic law. That refusal amounted to wilful obstruction of a constable in the execution of his duty:

"The law protects the liberty of the subject, but it must recognise that in certain circumstances . . . a constable may oblige persons to disobey a traffic regulation and not only in those cases that are explicitly dealt with by Parliament . . . a constable would be entitled, and indeed under a duty, to give such an instruction if it were reasonably necessary for the protection of life or property."

The courts have not gone so far as to say that whenever a police officer is acting in pursuance of some police objective or general duty, he is acting in the execution of his duty for the purposes of s 89. The better approach is revealed by Ashworth J in *R v Waterfield* (above):

"In most cases it is probably more convenient to consider what the police constable was actually doing and in particular whether such conduct was *prima facie* an unlawful interference with a person's liberty or property. If so, it is then relevant to consider whether (a) such conduct falls within the general scope of any duty imposed by statute or recognised at common law and (b) whether such conduct, albeit within the general scope of such a duty, involved an unjustifiable use of powers associated with the duty."

Thus, whenever a police officer interferes with the rights or liberties of a citizen he must be able to point to the proper exercise of power, and the focus shifts to the justification for interference. A constable who is acting unlawfully cannot at the same time be acting in the execution of his duty.

Justification for Interference

Justification for interference with the rights or liberties of the individual is usually found in statute, although the residual common law powers concerning breaches of the peace remain important.

Commonly, in instances of disorder, the justification for interference with the citizen's liberty or property is the common law power to deal with breaches of the peace. This is examined in Chapter 2. Failure properly to exercise these powers takes the constable outside the execution of his duty.

Public Safety

As has been seen, the emphasis in *Johnson v Phillips* was on the role of the police in ensuring public safety. The court there observed that:

> "It is [the officer's] general duty to protect life and property: see *Glasbrook Brothers Ltd v Glamorgan County Council* [1925] AC 270 where Viscount Finlay said: 'There is no doubt that it is the duty of the police to give adequate protection to all persons and their property.' Stemming from that duty is his duty to control traffic on public roads."

The principle which underpins *Johnson v Phillips* is sufficiently broad to apply to directions given by a police officer, to a citizen on foot, to move clear of an area or follow a particular route in the interests of public safety. Disobeying such an order would be a wilful obstruction of the police officer acting in the execution of his duty, or wilful obstruction of the highway – see below (*Samuelson v Bagnall*, 1985, unreported)).

Entry to Premises

A police officer who enters premises with consent, express or implied, must leave expeditiously when requested to do so by the owner or someone acting with authority. Failure to leave makes him a trespasser and takes him outside the execution of his duty (*Davies v Lisle* [1936] 2 KB 434; *Robson v Hallett* [1967] 2 QB 939, [1967] 3 WLR 28, [1967] 2 All ER 407 (DC); *McArdle v Wallace* [1964] Crim LR 467 (DC)).

Whether or not a constable has an implied licence to enter premises depends on the general law, but it is reasonably clear that approaching the front door of a house, or entering the public areas of business premises, is within the scope of implied licence (*Robson v Hallett*; *Davis v Lisle*; *Halliday v Nevill*, 1984, unreported). Leaving a front door open in the knowledge that a police officer is standing there may constitute implied licence by conduct (*Faulkner v Willets* [1982] RTR 159, [1982] Crim LR 453 (DC)).

The activation of a burglar alarm connected to a police station gives implied authority to the police to enter the premises to investigate the alarm (*Kay v Hibbert* [1977] Crim LR 226 (QBD)); and an attack, even by the occupier, before a reasonable time has elapsed, is an assault under s 89. It seems that this is so even where the occupier purports to revoke the licence and refuses to co-operate with an officer seeking to confirm his identity (*Kay v Hibbert*). *Kay v Hibbert* was applied in *Ledger v DPP* [1991] Crim LR 439 (DC), which concerned entry to premises under implied licence and a purported revocation by the occupier who refused to identify himself to the police. The wilful obstruction which subsequently occurred was an offence within s 89(3).

Revocation of an implied or express licence must be in clear and unequivocal terms; mere vulgar abuse may be insufficient (*Gilham v Breiden-*

bach [1982] RTR 328 (DC); *Snook v Mannion* [1982] Crim LR 601, [1982] RTR 321 (DC)). Such abuse may constitute an offence contrary to s 5 of the Public Order Act 1986 (see *DPP v Orum* [1989] 1 WLR 88, [1988] 3 All ER 449, (1989) 88 Cr App R 261 (QBD); see page 110). A failure expressly to countermand an earlier licence to enter cannot be taken to be revocation (*Riley v DPP* (1990) 91 Cr App R 14, (1990) 154 JP 453, [1990] Crim LR 422 (DC)).

Where consent for a police officer to enter or remain on premises has been terminated, the officer may nonetheless remain on the premises if he reasonably anticipates an actual or imminent breach of the peace; he need not vacate the premises and return (*Robson v Hallet* [1967] 2 QB 939, [1967] 3 WLR 28, [1967] 2 All ER 407 (DC); *Lamb v DPP* (1990) 154 JPN 172, (1990) 154 JP 381 (DC)).

A police officer invited on to premises by one co-occupier, such as a spouse or partner of a second co-occupier, is acting lawfully in remaining, despite a request from the second co-occupier that he should leave. The licence continues either until withdrawn by the party who gave it, or until the police officer satisfies himself that the spouse or partner (and presumably any children) is safe (*R v Thornley* (1981) 72 Cr App R 302, [1981] Crim LR 637 (CA)). This principle seems to extend even to non-owning co-occupiers (*R v Thornley*; *McGowan v Chief Constable of Hull* (1967) 117 NLJ 1138, [1967] Crim LR 34 (DC)).

A police officer may be invited into premises at which a party is taking place by one of the party-goers, and is there lawfully until the licence is properly revoked by the occupier or someone with authority (*Jones and Jones v Lloyd* [1981] Crim LR 340 (DC)). Knowledge or awareness of the authority is irrelevant to the question whether or not the police officer is acting in the execution of his duty.

Questioning and Detention Without Arrest

A police officer may address questions to a citizen and in doing so acts in the execution of his duty. It is otherwise if he detains the citizen with a view to asking the questions or pursuing enquiries of another (see *Bentley v Brudzinski* (1982) 75 Cr App R 217, [1982] Crim LR 825 (DC); *Ludlow v Burgess* [1971] Crim LR 238 (DC); *Kenlin v Gardiner* [1967] 2 QB 510, [1967] 2 WLR 129, [1966] 3 All ER 931 (DC)). In *Kenlin v Gardner*, the detention by police officers of two schoolboys was held to be unlawful since the police officers had not been attempting to arrest the boys; they had simply wanted to detain them to help with their enquiries. The simple availability, without more, of a power to arrest or to stop and search does not put an officer in execution of his duty; he must purport to *use* the power.

Whether or not a police officer has committed a battery or false imprisonment, and thereby taken himself outside the execution of his duty, is often a difficult issue of fact, but the law is reasonably clear and emerges from

Collins v Wilcock [1984] 1 WLR 1172, [1984] 3 All ER 374, (1984) 79 Cr App R 229 (DC). The same principles apply to police officers as to other citizens.

Touching another person, however slightly, may amount to a battery, subject to specific exceptions such as pursuant to a power of arrest. There is also a broader general exception allowing for the exigencies of everyday life. Although many of the physical contacts of ordinary life are not actionable because they are impliedly consented to, the courts prefer to treat them as falling within a general exception embracing all physical contact which is generally acceptable in the ordinary conduct of daily life (*Collins v Wilcock*).

Among the generally acceptable forms of conduct is touching a person, even more than once if appropriate, for the purpose of engaging his attention, though using no greater degree of physical contact than is reasonably necessary in the circumstances (see *Wiffin v Kincard* (1807) 2 Bos & Pul 471). But a distinction is drawn between a touch to attract a person's attention, which is generally acceptable, and a physical restraint, which is not (see *Rawlings v Till* (1837) 3 M & W 28, [1837] 150 ER 1042). Holding a person's arm to calm him down may not be sufficient to take the constable outside the execution of his duty (*Mepstead v DPP* (1995) 160 JP 475). If a police officer's use of physical contact in the face of non-cooperation persists beyond generally acceptable standards of conduct, his action becomes unlawful. And if a police officer restrains a person, then his action is unlawful unless he is lawfully exercising a power (*Collins v Wilcock*).

It has been said that not every trivial interference with the citizen amounts to a course of conduct which takes a police officer outside the execution of his duty: *Donnelly v Jackman* [1970] 1 WLR 562, [1970] 1 All ER 987, (1969) 114 SJ 130 (DC). The decision in that case was highly unusual and has not generally found judicial favour (see *Collins v Wilcock*). A police officer had repeatedly tapped a defendant on the shoulder even though he had already indicated that he did not wish to speak to the officer. The defendant, who struck the constable during the altercation, was convicted of assaulting the constable in the execution of his duty.

A police officer who reinforces a request with the threat, actual or implicit, to use force if the other person does not comply, acts unlawfully.

It is apparent from *Rice v Connolly* [1966] 2 QB 414, [1966] 3 WLR 17, [1966] 2 All ER 649 (DC), that refusal to help police with their enquiries is not something recognised at common law as a separate and distinct offence. In *R v Lemsatef* [1977] 1 WLR 812, [1977] 2 All ER 835, (1977) 64 Cr App R 242 (CA), the court stated that:

"First, it must be clearly understood that neither customs officers nor police officers have any right to detain somebody for the purposes of getting them to help with their enquiries. Police either arrest for an offence or they do not arrest at all . . . arrest can[not] be carried out without the accused person being told the offence for which he is being arrested.

There is no such thing as helping the police with their enquiries."
Police officers must guard against detaining an individual without authority.
Any decision to arrest should be communicated to the suspect and the necessary formalities carried out (Police and Criminal Evidence Act 1984, ss 28
and 31); and failure to do so takes the police officer outside the execution of
his duty (*R v Inwood* [1973] 1 WLR 647, [1973] 2 All ER 645, [1973] Crim
LR 290 (CA)).

Statutory Powers of the Police

Although police powers are outside the scope of this book, it is axiomatic
that powers should be exercised correctly. A failure by a police officer correctly to exercise powers under the Public Order Act 1986 or the Criminal
Justice and Public Order Act 1994 takes him outside the execution of his
duty, and any disobedience of an order made pursuant to a power which is
exercised incorrectly is not wilful obstruction.

Establishing the Legality of Police Action

Ordinarily, the legality of police intervention must be justified by direct evidence. Where the legality of police action depends on a chain of events, legality must be demonstrated throughout the chain of events. An inference of
legality may not be drawn where the police officers concerned are readily
identifiable and direct evidence to support the legality of the original arrest is
available:

- *McBean v Parker* [1983] Crim LR 399 (DC) (legality of prior stop-
  search has to be established);
- *Riley v DPP* (1990) 91 Cr App R 14, (1990) 154 JP 453, [1990] Crim
  LR 422 (DC);
- *Griffiths v DPP*, 1992, unreported;
- *Edwards (Deborah) v DPP* (1993) 97 Cr App R 301, [1993] Crim LR
  854, *The Times* 29 March 1993 (DC);
- *Odewale v DPP*, 28 November 2000, unreported (QBD) (legality of the
  arrest of a third party must be established in order to convict the defendant of obstructing a constable by interfering with a lawful arrest);
- *Chapman v DPP* (1989) 89 Cr App R 190, [1988] Crim LR 843, (1989)
  153 JP 27 (QBD) (legality of entry to premises must be established in
  order to convict the defendant of interfering with the entry or search).

A police officer's reasonable and genuine belief as to a particular state of affairs is insufficient (*Kerr v DPP* (1994) 158 JP 1048, [1995] Crim LR 394
(QBD)).

But where there has been a serious disturbance involving breaches of
the peace, the court may draw the inference from the circumstantial evidence
that an attempted arrest by an unidentified police officer is lawful, and accordingly interference with that arrest by another person amounts to an offence contrary to s 89 of the Police Act 1996 (*Plowden v DPP* [1991] Crim
LR 850 (DC)).

Assault

Assault includes battery, and requires the intentional or reckless application of unlawful force to the person, or threat causing another to fear the application of unlawful force, knowing it to be unlawful. Usually the assault comprises a positive act, but in certain instances an omission may suffice (see *Fagan v Metropolitan Police Commissioner* [1969] 1 QB 439, [1968] 3 WLR 1120, [1968] 3 All ER 442 (DC)).

In the light of the public policy issues concerning special protection for police officers (see *Blackburn v Bowering* [1994] 1 WLR 1324, [1994] 3 All ER 380, [1995] Crim LR 38 (CA)), knowledge, or recklessness as to the fact, that the person assaulted is a constable is not required; nor need the prosecution establish that the defendant knew that the police officer was acting in the execution of his duty (*R v Forbes and Webb* (1865) 10 Cox CC 362; *R v Maxwell and Clanchy* (1909) 2 Cr App R 26; *McBride v Turnock* (1964) 108 SJ 336, [1964] Crim LR 456 (DC); *R v Brightling* [1991] Crim LR 364 (CA)). There is thus an element of strict liability, mitigated only by the possible impact on a plea of self-defence of a genuine (even if unreasonable) belief that the other is not a police officer.

A defendant who, in self-defence or in defence of others, assaults a police officer, knowing that he is a police officer, in the genuine and reasonable belief that the police officer is acting outside the execution of his duty, when he is in fact within it, has no defence: *R v Bentley* (1850) 4 Cox CC 406; *R v Fennell* [1971] QB 428, [1970] 3 WLR 513, [1970] 3 All ER 215 (CA). See also *R v Ball* (1990) 90 Cr App R 378, [1989] Crim LR 579 (CA) on the consequence of a belief that police were using excessive force during an arrest. This is a mistake of law and does not excuse the defendant. A defendant who, knowing that another is a police officer, intervenes either in defence of others or himself is entitled to be acquitted only where the police officer is in law acting outside the execution of his duty. In such a case, the use of excessive force would lead to a charge of assault *simpliciter* rather than the more technically demanding s 89 offence.

A defendant who defends himself or another against the actions of a police officer, and who uses reasonable force in the circumstances, is not guilty of s 89 assault where he mistakenly believes that the police officer is not a police officer. Such a belief must be genuine but need not be reasonable (see *R v Williams (Gladstone)* [1987] 3 All ER 411, (1984) 78 Cr App R 276, [1984] Crim LR 163 (CA); *Beckford v R* [1988] AC 130, [1987] 3 WLR 611, [1987] 3 All ER 425; and *Blackburn v Bowering* (above)). This is a mistake of fact and the defendant must be judged by the facts as he mistakenly took them to be. The reasonableness of the belief is relevant only to the issue of its genuineness.

1.3 *"Wilful"*

"Wilful" has caused difficulties in a wide range of statutory contexts and has no fixed meaning. In s 89, "wilful" connotes something which is done intentionally. It must be shown that the defendant was aware that the person obstructed was a police officer (*Ostler v Elliott* [1980] Crim LR 584 (DC)). A reasonable belief that the other is not a police officer provides a sound defence.

The requirements in *Willmott v Atack* [1977] QB 498, [1977] Crim LR 187, that the act of the defendant should be hostile, and in *Hills v Ellis* [1983] QB 680, [1983] 2 WLR 234, [1983] 1 All ER 667 (DC), that the action should be aimed at the police, have been taken to be largely without substance, since motive and emotion are irrelevant in criminal law. "Wilful" requires no more than an intention to obstruct; the thing done must be done deliberately and with the knowledge and intention that it should have an obstructive effect (*Lewis v Cox* [1984] 3 WLR 875, [1984] 3 All ER 672, (1985) 80 Cr App R 1 (DC)). There must be deliberate acts with the intention of bringing about a state of affairs which, objectively viewed, amount to an obstruction: *Moore v Green* [1983] 1 All ER 663.

Interfering with a lawful arrest in the belief that it is unlawful is a wilful obstruction (*Hills v Ellis*, and *Lewis v Cox*, where the defendants were warned that their actions were making the task of the police more difficult).

1.4 *"Resist" and "Obstruct"*

The word "resist" has received no attention from the English courts in the reported cases, although there are several Australian decisions relating to similar provisions.

"Obstruction" was given its widest description in *Hinchcliffe v Sheldon* [1955] 1 WLR 1207, [1955] 3 All ER 406 (DC), where it was said to mean making it more difficult for the police to carry out their duties. The scope of that *dictum* has meant that obstruction may be by physical means (*Hinchcliffe v Sheldon*; *Lewis v Cox*), or by other means, including omissions, such as a refusal to cooperate (*Ledger v DPP* [1991] Crim LR 439 (DC); *Lunt v DPP* [1993] Crim LR 534, [1993] COD 430 (DC)).

In *Rice v Connolly* [1966] 2 QB 414, [1966] 3 WLR 17, [1966] 2 All ER 649, the Divisional Court regarded "wilful" as connoting something intentional and without lawful excuse. The reference in that case to the absence of lawful excuse belongs more properly to an analysis of the *actus reus* of the offence rather than to the *mens rea*, and the proposition advanced by the court serves only to confuse. In *Rice v Connolly*, the obstruction consisted of refusing to answer police enquiries or to accompany the officer to a police box so that further enquiries might be made. The lawful excuse was the absence of any legal duty to do so.

Following *Rice v Connolly*, it is not possible to maintain that obstruction cannot comprise omissions, even if there is to be a distinction between, on the one hand, refusals or failures to act, and, on the other hand, allowing the continuation of a state of affairs such as occurred in *Fagan v Metropoli-*

tan Police Commissioner [1969] 1 QB 439, [1968] 3 WLR 1120, [1968] 3 All ER 442 (DC); and *Duncan v Jones*. In *Johnson v Phillips* [1976] 1 WLR 65, [1975] 3 All ER 682, [1975] Crim LR 580 (DC), refusal to reverse down a one-way street was held to be an obstruction and to be wilful.

Despite *dicta* in *Dibble v Ingleton* [1972] 1 QB 480, [1972] 2 WLR 163, [1972] 1 All ER 275 (DC), it is not entirely convincing to say that a passive obstruction by omission is not an obstruction unless the law imposes an obligation to act, given the difficulty of forecasting in advance when such an obligation will arise. Nonetheless, *Dibble v Ingleton* has been applied in *Lunt v DPP* [1993] Crim LR 534, [1993] COD 430 (DC), with the result that a failure to open a door to the police who had a power to enter was a wilful obstruction.

There are situations where the law imposes, in response to the proper exercise of a power by the police (or others such as Customs and Excise), a positive duty on the citizen to act, and failure to do so is taken to be wilful obstruction. In other instances the law may simply impose a duty on the citizen in the absence of a police power. For example, a motorist, when requested to stop by a police officer in uniform exercising the power in s 163 of the Road Traffic Act 1988, must keep his vehicle at a standstill to give the police officer an opportunity to carry out his statutory enquiries, even though the Act does not confer a power on the constable to keep the vehicle there (*Lodwick v Saunders* [1985] 1 WLR 382, [1985] 1 All ER 577, (1985) 80 Cr App R 305 (DC)).

A positive act of obstruction need not be unlawful in itself to amount to an obstruction for the purposes of the Act; this is inherent in the offence under s 89 and was expressly accepted in *Dibble v Ingleton*, where it was held to be a wilful obstruction to drink whisky after a request for a breath test but before the test was taken.

Generally, refusal to answer questions is not a wilful obstruction (*Rice v Connolly*); doing so in abusive terms may be (*Ricketts v Cox* (1982) 74 Cr App R 298, [1982] Crim LR 184 (DC)), although in such an instance a charge under s 5 of the Public Order Act 1986 may be more appropriate. *Ricketts v Cox* was applied in *Ledger v DPP* (above) to a verbally aggressive, vulgar and generally unhelpful refusal to co-operate with the police. Advising someone of the right to remain silent is not wilful obstruction (*Green v DPP* (1991) 155 JP 816, [1991] Crim LR 782, (1991) 155 JPN 474 (DC)), subject presumably to the manner in which that advice is proffered.

1.5 Power of Arrest

There is no specific power of arrest in s 89, nor are the offences in s 89 arrestable offences. The offence under s 89(1) (assault) involves a breach of the peace and accordingly the common law power of arrest arises. The general power of arrest in s 25 of the Police and Criminal Evidence Act 1984 also applies. The offence in s 89(3) does not necessarily involve a breach of the peace and the common law power of arrest does not arise as a matter of course. According to *Wershof v Metropolitan Police Commissioner* [1978] 3 All ER 540, (1979) 68 Cr App R 82, [1978] Crim LR 424 (QBD), a police officer:

> "may only arrest without warrant anyone who wilfully obstructs him in the execution of his duty if the nature of that obstruction is such that he actually causes, or is likely to cause, a breach of the peace, or is calculated to prevent the lawful arrest or detention of another."

See also *Riley v DPP* (1990) 91 Cr App R 14, (1990) 154 JP 453, [1990] Crim LR 422 (DC); and *Gelberg v Miller* [1961] 1 WLR 153, [1961] 1 All ER 291 (DC), where the point was described as one of "grave constitutional importance", the Attorney-General expressly accepting the absence of any such power, except the power to arrest for breach of the peace.

2 Obstruction of the Highway

2.1 Use of the Highway

Following the decision of the House of Lords in *DPP v Jones* [1999] 2 AC 240, [1999] 2 All ER 257, [1999] 2 Cr App R 348 (HL), it is now possible to state as a general principle that the general public has a primary right to use the highway for purposes of passage and repassage, and for such reasonable and usual activities as are consistent with that primary right. Previous limitations on the use of the highway for purposes incidental or ancillary to the right of passage are no longer good law. The decision of the House of Lords was by a 3:2 majority in a case concerned with trespassory assembly on the highway, but the majority was of the opinion that there should be "a symmetry in the law between the activities on the public highway which may be trespassory and those which may amount to unlawful obstruction of the highway." (*per* Lord Irvine LC).

Generally, it is an offence both at common law and contrary to statute to obstruct the highway; obstruction of the highway is also capable of amounting to the common law offence of public nuisance (see page 212). The principles underpinning each are broadly similar and the authorities on the topic appear to be drawn freely from the range of offences.

Many other provisions relate more generally to activities permitted on or near the highway or to the use of the public highway (for example the Highways Act 1980; the Sexual Offences Act 1985, s 1 (kerb-crawling); the Control of Pollution Act 1974, s 62 (noise in streets from loudspeakers); or other locations, either nationally or locally (such as the power to make regulations in respect of Trafalgar Square and other open spaces in London), public or private (for example, the Military Lands Acts 1892–1903).

2.2 The Offence

Section 137(1) of the Highways Act 1980 states:

"If a person, without lawful authority or excuse, in any way wilfully obstructs the free passage along a highway he shall be guilty of an offence
and liable to a fine not exceeding level 3 on the standard scale."

The meaning of "highway" ascribed by the Act is to be found in s 328; it
"means the whole or a part of a highway other than a ferry or waterway".
"Highway" is a common law concept of a way, over which all members of
the public are entitled to pass and repass; it includes footpaths and bridleways as well as carriageways. The offence under s 137 is charged in many
instances of disorder, for example in respect of pickets, those who distribute
leaflets, "sit-down demonstrators", and those who otherwise assemble on the
highway.

For there to be an unlawful obstruction of the highway the prosecution
must demonstrate:
(a) the fact of obstruction;
(b) that it was wilful; and
(c) the absence of lawful authority or excuse.

Magistrates must consider all the elements (see *Hirst and Agu v Chief Constable of West Yorkshire* (1987) 151 JP 304, (1987) 85 Cr App R 143, [1987]
Crim LR 330 (DC)).

Obstruction

Except where the obstruction is so slight as to fall within the *de minimis*
principle, any stopping on the highway may be an obstruction: see *Hertfordshire County Council v Bolden* (1987) 151 LG Rev 290, (1987) 151 JP 252;
Seekings v Clarke (1961) 105 SJ 181, (1961) 59 LGR 268 (DC). See also
Wolverton UDC v Willis [1962] 1 WLR 205, [1962] 1 All ER 243, (1962)
106 SJ 153 (DC); and *Hinchon v Briggs* (1963) 61 LGR 315, [1963] Crim
LR 357 (DC) on the *de minimis* principle under other legislation.

It is sufficient to make out the offence to show that part of a road was
occupied, thereby interfering with the use of the road as a whole. Even the
presence of a single individual standing on the highway is capable of
amounting to an obstruction (see *Scarfe v Wood* (1969) 113 SJ 143, [1969]
Crim LR 265 (DC)). A slight obstruction created while addressing a crowd
is an obstruction even though there remains ample room for pedestrians to
pass unaffected by the obstruction (*Homer v Cadman* (1886) 55 LJMC 110;
Arrowsmith v Jenkins [1963] 2 QB 561, [1963] 2 WLR 856, [1963] 2 All ER
210 (DC)). Evidence that others were or were not inconvenienced by an obstruction serves only to illuminate whether or not the use of the highway was
unreasonable; it is not relevant to whether or not there was an obstruction.

Activities both on and off the highway may give rise to a charge under
s 137. For example, conducting a business on premises adjacent to the highway in such a way as to encourage a crowd to develop on the highway is capable of amounting to an unreasonable use of the highway and an offence
under statute or at common law, but not if the business is carried on in an or-

dinary way. The cases commonly cited in this context are *Fabbri v Morris* (1947) 176 LT 172, [1947] 1 All ER 315 (DC) and *Dwyer v Mansfield* [1946] KB 437, [1946] 2 All ER 247 (KBD), a civil case. See also *Pugh v Pigden & Powley* (1987) 151 JP 644, (1987) JPN 510 (DC), where the court considered that it was material that the stall in question had been situated in the same place for many years and that the respondents had used their best efforts to prevent the queue encroaching on the street.

Conduct falling within the section ranges from the commonplace to the absurd; thus it may be an obstruction to collect trolleys on the highway outside a supermarket (*Devon CC v Gateway Foodmarkets Ltd* (1990) 54 JP 557, [1990] COD 324, (1990) 154 JPN 442 (DC)); or to trade from a vehicle parked on the highway (*Nagy v Weston* [1965] 1 WLR 280, [1965] 1 All ER 78, (1965) 109 SJ 215 (DC); *Pitcher v Lockett* (1966) 64 LGR 477, [1966] Crim LR 283 (DC)); or to juggle with firesticks in a pedestrian precinct (*Waite v Taylor* (1985) 149 JP 551, (1985) 82 LS Gaz 1092 (DC)).

Picketing, even when conducted within relevant legislation, confers no immunity from the criminal law nor any lawful authority on the participants, who run the risk of obstructing the highway should they try to compel individuals to stop (*Broome v DPP* [1974] AC 587, [1974] 2 WLR 58, [1974] 1 All ER 314 (DC); *Kavanagh v Hiscock* [1974] QB 600, [1974] 2 WLR 421, [1974] 2 All ER 177 (DC)). The right to communicate peacefully does not exist alongside an obligation on others to stop and listen (*Broome v DPP*); and a picket may be compared with a hitchhiker standing alongside a road (*Broome v DPP, per* Lord Reid). Pushing through a police cordon at a picket line in order to stop a vehicle is a wilful obstruction of a constable acting in the execution of his duty (*Kavanagh v Hiscock*).

The same general principles apply to non-industrial picketing; see *Tynan v Balmer* [1967] 1 QB 91, [1966] 2 WLR 1181, [1966] 2 All ER 133 (DC) and *Hubbard v Pitt* [1976] QB 142, [1975] 3 WLR 201, [1975] All ER 1 (QBD) on the propriety of non-industrial picketing. It seems unlikely that the imposition of conditions on an assembly under s 14 POA 1986 (see page 160) would provide a lawful excuse, although it may be some evidence of reasonable user.

A club tout who approached groups of pedestrians to engage them briefly in conversation, thereby causing other pedestrians to walk off the narrow pavement and into the roadway, committed an obstruction (*Cooper v Metropolitan Police Commissioner* (1985) 82 Cr App R 238). Distributing leaflets or assembling with banners is capable of amounting to an obstruction (*Hirst and Agu v Chief Constable of West Yorkshire* (1987) 151 JP 304, (1987) 85 Cr App R 143, [1987] Crim LR 330 (DC)).

"Wilful"

To meet the test of "wilfulness", it is sufficient that the obstruction is deliberate; see *Arrowsmith v Jenkins* [1963] 2 QB 561, [1963] 2 WLR 856,

[1963] 2 All ER 210 (DC), where "wilful" was held to mean of one's own free will. In *Fearnley v Ormsby* (1879) 4 CPD 136, (1879) 43 JP 384, it was said that "wilful" means "purposely": "It amounts to this, that he knows what he is doing, and intends to do what he is doing, and is a free agent". There is no need for an intention to obstruct.

Lawful Authority or Excuse
"Lawful authority" relates to matters such as permits or licences granted under statutory authority. A reasonable and honestly held belief as to lawful authority is no defence (*Arrowsmith v Jenkins*), nor is the established practice of a local authority or the police in relation to a particular activity (*Redbridge London Borough v Jaques* [1970] 1 WLR 1064, [1971] 1 All ER 260, [1971] RTR 56 (DC); *Pugh v Pigden and Powley* (1987) 151 JP 644, (1987) JPN 510 (DC)).

On the other hand, lawful excuse frequently turns on the reasonableness of the user, and "excuse" and "reasonableness" have been equated (*Nagy v Weston* [1965] 1 WLR 280, [1965] 1 All ER 78, (1965) 109 SJ 215 (DC)). The classic description of "reasonable user" is found in *Nagy v Weston*. This was approved by Lord Denning in *Hubbard v Pitt* [1976] QB 142, [1975] 3 WLR 201, [1975] All ER 1 (QBD); and by the Court of Appeal in *Hipperson v Newbury Electoral Officer* [1985] QB 1060, [1985] 3 WLR 61, [1985] 2 All ER 456 (CA). It was applied in *Hirst and Agu v Chief Constable of West Yorkshire* (1987) 151 JP 304, (1987) 85 Cr App R 143, [1987] Crim LR 330 (DC), a decision expressly approved by the majority in *DPP v Jones* [1999] 2 AC 240, [1999] 2 All ER 257, [1999] 2 Cr App R 348 (HL):

"Whether or not the use amounting to an obstruction is or is not an unreasonable use of the highway is a question of fact. It depends upon all the circumstances, including the length of time the obstruction continues, the place where it occurs, the purpose for which it is done, and, of course, whether it does in fact cause an actual obstruction as opposed to a potential obstruction."

The question of unreasonable use may or may not relate to matters associated with passage. The reasonableness or otherwise of the use is distinct from whether or not there is an obstruction, and it is for the prosecution to demonstrate the unreasonableness of the use rather than for the defence to establish its reasonableness.

Thus, in *DPP v Jones* a peaceful, non-obstructive assembly of twenty or more persons on the highway did not necessarily exceed the public's right of access to the highway and did not amount to a trespassory assembly. On the other hand, a claim that an obstruction by lying down in the highway amounted to lawful excuse because the purpose was to prevent crime was rejected in *Birch (Stephen) v DPP, The Independent*, 13 January 2000 (QBD). The defendants had obstructed the highway outside a company's premises by lying down on it. They wished to call evidence that the activities of the company were unlawful and that they had a lawful excuse to obstruct the highway in the prevention of crime. The Divisional Court accepted that there might be circumstances where obstruction of the highway could be justified by reference to prevention of a crime. But simply obstructing the highway to prevent the passage of a vehicle which might contribute to what was alleged to be a crime was not a lawful excuse; it was intended only to draw attention to what was believed to be a potential crime and no more. The magistrate who refused to hear evidence as to the allegations of potential crime had been entitled to do so.

For there to be lawful excuse, the activity complained of must be inherently lawful, and, for example, unlawful picketing cannot be said to be an activity for which there is a lawful excuse (*Hirst and Agu v Chief Constable of West Yorkshire*, above). The appropriate approach for the court is to consider, first, whether or not there was an obstruction; secondly, whether or not it was wilful; and thirdly, whether or not the prosecution has proved the action in question was without lawful authority or without lawful excuse.

The importance of freedom of speech and protest was recognised by Lord Denning in *Hubbard v Pitt* (above, a civil case relating to the grant of an interlocutory injunction) and *Hirst and Agu v Chief Constable of West Yorkshire* (above), where the words of Lord Denning were expressly applied to the offence under the Highways Act:

"[The courts] should not interfere by interlocutory injunction with the right to demonstrate and to protest any more than they interfere with the right of free speech; provided that everything is done peaceably and in good order."

2.3 Arrest

There is no longer a specific power to arrest for obstruction of the highway, although unlawful obstruction of the highway is one of the general conditions for arrest in s 25 of the Police and Criminal Evidence Act 1984:

"(1) Where a constable has reasonable grounds for suspecting that any offence which is not an arrestable offence has been committed or attempted, or is being committed or attempted, he may arrest the relevant person if it appears to him that service of a summons is impracticable or inappropriate because any of the general arrest conditions is satisfied.

(2) In this section "the relevant person" means any person whom the constable has reasonable grounds to suspect of having committed or having attempted to commit the offence or of being in the course of committing or attempting to commit it.

(3) The general arrest conditions are– . . .

(d) that the constable has reasonable grounds for believing that arrest is necessary to prevent the relevant person– . . .

(v) causing an unlawful obstruction of the highway."

2.4   Conclusion

The conclusion which seems to flow from *DPP v Jones* and *Hirst and Agu v Chief Constable of West Yorkshire* is that whether or not there has been an offence is effectively a matter for the magistrates, before whom robust pleas of freedom of speech, rights of protest and general liberties may have more, or less, success.

Section 137(1) of the Highways Act 1980 is quite capable of use as a tool both of practical preventive justice and censorship, by both the police and the magistracy. The threat to move on or be arrested often deprives a protest of its efficacy, and a conviction subject to a suitable penalty such as conditional discharge or binding over may provide a potent disincentive.

In connection with processions and assemblies, s 137 provides a useful additional power which may well bypass the provisions of the Public Order Act 1986. On the other hand the Human Rights Act 1998 requires that courts dealing with cases involving the use of the highway for protest should consider carefully the rights under that Act and the exercise of police discretion, and public rights of passage and protest should be balanced in the light of those rights.

3   Police Powers to Prevent Obstruction

3.1   In London

Under s 52 of the Metropolitan Police Act 1839 and s 22 of the City of London Police Act 1839, the Commissioner of Police may make regulations and give directions to prevent the obstruction of streets in the Metropolitan Police District, eg by assemblies or processions which are capable of giving rise to obstruction of the streets or to disorder or annoyance of a kind likely to lead to breaches of the peace. For the construction of the provision, see *Papworth v Coventry* [1967] 1 WLR 663, [1967] 2 All ER 41, (1967) 111 SJ 316 (DC). These regulations and directions provide a useful form of control over processions and assemblies and have been used to counter novel types of disorder such as the "Stop the City" demonstrations in 1983–84.

3.2   Elsewhere

The Town Police Clauses Act 1847, s 21 is of similar effect and applies in certain areas outside the metropolitan police district. The local authority has power in limited instances to make orders as to the routes vehicles should follow, in order to prevent obstructions. The instances are "in all times of public processions, rejoicings, or illuminations, and in any case when the streets are thronged or liable to be obstructed". The phrase "in any case" is to be construed *eiusdem generis* with public processions, etc (see *Brownsea Haven Properties v Poole Corporation* [1958] Ch 574, [1958] 2 WLR 137, [1958] 1 All ER 205).

Both s 28 of the Town Police Clauses Act 1847 and s 54 of the Metropolitan Police Act 1839 create summary offences of obstruction of footpaths or thoroughfares. "Obstruction" in the context of this legislation has been interpreted more restrictively than under the 1980 Act, and requires actual obstruction.

3.3 The House of Commons

The sessional orders of the House of Commons require police constables to prevent obstruction of the streets leading to the House. Obstructing the police acting pursuant to these measures is an offence contrary to s 89 of the Police Act 1996 (see *Pankhurst v Jarvis* (1910) 101 LT 946, (1910) 74 JP 64, (1910) 26 TLR 118, and *Despard v Wilcox* (1910) 102 LT 103, (1910) 74 JP 115, (1910) 26 TLR 226).

4 Public Nuisance

Public nuisance is a crime at common law but may be remedied by injunction at the instance of the Attorney-General in a relator action brought by an affected party, or at the instance of a local authority exercising its rights, under s 222 of the Local Government Act 1972, to protect the local community (see generally *Attorney-General v PYA Quarries* [1957] 2 QB 169, [1957] 2 WLR 770, [1957] 1 All ER 894 (CA)). Where an individual suffers particular damage above and beyond that suffered by the community as a whole, that individual is able to maintain an action in tort. It is perhaps in the civil context rather than in the criminal context that public nuisance is most commonly encountered as a means of controlling public assemblies or activities on or nearby the highway.

The offence is broadly defined and versatile, and the conduct which has been held to amount to the offence is of such diversity as to defy categorisation; it ranges from public order matters to public health matters, from matters of public decency to matters of public safety. In *R v Coventry City Council ex p Phoenix Aviation* [1995] 3 All ER 37, [1995] COD 300, (1995) NLJ 559 (QBD), a judicial review decision, Simon Brown LJ said that:

> "The precise point at which the right of public demonstration ends and the criminal offence of public nuisance begins may be difficult to detect. But not only is all violent conduct unlawful; so too is any activity which substantially inconveniences the public at large and disrupts the rights of others to go about their lawful business."

Public nuisance is sufficiently broad to encompass many activities of modern life which affect the public at large, and its application in these circumstances reflects long-standing principles. The offence has been considered in the contexts of:

- bomb hoaxes (*R v Madden* [1975] 1 WLR 1379, [1975] 3 All ER 155, 61 Cr App R 254 (CA));
- acid house parties (*R v Shorrock (Peter)* [1994] QB 279, [1993] 3 WLR 698, [1993] 3 All ER 917 (CA) – fine of £2,500 imposed on owner of a

field let for an acid house party; *R v Ruffell (David Ian)* (1992) 13 Cr App R(S) 204 (CA) – 12 months' imprisonment, suspended, for the organiser of an acid house party; *R v Taylor* (1992) 13 Cr App R(S) 466 – £5,000 fine on organiser of an acid house party); and

- joy riders (*R v Mason* (1995) CAOI, 3rd, 214 – 30 months' imprisonment for a joy rider whose activities attracted large crowds of onlookers antagonistic to the police).

As far as public order is concerned, much of what falls within the crime of public nuisance is also provided for in bye-laws, eg relating to the making of noise or the playing of instruments.

4.1 Definition

Stephen's Digest of the Criminal Law (9th edn, 1950) defines public nuisance as "an act not warranted by law or an omission to carry out a legal duty, which act or omission obstructs or causes inconvenience or damage to the public in the exercise of rights common to all His Majesty's subjects".

In *Blackstone's Commentaries* (3 BL COM, 1st edn, 1768) it is said that:

"Nuisance . . . signifies any thing that works hurt, inconvenience, or damage. And nuisances are of two kinds; public and common nuisances, which affect the public, and are an annoyance to all the king's subjects; for which reason we must refer them to the class of public wrongs, or crimes and misdemeanours; and private nuisances . . ."

In *Gillingham Borough Council v Medway (Chatham) Dock Co Ltd* [1993] QB 343, [1992] 3 WLR 449, [1992] 3 All ER 923 (QBD), Buckley J, in the High Court, considered that, contrary to the definition in *Stephen's Digest,* it was not necessary that public nuisance should involve an otherwise unlawful activity. In so far as the use of the highway is concerned, the point is not material since misuse of the highway is unlawful.

To constitute the offence, the activity must be sufficiently far-reaching as to affect the neighbourhood. In *Attorney-General v PYA Quarries* it was said that:

"any nuisance is 'public' which materially affects the reasonable comfort and convenience of life of a class of Her Majesty's subjects. The sphere of the nuisance may be described generally as 'the neighbourhood'; but the question whether the local community within that sphere comprises a sufficient number of persons to constitute a class of the public is a question of fact in every case. It is not necessary, in our judgment, to prove that every member of the class has been injuriously affected; it is sufficient to show that a representative cross-section of the class has been so affected for an injunction to issue."

In *Soltau v De Held* (1851) 2 Sim (NS) 133 Kindersley VC, said:

"I conceive that, to constitute a public nuisance, the thing must be such as, in its nature or its consequences, is a nuisance – an injury or a damage, to all persons who come within the sphere of its operation, though it may be so in a greater degree to some than it is to others."

In *R v Lloyd* (1802) 4 Esp 200 176 an indictment for a nuisance by noise was preferred by the Society of Clifford's Inn, but since the noise complained of affected only three houses in the Inn, the indictment could not be sustained.

The Highway

It is generally accepted that it is only *unreasonable* use of the highway which amounts to a public nuisance (*R v Train* (1862) 3 F&F 22, (1862) 2 B&S 640). In *Jacobs v London County Council* [1950] AC 361, [1950] 1 All ER 737 (HL), public nuisance was said to be "Any wrongful act or omission upon or near a highway, whereby the public is prevented from freely, safely and conveniently passing along it". And in *Lowdens v Keaveney* (1902) 67 JP 378, it was said that "Where the use of the highway is unreasonable and excessive, that is a nuisance, irrespective of any guilty or wrongful intent".

In *Tynan v Balmer* [1967] 1 QB 91, [1966] 2 WLR 1181, [1966] 2 All ER 133 (DC), pickets moving in a circle on the highway outside a factory were told by police to stop, and when they did not they were arrested and charged with wilful obstruction contrary to s 89(3). It was held that the circling amounted to an unreasonable use of the highway and that the police were acting in the execution of their duty.

Demonstrations, pickets and other assemblies, usually occurring on or about the highway, may amount to the common law offence of public nuisance (see *R v Clark* (1963) 47 Cr App R 203; *R v Moule* (1964) 108 SJ 100, [1964] Crim LR 303 (CCA); *R v Adler* [1964] Crim LR 304 (CCA); and *Hubbard v Pitt* [1976] QB 142, [1975] 3 WLR 201, [1975] All ER 1 (QBD), a civil case). Although picketing does not necessarily constitute the offence (but see *Tynan v Balmer*), mass picketing does. In *Thomas v NUM (South Wales) Area* [1986] Ch 20, [1985] 2 WLR 1081, [1985] 2 All ER 1 (Ch D), Scott J remarked:

> ". . . if picketing . . . is peacefully and responsibly conducted . . . I can see no reason at all why it should be regarded *per se* as a common law nuisance . . . In my judgment, mass picketing is clearly . . . common law nuisance . . ."

As is the case under the Highways Act 1980, activities on premises adjacent to the highway are capable of amounting to public nuisances, for example the exhibition of certain items in a window which attracts a large crowd, thereby blocking the highway, as in *R v Carlile* (1834) 6 C&P 636 (an anti-clerical protest involving the display of effigies of bishops); and adopting an unreasonable method of running a shop adjacent to the highway, eg *Lyons, Sons & Co v Gulliver* [1914] 1 Ch 631, [1914] 83 LJ Ch 281, (1914) 110 LT 284; a theatre queue, *Wagstaff v Edison Bell Phonograph Corpn Ltd* (1893) 10 TLR 80; *R v Moore* [1824–1834] All ER Rep 527.

4.2   Mens Rea

The *mens rea* of the offence had received little consideration until the position was clarified in *R v Shorrock (Peter)* [1994] QB 279, [1993] 3 WLR 698, [1993] 3 All ER 917 (CA), drawing support from *R v Moore* (above). In *Shorrock,* the defendant let his field for a weekend to three individuals who held an acid house party which caused great disturbance over a wide area. Although he denied specific knowledge of the purposes of the licensees, he was convicted. On appeal on the question of the judge's direction on *mens rea*, the conviction was upheld, the Court of Appeal holding that, *per* Rattee J:

> ". . . the appellant was guilty of the offence . . . if either he knew or ought to have known, in the sense that the means of knowledge were available to him, that there was a real risk that the consequences of the licence granted by him in respect of his field would be to create the sort of nuisance that in fact occurred . . ."

In reaching its decision on the relevant *mens rea*, the court concluded that the basis of liability in both criminal and civil jurisdictions is the same.

Chapter 8

Weapons, Explosives and Air Rage

1   Blades and Pointed Articles

Checklist
- no *mens rea* needed for an offence under s 139, Criminal Justice Act 1988;
- s 139 applies to blades and sharply pointed instruments;
- a lock knife is always within the section;
- a folding pocket-knife is within the section only if the blade is over three inches long;
- fruit peeling is not a defence in respect of a blade over three inches;
- there are defences of national costume, religious reason and use at work;
- Magistrates' Association guideline sentence is custody;
- particular provisions for schools.

Section 139 of the Criminal Justice Act 1988 provides:
"(1)   Subject to subsections (4) and (5) below, any person who has an article to which this section applies with him in a public place shall be guilty of an offence.
(2)   Subject to subsection (3) below, this section applies to any article which has a blade or is sharply pointed except a folding pocket-knife.
(3)   This section applies to a folding pocket-knife if the cutting edge of its blade exceeds three inches.
(4)   It shall be a defence for a person charged with an offence under this section to prove that he had good reason or lawful excuse for having the article with him in a public place.
(5)   Without prejudice to the generality of subsection (4) above, it shall be a defence for a person charged with an offence under this section to prove that he had the article with him–
    (a) for use at work;
    (b) for religious reasons; or
    (c) as part of any national costume.
(6)   A person guilty of an offence under subsection (1) shall be liable on conviction to imprisonment for up to six months or a fine.
(7)   In this section "public" place includes any place to which at the material time the public have or are permitted access, whether on payment or otherwise."

Section 139A Criminal Justice Act 1988 makes it an offence for any person to have an article to which s 139 applies with him on school premises (s 139A(1)). It is also an offence to have on school premises an offensive weapon within the meaning of s 1 Prevention of Crime Act 1953 (s 139A(2)).

It is a defence to either charge for the defendant to prove that he had the article or offensive weapon with him for good reason or with lawful authority (s 139A(3)). There are other defences, mirroring those under s 139: that the defendant had the article or weapon for use at work, for educational purposes, for religious reasons or as part of a national costume (s 139A(4)).

On conviction in the magistrates' court, the defendant is liable to up to six months imprisonment or a fine; or, in the Crown Court, to two years imprisonment and/or a fine for an offence under s 139A(1), or up to four years for an offence contrary to s 139A(2).

"School premises" means land used for the purposes of a school, excluding any land occupied solely as a dwelling by a person employed at the school (s 139A(6)).

Section 139B Criminal Justice Act 1988 authorises a constable to enter school premises and search those premises and any person on those premises for any article to which s 139 applies or for any offensive weapon if he has reasonable grounds for believing that an offence under s 139A is being, or has been, committed. If he discovers such an article or weapon he may seize and retain it. He is permitted to use reasonable force in the exercise of the power of entry.

1.1   Blade or Sharply Pointed Instrument

Section 139 of the Criminal Justice Act 1988 is aimed at those who choose to carry bladed or sharply pointed instruments which may not fall within the definition of "offensive weapon" (see page 220), yet might give rise to a risk of injury or of use to the detriment of public order. No *mens rea* is required. If an implement falls within the definition and none of the defences applies, the offence is made out. A *Stanley* knife would be caught; it is not a pocket knife, but it is bladed. In the absence of one of the defences, it is covered by the section, whether or not it was carried with offensive intent. A comb with a sharpened edge or a sharply pointed end is also covered.

1.2   Public Place

There is a definition of "public place" in s 7, but this is not an exclusive definition. There has been a number of cases dealing with whether or not particular places are public places. A staircase adjoining a block of flats is a public place if there is nothing preventing the public from using it (*Knox v Anderton* (1983) 76 Cr App R 156, (1983) 147 JP 340 (QBD)). A garden is not "public" merely because there is access to a house through it where the access was for a visitor rather than for the public at large (*R v Edwards and*

Roberts (1978) 122 SJ 177, (1978) 67 Cr App R 228, [1978] Crim LR 564 (CA)). A public house car park with a "patrons only" sign is not public (*Sandy v Martin* [1974] RTR 263, [1974] Crim LR 258 (DC)). Well after a shop has closed, its car park is not public (*Marsh v Arscott* (1982) 75 Cr App R 211, [1982] Crim LR 827 (QBD)). That a place is a public place is best demonstrated by the fact that the public in fact has access to it.

1.3 "Has with him"

This formula is not to be taken as meaning precisely the same as "possession". It has a connotation of more proximate connection than the word "possession": "There must be a very close physical link and a degree of immediate control . . ." *per* Scarman LJ (*R v Kelt* [1977] 1 WLR 1365, [1977] 3 All ER 1099, (1997) 65 Cr App R 74 (CA)). It is aimed at the person who has the article in question in a pocket or with him in a vehicle. Anything much beyond that in terms of proximity is unlikely to fall within the definition.

It remains an unresolved question whether "has with him " is satisfied where the prosecution can prove that the defendant knew that he had the offending article with him, but did not know that it was a weapon (*R v Densu* [1998] Cr App R 400, (1997) 141 SJLB 250, *The Times* 10 December 1997 (CA)).

1.4 Folding Pocket Knife

The folding pocket knife is given its own definition to avoid an absolute prohibition on carrying pocket knives. For a folding pocket knife to be caught by the Act it must have a "cutting edge of its blade" which is more than three inches long. The cutting edge is that part of the blade that is sharpened. Only the sharpened edge should be measured, and only that part of the sharpened edge which is actually sharpened to cut. That part of that edge towards the handle which has not been sharpened should not be included.

"Folding pocket knife" does not include a lock knife. A lock knife is not readily and immediately foldable at all times. A lock knife needs the trigger mechanism to be used to close it. The length of a lock knife does not matter because it is not treated as a folding pocket knife (*Harris v DPP* [1993] 1 WLR 82, [1993] 1 All ER 562, (1993) 96 Cr App R 235 (DC)).

1.5 Defences

Good Reason

It appears that it is for the defendant to provide evidence of the defence and then for the prosecution to disprove it beyond reasonable doubt (*R v Lambert*; see page 91). The issue of reasonable excuse is one of fact and depends on the circumstances of the case. As a matter of public policy the courts are not easily persuaded that carrying articles for self-defence in any context can be reasonable. A common defence in relation to folding pocket knives is that they are used, and needed, for peeling fruit and similar non-hazardous practicalities. This is not a valid defence in respect of either a pocket knife with a blade over three inches or a lock knife. In each case there is no necessity for the particular type of knife, and therefore there is no good reason for having it. It is as easy to peel an apple with a two inch blade as it is with a three inch one, and a lock provides no assistance for such routine tasks in the absence of special and particular evidence.

A person's forgetting that an article is in his possession was thought not to amount to a defence of good reason (*DPP v Gregson* (1993) 96 Cr App R 240, (1993) 157 JP 201 (DC)). As a result of the decision in *R v Glidewell (Raymond)* (1999) 163 JP 557 (QBD), which develops the judgment in *R v McCalla* (1988) 87 Cr App R 372, (1988) 152 JP 481, (1988) 152 JPN 494 (CA), the position is clearer. In *Glidewell* a taxi driver aged 53 and of good character had his attention drawn to two weapons in the back of his taxi, and placed them in the front with a view to removing them after work. Through working late he forgot, and they were later found in the footwell of the taxi. At first instance the judge said to the jury "I have told you that forgetting is not an excuse in law", and Mr Glidewell was convicted.

On appeal, the Vice President referred back to the *McCalla* case where, on appeal, it had been said:

". . . we are quite satisfied that to have forgotten that one has an offensive weapon in the car . . . is not a reasonable excuse under the Act. But when such forgetfulness is coupled with particular circumstances relating to the original acquisition of the article, the combination of the original acquisition and the subsequent forgetfulness . . . may . . . be a reasonable excuse."

McCalla lost his appeal because he had himself originally introduced the offensive weapon into the vehicle some time before. Mr Glidewell's position was quite different and in his case the combination of the original circumstances, his heavy workload, the short time lapse and his forgetfulness did amount to a reasonable excuse. His appeal against conviction was successful.

Lawful Authority
This defence seems to apply only to "those people who from time to time carry an offensive weapon as a matter of duty – the soldier with his rifle and the police officer with his truncheon", *per* Lord Widgery CJ in *Bryan v Mott* (1975) 119 SJ 743, (1975) 62 Cr App R 71, [1976] Crim LR 64 (DC). Thus, a soldier's bayonet would not be caught by the provision, but if he were carrying an article not authorised as part of his kit he would be guilty.

Use at Work
This defence is designed to protect those who need to carry, for their work, articles that would fall within the Act. Thus a *Stanley* knife might well be a

legitimate tool carried by some workers, as might any other sharp or bladed instrument such as a saw, chisel or bradawl. There is no general permission to carry such items, and a person who is carrying them other than en route to and from work should expect the additional burden of proving the need to carry them on other occasions. Such proof is not impossible for people who might be on call, but ought not to be available to a person who has merely left his tools in a vehicle for convenience.

Religious Reasons

This defence is designed to protect religious groups such as Sikhs who, as part of their religion, are in certain circumstances required to carry a bladed article which might otherwise contravene the section. Each case must be looked at on its merits to determine whether there is such a religious reason, and whether that was in fact the reason of the person concerned.

National Costume

This defence is aimed at those, such as the Scots, who might have a bladed article in the sock as part of national costume. Again, each case must be assessed on its merits to determine whether the national costume requires the article and whether the person was actually carrying the article as part of a national costume.

Generally

Each defence must be proved on a balance of probabilities. Once the elements of the offence are made out, then, in the absence of one of the statutory defences, the person is guilty (*Goodwin v DPP* (1992) 156 JP 643).

2 Offensive Weapons

Checklist

- "Offensive" *per se* means designed or adapted to injure people;
- intent to injure is required for items which are not offensive *per se;*
- "public place" has a wide meaning;
- the accused must know he has the article;
- transferred burden of proof in respect of reasonable excuse and lawful authority;
- Magistrates' Association guideline sentence is custody.

Section 1(1) of the Prevention of Crime Act 1953, as amended, provides:

"(1) Any person who without lawful authority or reasonable excuse, the proof whereof shall lie on him, has with him in any public place any offensive weapon shall be guilty of an offence, and shall be liable–

(a) on summary conviction, to imprisonment for a term not exceeding [six months] or a fine not exceeding [the prescribed sum] or both;

(b) on conviction on indictment, to imprisonment for a term not exceeding two years or a fine ... or both.

(2) Where any person is convicted of an offence under subsection (1) of this section, the court may make an order for the forfeiture or disposal of any weapon in respect of which the offence was committed . . .

(4) In this section 'public place' includes any highway and any other premises or place to which at the material time the public have or are permitted to have access, whether on payment or otherwise; and 'offensive weapon' means any article made or adapted for use for causing injury to the person, or intended by the person having it with him for such use by him or by some other person."

2.1 Offensive per se

The first category of offensive weapon is those specifically designed or adapted to cause injury to the person. Whether an article is offensive *per se* is a question of fact, but certain articles are automatically offensive *per se*. Flick knives are offensive *per se,* as are any of the articles set out in the schedule to s 141 of the Criminal Justice Act 1988. This schedule sets out the articles which it is an offence to manufacture, sell or hire, and includes "death stars", knuckledusters and swordsticks. These objects have no purpose but to injure and so are offensive *per se*. The position in respect of articles which have been privately adapted may be less clear. A stave with a nail through it might have been adapted for a reason other than to cause injury, and it is for the tribunal of fact to determine from the evidence the purpose of such manufacture or adaptation. *R v Allamby* [1974] 1 WLR 1494, [1974] 3 All ER 126, [1975] Crim LR 39 (CA) confirms that carrying such obvious items as flick knives demonstrates a conditional intention to use them, and that is sufficient for the section. In *DPP v Hynde* [1998] 1 All ER 649 (QBD), the court found that a butterfly knife had been adapted so as to cause injury and so fell within the provision.

2.2 Not Offensive per se

The second category of offensive weapon comprises articles intended to be used, by those having them or somebody else, for causing injury to the person. Thus a non-offensive article becomes an offensive weapon if the person intends it to cause harm. A baseball bat in a car may be an offensive weapon not because it is capable of injuring a person, but because the person who has it intends to use it for that purpose. Many other articles have been deemed offensive weapons in particular contexts:

- belts with studs (*McMahon v Dollard* [1965] Crim LR 238 (DC));
- workmen's tools (*R v Dayle* [1974] 1 WLR 181, [1973] 3 All ER 1151, (1973) 117 SJ 852 (CA)); and
- kitchen knives (*R v Rapier* (1980) 70 Cr App R 17, [1980] Crim LR 48 (CA)).

For reasons of public policy courts are unwilling to permit the public at large to arm themselves for their own protection. That is the job of the police.

Thus, carrying an object with the provisional intention of using it, ie if someone attacks, is generally deemed sufficient to make an object an offensive weapon.

The problem in court is that if the article is not offensive *per se*, and the defendant denies carrying it for reasons of self-protection, then, in the absence of telling circumstantial evidence, there is little basis for finding the necessary intent. In practice, however, many such cases are proved because, in interview, the person denies an offensive intent but admits a defensive intent; this provides the conditional intention to use, which is sufficient for a conviction.

2.3 Injury to the Person

In most cases the fact that an object is to cause injury is apparent from the evidence. "Injury" means physical injury caused by the object itself. The only difficulty in this context relates to the person who has with him an offensive weapon to frighten or intimidate, but not to cause injury. Tribunals of fact generally find it difficult to accept that an object was for intimidation and not to injure. It would also be difficult to ignore the notion of conditional intention – if a person carries an object he has it in mind to use it if required. For public policy reasons, the courts have been slow to develop a distinction between intimidation and injury (see *Woodward v Koessler* [1958] 1 WLR 1255, [1958] 3 All ER 557 (DC) and *R v Edmonds* [1963] 2 QB 142, [1963] 2 WLR 715, [1963] 1 All ER 828).

2.4 "Has with him in a public place"

See page 218 for the meaning of "has with him", and page 217 on "public" places. The section incorporates the expression "at the material time". It follows that a place may be public at one time and not at another. The issue is whether the public has free or paying access at the material time.

2.5 Intent

There is no offence unless the defendant had the offensive weapon knowingly (*R v Cugullere* [1961] 1 WLR 858, [1961] 2 All ER 343, (1961) 105 SJ 386 (CA)). If a person does not know the nature of the article in his possession he is not guilty (*R v Densu* [1998] Cr App R 400, (1997) 141 SJLB 250 *The Times* 10 December 1997 (CA), where the defendant had a baton in his possession). The issue was whether he understood its nature. If he did not, he could not be guilty.

Where more than one person has a weapon or weapons, it is necessary to show that each person knew about the weapons which the other(s) had and that they had common purpose (*R v Edmonds*, above). Intent is shown by conduct that may be irrefutable, or by words. The law relating to interviews and giving evidence has been modified (CJPOA 1994, ss 34, 35 and 36). It may be easier to prove possession of an offensive weapon if persons in possession of suspect articles answer questions in interview or in court, so avoiding the drawing of adverse inferences.

2.6 Defences

For the defences of lawful authority and reasonable excuse, see pages 218 and 219, but the prosecution must first demonstrate the elements of the offence (*R v Petrie* [1961] 1 WLR 358, [1961] 1 All ER 466, 45 Cr App R 72 (CCA)). The fact that a person has forgotten he has an article with him does not amount to the defence of reasonable excuse (*R v McCalla* (1988) 87 Cr App R 372, (1988) 152 JP 481, (1988) 152 JPN 494 (CA)). See *R v Lambert* (page 91) on the transferred burden of proof.

2.7 Mode of Trial

The guideline penalty is custody. In relation to mode of trial, the general rule is that, except where otherwise stated, either way offences should be tried summarily. It is hard to reconcile this with the gravity of carrying articles such as flick knives and purpose-designed coshes which, subject to the circumstances of a case, give rise to the risk of an immediate and significant custodial sentence, above the maximum available in the magistrates' court.

2.8 The Sale of Offensive Weapons

Section 141 of the Criminal Justice Act 1988 makes it an offence for:
> "any person to manufacture, sell or hire or offer for sale or hire, or expose or have in his possession for the purpose of sale or hire, or to lend or give to any other person, a weapon to which this section applies".

The penalty is imprisonment for up to six months or a fine up to level 5. The Secretary of State may direct the section to apply to any weapon, except crossbows and weapons subject to the Firearms Act 1968. The list of weapons falling within s 141 is set out in the schedule to the Act and includes knuckledusters, swordsticks and telescopic truncheons. See also the Restriction of Offensive Weapons Act 1959 s 1 and the Criminal Justice Act 1988 s 141A on the sale of knives to sixteen-year-olds.

3 Knives

The Knives Act 1997 was enacted to deal with knives marketed in a way which links them to combat or violence, and the inevitability that, as a consequence, they may be used for violence generally and in incidents of public disorder. Whether the new provisions have affected or will affect the carrying of knives in general is a different issue, but the government view was that it is correct to challenge every aspect of any culture of violence.

3.1 The Offences

Section 1 provides that a person is guilty of an offence if he markets a knife in a way which indicates or suggests that it is suitable for combat. He is also guilty if he markets it in a way that will stimulate or encourage violent behaviour involving the use of the knife as a weapon.

The section anticipates the risk as arising from the name or description applied to the knife, its packaging or any advertisement. People who sell, offer or expose for sale, or possess for the purpose of sale or hire, are all caught by the Act. On summary conviction, the penalty is up to six months imprisonment or a fine. On indictment, the penalty is imprisonment for up to two years, a fine or both.

Section 2 makes it an offence to publish written or pictorial material in connection with the marketing of knives if that material indicates or suggests a purpose of combat, or if it may stimulate or encourage violent behaviour. The penalties for the offence under s 2 are the same as for the offence under s 1.

3.2   Defences

There are statutory defences:

- to protect sellers who are marketing items to be used by the armed forces, or selling antiques or curios. There is a power to prescribe other categories to be excluded;
- where it was reasonable to market the knife in the particular way;
- where there was "no reasonable ground for suspecting that a person into whose possession the knife might come . . . would use it for an unlawful purpose".

Publishers also have statutory defences, where:

- the publication was in connection with one of the exempted categories (sales to the armed forces etc, above);
- it was reasonable to market the knife in the particular way;
- there was no reasonable ground for suspecting use for an unlawful purpose.

Section 4 provides additional offences for those charged under s 1:

- where the defendant did not know or suspect, and had no reasonable grounds for suspecting, that the way the knife was marketed fell into any of the categories making it an offence;
- the defendant took all reasonable precautions and exercised all due diligence to avoid committing the offence.

Section 5 contains provisions on warrants and seizure, and s 6 provides for forfeiture.

Section 10 defines a knife as "an instrument which has a blade or which is sharply pointed".

4   Stop and Search; Concealment of Identity

There is a wide range of stop and search powers in UK law (s 1 PACE, s 47 Firearms Act etc). Any of these powers may from time to time impact on public order law, but specific anxieties about policing disorder led to the use of s 60 CJPOA (powers to stop and search in anticipation of violence) in its amended form as a means of restraining people engaged in or intent on public disorder by requiring the removal of masks. Its original purpose had been to play a part in the fight against street crime and the use of knives in street robberies, rather than as a means of making protestors remove masks.

The use of masks for concealing identity is a growing feature of public order disturbances and results from the increasing number of cameras and video recorders being used, by the public authorities and other interested parties, to monitor such events. Section 60 CJPOA 1994 provides a mechanism whereby relatively tightly controlled arrangements can be made for stop and search to be used as a crime-fighting tactic in a particular geographical area for a limited time. Historically, stop and search had been perceived as inappropriately directed at young men from ethnic minorities. It was hoped that the revised section would facilitate a more focused approach, with the emphasis on area, and not skin colour or gender. To that end, Home Office Circular 7/99 emphasises, in relation to face coverings, that sensitivity has to be used when they are worn on religious grounds, for example veils worn by Muslim women. Code A under the Police and Criminal Evidence Act 1984 has been modified to control the conduct of stop and search, and now contains non-discrimination requirements. Section 60 is not expressly a public order provision – it has been used in relation to risks of knife attacks and in areas where street robbery has been a particular problem. Nevertheless it has a public order resonance because of the risks of confrontation between different groups that occur from time to time.

The power under s 60 can be triggered either by the reasonable belief of a police inspector or above that incidents involving serious violence may take place, or that people are carrying dangerous implements or offensive weapons in the locality. The power can operate for 24 hours; must be recorded in writing, specifying the time, location and reason; and can be extended for a further 24 hours by a police superintendent. Once in place, it authorises stop and search for "dangerous instruments or offensive weapons".

Section 25 Crime and Disorder Act 1998 amended s 60 CJPOA to give a constable in uniform the power to require the removal of any item which he reasonably believes a person is wearing wholly or mainly for the purpose of concealing his identity. The constable has power to seize any item which he reasonably believes is to be worn for that purpose. There is no power to stop and search for such items, but if they are found during a search or if they are seen being carried, then the constable can seize them. When the constable has required an item to be removed he must decide whether he has reasonable grounds to seize the item. Does he reasonably believe that the person still intends to wear the item wholly or mainly to conceal identity? If so, he has power to seize.

Non-compliance with a requirement, under s 60, to stop a vehicle or remove an item used to conceal identity, is an arrestable offence. It carries a penalty of imprisonment for up to one month or a fine up to level 3 or both. An item for concealing identity which is seized must be retained by the police for two months.

It is anticipated that face paint will not be caught by the provision as it is unlikely to meet the definition of "an item".

5 Explosives

Offences contrary to the Explosive Substances Act 1883 may not be instituted without the consent of the Attorney-General (s 7, Explosive Substances Act 1883). The proceedings are "instituted" when the accused goes to court to answer a charge (*R v Elliot* (1985) 81 Cr App R 115, [1985] Crim LR 310 (CA); see also *R v Bates* [1911] 1 KB 964, (1911) 55 Sol Jo 410, (1911) 104 LT 688 and *R v Cain and Schollick* [1976] QB 496, [1975] 3 WLR 131, [1975] 2 All ER 900 (CA) on the question of consent, which may be given in general terms, but if it is missing it invalidates the proceedings). Historically, the possession of explosives has been regarded as related to public order law. These are serious offences and those who commit them in the context of public disorder place themselves at risk of immediate long-term prison sentences, whatever their motives.

5.1 The Offences

Section 2 makes it an offence if any person:

"unlawfully and maliciously causes by any explosive substance an explosion of a nature likely to endanger life or to cause serious injury to property."

Section 3 makes it an offence if a person:

"(a) does any act with intent to cause, or conspires to cause, by an explosive substance an explosion of a nature likely to endanger life, or cause serious injury to property whether in the United Kingdom or the Republic of Ireland, or makes or has in his possession or under his control an explosive substance with intent by means thereof to endanger life, or cause serious injury to property, whether in the United Kingdom or the Republic of Ireland or to enable any other person so to do."

Section 4 states:

"Any person who makes or knowingly has in his possession or under his control any explosive substance, under such circumstances as to give rise to a reasonable suspicion that he is not making it or does not have it in his possession or under his control for a lawful object, shall, unless he can show that he made it or had it in his possession or under his control for a lawful object be guilty of a felony . . ."

Sections 2 and 3 carry life imprisonment and s 4 carries up to fourteen years' imprisonment.

5.2 *"Explosive Substance"*

"Explosive substance" is widely defined in the 1883 Act. It includes anything used in the making of any explosive substances, and, for example, the ingredients of, and the equipment for manufacturing, petrol bombs (*R v Elliot,* above).

5.3 *Lawful Object*

The words "lawful object" in s 4 might protect Her Majesty's forces in certain circumstances. In relation to the ordinary citizen, it has been reviewed in the context of self defence where a person made petrol bombs for self-protection following riots. So long as he can demonstrate, on a balance of probabilities, that his object was the protection of self, family or property from imminent attack, by means which he believed were no more than those reasonably needed to meet the particular type of attack, then he has a lawful object (*Attorney-General's Reference (No 2 of 1983)* [1984] AC 456, [1984] 2 WLR 465, [1984] 1 All ER 988, (CA)).

The burden of proving a lawful object falls on the defendant (but see page 91 on the transferred burden of proof), and to that extent differs from the remaining provisions of the Explosive Substances Act.

Sections 2 and 3 extend to acts committed outside the UK which would be offences in the UK; "lawful object" is therefore not limited to a purpose taking place in the UK (*R v Berry* [1985] AC 246, [1984] 3 WLR 1274, [1984] 3 All ER 1008 (HL)).

5.4 *Knowledge*

Section 4 calls for proof that the accused knew he had the substance, and knew that the substance was a defined explosive substance under s 9. Knowledge may be inferred from the circumstances (*R v Hallam* [1957] 1 QB 569, [1957] 2 WLR 521, [1957] 1 All ER 665 (CCA)). It must also be proved that the possession was in circumstances that gave rise to the required suspicion.

5.5 *"Unlawfully and maliciously"*

Legitimate demolition using explosives is not the target of ss 2 and 3 of the 1883 Act, nor is the use of explosives by Her Majesty's forces in appropriate circumstances. Those uses are not unlawful. The reason for the word "maliciously" is less clear in that it incorporates into the sections a level of intent requiring proof. The implication is that there is a category of explosion which are unlawful but not malicious and so would not warrant the penalties under these sections.

6 Football Grounds

Section 2A of the Public Order Act 1986 provides, among other things:

"A person who without lawful authority possesses a designated article in or whilst trying to enter a designated ground or in any area of a ground from which the event may be directly viewed commits an offence."

Section 2A(3) prohibits possession of:

"any article or substance whose main purpose is the emission of a flare for purposes of illuminating or signalling (as opposed to lighting or heating) or the emission of smoke or a visible gas; and in particular applies to distress flares, fog signals, and pellets and capsules intended to be used as fumigators or for testing pipes, but not to matches, cigarette lighters or heaters."

There are powers to enter grounds; to search designated vehicles and people; and to arrest on reasonable grounds for believing an offence is being or has been committed. The purpose of these provisions is to reduce the risk of fire. There has been at least one case where such an item, fired recklessly, caused death.

7   Firearms

The subject of firearms is increasingly relevant as firearms are more widely available. Most of the law on firearms is not sufficiently connected to the law relating to public disorder to justify detailed analysis here. The provisions set out below deal with those parts of the law most directly connected with the protection of public order. All firearms offences are treated seriously and do not appear in the National Mode of Trial Guidelines or in the Magistrates' Association Sentencing Guidelines. This is no doubt because of the presumption that either way cases involving firearms will be dealt with in the Crown Court except in the most exceptional of cases.

7.1   The Offences

Section 16 of the Firearms Act 1968 provides:

"It is an offence for a person to have in his possession any firearm or ammunition with intent by means thereof to endanger life . . . or to enable another person by means thereof to endanger life . . . whether any injury . . . has been caused or not."

Section 16A provides:

"It is an offence for a person to have in his possession any firearm or imitation firearm with intent–

(a) by means thereof to cause, or

(b) to enable another person by means thereof to cause,

any person to believe that unlawful violence will be used against him or another person."

Section 19 provides:

"A person commits an offence if, without lawful authority or reasonable excuse (the proof whereof lies on him) he has with him in a public place a loaded shot gun or loaded air weapon, or any other firearm (whether loaded or not) together with ammunition suitable for use in that firearm."

Section 20 provides:

"(1) A person commits an offence if, while he has a firearm (or imitation firearm) with him, he enters or is in any building or part of a building as a trespasser and without reasonable excuse (the proof whereof lies on him).

(2) A person commits an offence if, while he has a firearm (or imitation firearm) with him, he enters or is on any land as a trespasser and without reasonable excuse (the proof whereof lies on him)."

7.2   The Elements of the Offences

A person has a firearm with him if there is a close physical connection, not necessarily that he actually carried it. It might be in a holdall at his feet or in some equally proximate place (*R v Kelt* [1977] 1 WLR 1365, [1977] 3 All ER 1099, (1997) 65 Cr App R 74 (CA); *R v Pawlicki and Swindell* [1992] 1 WLR 827, [1992] 3 All ER 902, (1992) 95 Cr App R 246 (CA)). For "lawful authority" and "reasonable excuse" see pages 219 and 218. The burden of proving lawful authority or reasonable excuse is on the defendant, on a balance of probabilities (*R v Carr-Briant* [1943] KB 607, [1943] 2 All ER 156, (1943) 169 LT 175 (CCA)), but see page 91 on the transferred burden of proof. Thus if he could persuade a court that he was, for example, a member of the forces acting in the course of his duties (lawful authority), or that he had found the item and was on his way to surrender it to the police (reasonable excuse), he would be entitled to an acquittal.

7.3   Penalties

The maximum penalties are as follows:

- section 16 (indictable only): life imprisonment, a fine or both;
- section 16A (indictable only): ten years imprisonment, a fine or both;
- section 19: on summary conviction, six months imprisonment, a fine or both; on indictment, seven years imprisonment, a fine or both;
- section 20(1): on summary conviction, six months imprisonment, a fine or both; on indictment, seven years imprisonment, a fine or both;
- section 20(2): on summary conviction, six months imprisonment, a level 4 fine or both.

8   "Air Rage"

Air rage is a relatively recent phenomenon and why it occurs now is a contentious issue. What might be a relatively minor matter on the ground takes on a seriousness all its own when committed in the air, because of the risk to other passengers and crew in the confined space of the aircraft. There have been instances where courts have queried the maximum sentences available. There have also been instances when courts, realising they have the power only to fine, have sought to allow alternative, more serious, charges, opening the door to the penalty of imprisonment. It is certainly anomalous that in some cases of such gravity, the defendant can preclude the risk of prison by indicating a guilty plea, thereby forestalling a mode of trial adjudication.

Public order offences on aircraft were created by the Air Navigation (No 2) Order 1995 (SI 1995 No 1970), and are described below. There are no guidelines for them in the Magistrates' Association Sentencing Guidelines.

Article 57(1) of the Air Navigation (No 2) Order 1995 creates the offence of being drunk in an aircraft: "A person shall not enter any aircraft when drunk, or be drunk in any aircraft". This offence is triable either way. The maximum penalty in the magistrates' court is a fine on level 5, and in the Crown Court, two years imprisonment. The maximum sentences should be kept in mind at mode of trial stage.

Article 59A(a) creates the offence of using threatening, abusive or insulting words towards the crew of an aircraft. It is a summary only offence, with a maximum penalty of a fine on level 4.

Article 59A(b) creates the offence of behaving in a threatening, abusive, insulting or disorderly manner towards crew. It is a summary only offence with a maximum penalty of a fine on level 4.

Article 59A(c) creates the offence of intentionally interfering with the duties of crew members. It is triable either way with a maximum penalty of a fine on level 5 in the magistrates' court and imprisonment for up to two years in the Crown Court. In a court dealing with a high volume of aircraft cases the local guideline penalty is custody, implying that if a defendant does not indicate a guilty plea, the case should be committed to the Crown Court. This is an anomaly, and the statutory mechanism may not fully comply with the Human Rights Act 1998. The net effect is to force some defendants to indicate a guilty plea to avoid committal and the high risk of imprisonment by the Crown Court.

Article 55 creates the offence of endangering safety on an aircraft: "A person shall not recklessly or negligently act in a manner likely to endanger an aircraft or any person therein". This is triable either way with a maximum sentence of a level 5 fine in the magistrates' court, and two years imprisonment by the Crown Court. It raises the same dilemma as the two preceding offences. In *R v Whitehouse* [2000] Crim LR 172, the Court of Appeal indicated that the word "likely" meant "is there a real risk that should not be ignored?" It does not mean "probably".

Article 58(2) of the 1995 Order creates the offence of smoking on an aircraft: "A person shall not smoke in any compartment of an aircraft . . . at a time when smoking is prohibited in that compartment by a notice exhibited . .". It is triable only summarily and the maximum penalty is a level 4 fine.

Chapter 9

Other Offences

1 Football Matches

1.1 Introduction

In recent years the law relating to sports grounds in general, and football matches in particular, has undergone radical change. The changes have been necessitated not only by tragic events at sports grounds but also by concern over public disorder related to matches both national and international. The police have developed strategies and tactics operating in tandem with the new statutory provisions, which have led to a decrease in the number of offences in connection with football matches. Not all the legislation has been implemented fully, and the national football membership scheme created by Part I of the Football Spectators Act 1989 seem unlikely ever to be brought into force.

The Football (Disorder) Act 2000 made considerable changes to Part II of and Sch 1 to the Football Spectators Act 1989. It also repealed and replaced many (but not all) parts of the Football (Offences and Disorder) Act 1999, and repealed and replaced ss 30–34 and 36 of the Public Order Act 1986 (which relate to the now defunct exclusion orders).

As to the safety issues, see the Safety of Sports Grounds Act 1975, as amended by the Fire Safety and Safety of Places of Sport Act 1987 and the Home Office *Guide to Safety at Sports Grounds* (the "Green Guide").

The unauthorised selling, offering or exposing for sale of tickets for designated football matches is now an arrestable offence under s 24(2)(h) of the Police and Criminal Evidence Act 1984 (see the Criminal Justice and Public Order Act 1994, s 166, as amended by s 10, Football (Offences and Disorder) Act 1999). This reflects the concern expressed in the Taylor Report into the Hillsborough disaster about the impact of touts on the safety of spectators, and the risk of violence if rival supporters are not segregated.

There is an important Home Office publication, *Guidance on Football Related Legislation*, HOC 34/2000. This contains specimen forms and details of procedures and legislation.

1.2 The Control of Alcohol

The Sporting Events (Control of Alcohol etc) Act 1985, as amended, makes extensive provision for specific offences in connection with the possession of alcohol at football matches or on journeys to football matches. Offences in connection with the possession of other items at football matches were also created.

The football matches or grounds to which the above provisions apply are designated by order made by the Secretary of State (see the Sports Grounds and Sporting Events (Designation) Order 1985 (SI 1985 No 1151), as amended by the Sports Grounds and Sporting Events (Designation) (Amendment) Order 1987 (SI 1987 No 1520) and the Sports Grounds and Football (Amendment of Various Orders) Order 1992 (SI 1992 No 1554)). Essentially, the "relevant grounds" are the home grounds of association football clubs which are members of the Football Association in England or Wales, Wembley Stadium and any other ground used for international football matches; the "relevant" matches are those in which a team which is a member of the Football League or the FA Premier Division plays, and include international games and games in the European Cup Winners Cup, UEFA Cup or the European Champions Cup. Designation also extends to football matches abroad at which English and Welsh clubs play. Matches played in Scotland are caught to the extent that anyone travelling to a Scottish FA match would fall within the Act until he reaches the border, after which the Criminal Justice (Scotland) Act 1980 would apply.

Alcohol in Vehicles
The offences under ss 1 and 1A of the Sporting Events (Control of Alcohol etc) Act 1985 concern alcohol on coaches, trains and certain other vehicles. Section 1 applies to public service vehicles or railway passenger vehicles being used for the principal purpose of carrying passengers for the whole or part of a journey to or from a designated sporting event. Section 1A applies to any motor vehicle which is not a public service vehicle but which is adapted to carry more than eight passengers and is being so used to carry two or more passengers on a journey to or from a designated sporting event.

It is an offence knowingly to cause or permit intoxicating liquor to be carried in such vehicles. The offence may be committed by the operator of a public service vehicle (or his servant or agent) (s 1(2)(a), (b)); or, where the vehicle falls within s 1A, by the driver or keeper (or his servant or agent) or any other person to whom the vehicle is made available (or his servant or agent) (s 1A(2)(a), (b)). It is also an offence to be in possession of intoxicating liquor when in such a vehicle (ss 1(3) and 1A(3)), or to be drunk in such a vehicle (ss 1(4) and 1A(4)).

Section 7(3) of the Sporting Events (Control of Alcohol etc) Act 1985 contains the power for a constable to stop and search a vehicle which falls within the Act, on reasonable suspicion that an offence is being or has been committed in respect of that vehicle.

Possession of Alcohol at Sports Grounds
It is an offence for a person to be in possession of intoxicating liquor or a

"relevant article" at any time during the "relevant period" of a designated sporting event, when he is in any area of a designated ground from which the event may be directly viewed (s 2(1)(a)). The "relevant period" commences two hours prior to the event and ends one hour after the event (s 9(4)); there are additional provisions in respect of postponed or cancelled matches (s 9(4)(a), (b)). The offence in s 2(1)(a) is subject to s 5A(l) which prescribes a different period in respect of private boxes at sports grounds.

It is also an offence for a person to be in possession of alcohol or a relevant article while entering or trying to enter a designated sports ground during the relevant period.

"Relevant article" is any article which is capable of causing injury to a person struck by it and which is a bottle, can or portable container used to hold drink, and which is usually discarded or left to be recovered by the supplier (s 2(3)).

It is an offence for a person to be drunk in a designated sports ground at any time during the relevant period, or to be drunk while entering or trying to enter a designated sports ground during the relevant period (s 2(2)).

Section 2A of the 1985 Act was inserted by the 1986 Public Order Act and makes it an offence to possess, in specified circumstances, certain other articles whose main purpose is the emission of a flare or smoke or visible gas, or which is a firework; see s 2A(1)–(4) and page 227. Where such a device causes death or injury, it may be appropriate to consider what other offences may have been committed.

Additional Police Powers

A constable has power to enter any part of a designated sports ground at any time during the relevant period of a designated sporting event for the purpose of enforcing the provisions of the Sporting Events (Control of Alcohol etc) Act 1985, s 7(1). A constable also has power to search a person he reasonably suspects is committing or has committed an offence under s 7(2) of the Act. A constable may, when acting in support of the relevant football club, carry out a search, with the consent of the person searched, where such a search is a condition of entry. A constable has power to arrest a person he reasonably suspects is committing or has committed an offence under the Act (s 7(2)).

There is no specific provision to use force in connection with s 7, and s 117 of the Police and Criminal Evidence Act 1984 (which authorises the use of reasonable force in connection with powers in the 1984 Act) does not apply, although s 3 of the Criminal Law Act 1967 may justify the use of force in appropriate circumstances.

1.3   Offences under the Football Offences Act 1991

There are three offences under the Football Offences Act 1991, now amended by s 9 Football (Offences and Disorder) Act 1999. The offences may be committed only in relation to designated football matches, ie an association football match, or a match of a description designated by order of the Secretary of State (s 1(1)), see the Football (Offences) (Designation of Football Matches) Order 2000 (SI 2000 No 2329). Essentially, these are the same as for the Sporting Events (Control of Alcohol etc) Act 1985 (see the Football (Offences) (Designation of Football Matches) Order 1991 (SI 1991 No 1565) as amended by the Sports Grounds and Football (Amendment of Various Orders) Order 1992 (SI 1992 No 1554)).

The "relevant period" for the purposes of these offences is the period beginning two hours before the start of the match or (if earlier) two hours before the time at which it is advertised to start, and ending one hour after the end of it (s 1(2)).

The three offences are:

(a) throwing missiles without lawful authority or excuse at or towards either:

   (i) the playing area or any area adjacent to the playing area to which spectators are not generally admitted, or

   (ii) any area in which spectators or other persons may be present (s 2);

(b) engaging in or taking part in chanting of an indecent or racialist nature at a designated football match (s 3).

   "Chanting" is the repeated uttering of any words or sounds whether alone or in concert with one or more others. "Racialist nature" means consisting of or including matter which is threatening, abusive or insulting to a person by reason of his colour, race, nationality (including citizenship) or ethnic or national origins (s 3(2)(b)). "Threatening", "abusive" or "insulting" are considered at page 113;

(c) without lawful authority or excuse going on to the playing area or on to any area adjacent to the playing area to which spectators are not generally admitted (s 4).

The burden of proving lawful authority or excuse under s 2 or 4 is on the defendant.

The offences are arrestable offences under s 24 of the Police and Criminal Evidence Act, which brings into play the extensive provisions on arrest pursuant under that Act (s 5(1)), including the power of ordinary citizens to arrest in the limited circumstances set out in s 24(4) and (5). They are triable summarily only and are subject to a fine not exceeding level 3 on the standard scale (s 5(2)).

1.4 Banning Orders

The schemes of orders (known from time to time as exclusion orders, domestic banning orders and international banning orders) previously found in ss 30–34 of the Public Order Act 1986 (as amended) and ss 14–17 of the Football Spectators Act 1989 (as amended) have been repealed. The Football (Disorder) Act 2000 inserts into the Football Spectators Act 1989 new ss 14,

14A–14J, 21A–21D and a new Sch 1. The 1989 Act remains the statutory source of the powers, but the new scheme considerably extends the powers of the courts and the police both to seek orders, and the circumstances in which an order may be made.

The Football Spectators Act 1989 also enables the court to make orders against those convicted of corresponding offences committed in other countries in respect of which an Order in Council has been made. The Football Banning Orders Authority provides the details to the relevant chief officer who then decides whether or not to lay an information for a summons or warrant to bring the individual before the court.

The power of a magistrates' court to make "declarations of relevance" (see below) and to order photographs of a person subject to a banning order is preserved, subject to minor changes to reflect the new terminology.

The Football (Disorder) Act 2000 has had the following overall impact (s 1(1)):

- banning orders combine the effect of the former domestic banning orders and international football banning orders, including the surrender of passports;
- in certain instances, the enforcing authority must require those subject to banning orders to surrender their passports;
- a constable may compel attendance at a magistrates' court to answer a complaint for the making of a banning order;
- magistrates may make a banning order on complaint as well as on conviction for certain offences;
- in the context of overseas matches a constable may summarily detain a person with a view to compelling him to attend court to answer a complaint seeking a banning order.

Regulated Football Match

The new measures under the Football Spectators Act 1989 apply in respect of "regulated football matches". These are association football matches (in England and Wales or elsewhere) which are prescribed or of a prescribed description. The Football Spectators (Prescription) Order 2000 (SI 2000 No 2126) sets out the details in full in respect of football matches in England and Wales (art 3 and Sch 2) and football matches outside England and Wales (art 4 and Sch 3). Thus, in England and Wales a "regulated football match" is an association football match:

> "in which one or both of the participating teams represents a club which is a full or associate member of the Football League, the Football Association Premier League or the Football Conference or represents a club from outside England and Wales or represents a country or territory and which is played either–
>
> (i) at a sports ground designated under s 1(1) of the Safety of Sports Ground Act 1975, or registered with the Football League or the

Football Association Premier League as the Home Ground of a club which is a member of either, or

(ii) in the FA Cup (except in a preliminary or qualifying round)."

Outside England and Wales, a regulated football match is one in which a national team, appointed by the FA to represent England or by the FA of Wales to represent Wales, or a team representing a club which is a full or associate member of the Football League or the Football Association Premier League, plays.

The Prohibition under a Banning Order

A banning order is an order which, in relation to a regulated football match:
- in England and Wales prohibits the person subject to the order from entering premises for the purpose of attending such matches, or which
- outside England and Wales requires the person subject to the order to report to a police station.

Control Period

The scheme in respect of matches outside England and Wales includes powers of detention and summary reference to a court (s 21A). These powers are available during the "control period", which means a period beginning five days before the day of the match and ending when the match is finished or cancelled. In respect of an external tournament (a football competition which includes regulated football matches outside England and Wales) it means any period described in an order made by the Secretary of State.

Relevant Offence

A banning order may be imposed on conviction of a "relevant offence" as set out in the substituted Sch 1 Football Spectators Act 1989, art 1(a) – (u) (or a corresponding offence committed abroad and identified in the relevant Order in Council). This very detailed schedule extends to attempts, conspiracy or incitement, aiding and abetting, and counselling and procuring the listed offences. In brief, the schedule includes offences:
- involving the use or threat of violence at, or on journeys to, a regulated match;
- under the Football (Offences) Act 1991, the Football Spectators Act 1989 and the Sporting Events (Control of Alcohol etc) Act;
- under s 5 or Part III (racial hatred) Public Order Act 1986 committed during a relevant period;
- involving the use, carrying or possession of an offensive weapon or firearm;
- where a "declaration of relevance" has been made.

Declaration of Relevance

Declarations of relevance are governed by s 23 Football Spectators Act 1989 (as amended by the Football (Offences and Disorder) Act 1999). Where certain offences are committed away from a ground or not on a journey, but are committed during a "relevant period", the court may on conviction make a declaration of relevance that the offence related to that or any other match in that relevant period. Five days notice of the prosecution's intention to seek such a declaration must be given.

Relevant Period

"Relevant period" for these purposes is defined by s 1(8) and (8A) of the Football Spectators Act 1989 (as amended). It is generally a period beginning two hours before the scheduled start of the match and ending one hour after the match ends. In some instances within s 1(8A) (as amended by Sch 2, Football (Disorder) Act 2000) the period is extended to 24 hours; see Sch 1 (q)–(t).

Violence and Disorder

Violence and disorder, as the basis for a banning order, are not restricted to violence or disorder in connection with football (s 14C(3)). "Violence" is defined as violence against persons or property and includes threatening violence and doing anything which endangers the life of any person (s 14C(1)). "Disorder" is defined in s 14C(2) as including:

(a) stirring up hatred against a group of persons defined by reference to colour, race, nationality (including citizenship) or ethnic or national origins, or against an individual as a member of a group,

(b) using threatening, abusive or insulting words or behaviour or disorderly behaviour,

(c) displaying any writing or other thing which is threatening, abusive or insulting.

Banning Order on Conviction

If the court (including a Crown Court on committal for sentence) convicts a person of a relevant offence and is satisfied that there are reasonable grounds to believe that making a banning order would help to prevent violence or disorder at or in connection with any regulated football matches, then, provided it imposes a sentence or conditionally discharges the offender, it must impose a banning order. Should a court not be so satisfied then it must state that fact in open court and give its reasons (s 14A).

Banning Order on Complaint and Summary Detention

The provisions for imposing a banning order on complaint, and for summary detention (s 21A), are temporary and will expire on 28 August 2002 (see the Football (Disorder) (Duration of Powers) Order 2001, SI 2001 No 2646).

The chief officer of police for the area where a respondent resides or appears to reside may apply to a magistrates' court by complaint for a banning order if it appears to him that the respondent has at any time caused or contributed to any violence or disorder in the United Kingdom or elsewhere. If it is proved that the condition is met and the court is satisfied that there are reasonable grounds to believe that making a banning order would help to prevent violence or disorder at or in connection with any regulated football matches then, provided it imposes a sentence or conditionally discharges the offender, it must impose a banning order (s 14B).

The magistrates' court may not take into account anything done ten years or more before the application, but may take into account the following matters (among others) so far as they considers it appropriate:

- any decision of a court or tribunal outside the UK;
- deportation or exclusion from a country outside the UK;
- removal or exclusion from premises used for playing football whether in the UK or elsewhere;
- conduct recorded on video or other means;
- before taking into account a conviction for a relevant offence, any statement made under s 14A(3) or 15(2A) when a court has declined to make a banning order.

Section 14D deals with appeals against the making of a banning order on complaint.

In addition to this procedure, a constable in uniform has power under ss 21A–21D of the 1989 Act to detain an individual for up to four hours (six, with higher authority) with a view to issuing a notice compelling him to attend a magistrates' court within 24 hours as if to answer a complaint under s 14B. The police officer may arrest and detain the individual with a view to achieving compliance with the notice (s 21B(6)). This power exists only in connection with the control period in respect of football matches outside England and Wales (s 21A). Failure to comply is a criminal offence (s 21C). There are provisions for compensation out of central funds if an order was refused (s 21D).

Sections 14A and B were considered in *Gough v Chief Constable of Derbyshire*, 13 July 2001, DC, where the question arose whether the sections were in breach of art 7 of the European Convention on Human Rights (prohibition on restrospectivity). Treating both sections in the same way, the court held that there was no breach of art 7 since a banning order made under either section could not be described as a "penalty" within the meaning of art 7 as developed in Convention cases. The court also held that there had been no breach of European Community law in respect of either freedom of movement or procedural standards.

The Order
The court must explain in ordinary language the effect of a banning order to the person subject to the order. The Home Office Guidance HOC 34/2000 identifies some of the matters to which the court might wish to draw attention, eg the purpose of the order; the power of arrest for breach; the potential punishment for breach; that any passport will be required to be handed in; and that the individual should report to the named police station within five days.

The order must require the person subject to it to report to a police station specified in the order within five days beginning with the day the order is made.

The order must require the person to surrender his passport in connection with regulated football matches outside the UK unless it appears to the court that there are exceptional circumstances. If there are, they must be stated in open court. This requirement comes into effect when the enforcing authority issues the banned person with a notice relating to a match outside the UK and requiring the person to surrender his passport at a particular police station.

There are provisions for making banning orders in respect of persons detained in custody.

A court making a banning order may impose additional requirements in relation to any regulated football matches, and the person subject to the order or the prosecutor may apply to vary the order so as to impose, replace or omit such a requirement.

The new s 14J creates offences in connection with failure to comply with banning orders, punishable by up to six months imprisonment or a fine up to level 5. A constable has no power to arrest someone he reasonably suspects is about to commit an offence, although entry to a match could be denied by the club or by the constable if he reasonably anticipates a breach of the peace.

Duration

A banning order:
- made on conviction and sentence of immediate imprisonment must be for a period of between six and ten years;
- made on conviction but without immediate imprisonment must be for a period of between three and five years;
- made on complaint must be for a period between two and three years.

Where a banning order has been in place for at least two thirds of its duration, the person subject to it may apply for its termination. The court hearing the application should have regard to the person's character; his conduct since the banning order was made; the nature of the offence or conduct which led to it; and other relevant circumstances. The court may terminate the order as from a specific date or refuse the application. In the event of a refusal no further application may be made for six months. Cost may be awarded against the applicant. See ss 14F and 14H, Football Spectators Act 1989.

Notice of Order

Section 18 of the Football Spectators Act 1989 (as amended) continues in force although s 34 of the Public Order Act was repealed by the Football (Disorder) Act 2000.

When a banning order has been made, the clerk or appropriate officer in the Crown Court should give a copy to the person to whom it relates, and, as soon as reasonably practicable, send copies to:

- the enforcing authority (the Football Banning Orders Authority, see s 57 Police Act 1996 and the Football Spectators (Prescription) Order 2000, SI 2000 No 2126), and any prescribed person – the chief executive of the Football Association Ltd;
- the officer responsible at the police station at which the person is to report initially;
- the person in whose custody the person subject to the order is detained. That person should then notify the enforcing authority where the person is released not less than five days before the expiry of the order.

If an order is terminated in accordance with s 14H, the terminating order should be given to those identified above (but not to the officer responsible for the police station).

Enforcement

Section 19 sets out the functions of the enforcing authority and the police, and creates offences in connection with failure to comply with the requirements of a banning order. Section 19 provides very broadly for the requirements which might be imposed by the enforcing authority: "such requirements . . . as are determined by the enforcing authority to be necessary or expedient for giving effect to banning orders." Failure to comply is an offence (s 19(6)).

Section 20 provides for exemptions from requirements to report. An application for such exemption should be made to the enforcing authority, but the police may grant exemption in certain circumstances (s 20(2), (3)). There is a right of appeal by way of complaint to a magistrates' court against refusal. The Home Office Guidance gives full details of relevant forms and procedures required by the enforcing authority.

Photographs

The taking of photographs remains governed by s 35, Public Order Act 1986 (as amended) and by PACE Code of Practice D. The procedures are similar to those under the Licensed Premises (Exclusion of Certain Persons) Act 1980. The form of order in the Home Office Guidance reflects the practice of the enforcing authority to require the production by the convicted person of three passport-sized photographs, proof of identity and current address.

The court which makes a banning order may, on the application of the prosecutor or complainant under s 14B of the Football Spectators Act 1989, make an order requiring a constable to take a photograph of the defendant or to cause it to be taken, and requiring the person to whom it relates to attend a police station within seven days to have his photograph taken (s 35(1)).

A constable may arrest without warrant any person who fails to comply with the order so that his photograph may be taken (s 35(4)). Arrest may be for no other purpose and failure to comply with the order is not an offence under the Act, although it may be wilful obstruction of a constable in the execution of his duty. The arresting constable may not be protected if he arrests the defendant when the defendant has in fact complied with the order, even if the constable acted on reasonable suspicion that he had not. In similar cases under different legislation the courts have been willing to take a somewhat relaxed view of this type of problem, see for example *Wills v Bowley* [1983] 1 AC 57, but that and similar cases concerned arrest for a suspected offence where public policy favoured a more lenient interpretation; here there is breach of something more akin to an administrative direction.

Arrest under s 35 is not an arrest for an offence and a person arrested under s 35 is not in police detention for the purposes of the Police and Criminal Evidence Act 1984 (see s 118 of the 1984 Act). Arrest under s 35 is akin to the power in the 1984 Act to arrest for breach of a requirement to attend a police station to be finger-printed. Section 28 (information to be given on arrest) and s 32(1) and (2)(a) (search upon arrest) of the 1984 Act apply to arrest under s 35. The detention provisions of the 1984 Act (ss 34, 37–46) do not apply, and neither does s 30 (duty to take to a police station) because there has not been an arrest for an offence. However, the common law applies, and the arrested person should be dealt with reasonably by taking him to a police station without delay for the photograph to be taken. Sections 54 (duty of custody officer to record details of possessions), 56 and 58 (right to have someone informed of arrest and access to legal advice) and the Code of Practice on Detention apply to arrest under s 35.

There is no express provision for the use of force to conduct the photographic session. Merely photographing a person is not a trespass, but restraining him or compelling him to remain to have a photograph taken would amount to a trespass and would take the officer(s) concerned beyond the execution of duty. The better view is that the use of reasonable force is implied, otherwise the section would be defective.

The Act refers to "a photograph" and "his photograph'; it does use the words "to be photographed". Strictly construed, this may mean that only one photograph may be taken without the consent of the individual. In common parlance, however, the phrase may mean no more than "be photographed". The Home Office Guidance HOC 34/2000 asserts that the enforcing authority requires that "a photograph" may mean a photograph which is not blurred or otherwise defective. Deliberately making it more difficult to take a photograph amounts to an offence contrary to s 51(3) of the Police Act 1964.

Offences Outside England and Wales
Orders in Council may identify offences in foreign countries which correspond to football-related offences in England and Wales. Where information is received that a person has been convicted of such an offence, the enforcing authority informs the appropriate chief officer, who may then lay an in-

formation against the person with a view to obtaining a football banning order (s 22).

The Future
The complex regulatory scheme envisaged by the 1989 Act centres on a national membership authority which would administer and enforce the membership scheme under which access to football grounds would be regulated. The 1989 Act was passed prior to the Hillsborough disaster and the consequent report of Lord Justice Taylor. In the light of that report, it is thought unlikely that the provisions in ss 2–7 of the 1989 Act will be implemented in their existing form, if at all. Accordingly, no further description of the scheme is thought to be necessary at this stage.

For the most part, the provisions of the 1989 Act relating to licences to admit spectators (ss 8–14) have been brought into force. "Designated football matches" for this purpose are defined by the Football Spectators (Designation of Football Matches in England and Wales) Order 2000, SI 2000 No 3331. Further discussion is beyond the scope of this text.

2   Intimidation

Section 241 of the Trade Union and Labour Relations (Consolidation) Act 1992 states that:

"(1) A person commits an offence who, with a view to compelling another person to abstain from doing or to do any act which that person has a legal right to do or abstain from doing, wrongfully and without legal authority–

(a) uses violence to or intimidates that person or his wife or children, or injures his property,

(b) persistently follows that person about from place to place,

(c) hides any tools, clothes or other property owned or used by that person, or deprives him of or hinders him in the use thereof,

(d) watches or besets the house or other place where that person resides, works, carries on business or happens to be, or the approach to any such house or place,

(e) follows that person with two or more other persons in a disorderly manner in or through any street or road.

(2) A person guilty of an offence under this section is liable on summary conviction to imprisonment for a term not exceeding six months or a fine not exceeding level 5 on the standard scale, or both.

(3) A constable may arrest without warrant anyone he reasonably suspects is committing an offence under this section."

Before consolidation of the legislation, this offence was to be found in s 7 of the Conspiracy and Protection of Property Act 1875. It has to be read together with s 220 of the Trade Union and Labour Relations (Consolidation) Act 1992, which now governs the legality of picketing at or near premises where pickets are employed. Section 220 does not provide immunity at either criminal or civil law save to the very limited extent of legalising peaceful picketing at such sites.

The scope of s 241 extends beyond the context of industrial disputes (see *DPP v Fidler* [1992] 1 WLR 91, (1992) 94 Cr App R 286, [1992] Crim LR 62 (DC)), but in the light of the decision in that case, police often prefer to invoke their statutory or common law preventive powers, or the statutory provisions on harassment (see page 125).

2.1 Common Features

The common features of the offences set out above are that the prohibited act is done "with a view to compel any other person to abstain from doing or to do any act which that person has a legal right to do or abstain from doing", and is done "wrongfully and without legal authority".

The phrase "with a view to compel" was considered in *DPP v Fidler*. What matters is the purpose behind the activity rather than the motive. Where the purpose of watching and besetting contrary to s 7(4) is to embarrass and shock and shame, this amounts to a purpose to dissuade rather than compel, and falls outside the scope of the legislation (*DPP v Fidler*, approving *R v Bonsall* [1985] Crim LR 150). Compulsion, not mere persuasion, is the necessary ingredient of the offence. The compulsion need not be successful, since what matters is the intention of the defendant. The means employed by the defendant may assist the court in establishing the purpose; thus in *DPP v Fidler*, the means adopted to confront women attending an abortion clinic were confined to verbal abuse and reproach and shocking reminders of the physical consequences of abortion. The police were in control of the situation and there was no attempt to use or threaten physical force. As to other charges in the context of abortion protests, see page 111.

The phrase "such other person" has, rather confusingly, been held to refer to *any* other person such as an employer, colleague or supplier, even if not the immediate subject of the offending behaviour (see *J Lyons & Sons v Wilkins* [1899] 1 Ch 255, (1899) 68 LJ Ch 146, (1899) 79 LT 709). This curious reading widens the scope of the offence.

There remains some confusion over the expression "wrongfully and without legal authority". It is probably now the case that it must be shown that the activity is unlawful outside the statute, eg as a tortious obstruction or nuisance. See *Thomas v NUM (South Wales) Area* [1986] Ch 20, [1985] 2 WLR 1081, [1985] 2 All ER 1 (Ch D) and *Ward, Lock & Co v Operative Printers' Assistants' Society* [1906] 2 Ch 550, (1906) 95 LT 345, (1906) 22 TLR 7. *J Lyons & Sons v Wilkins* (above) tended to the opposite view.

2.2 Offensive Behaviour

The behaviour which falls within s 7 has received little judicial attention and the issues are principally issues of fact, eg as to whether or not following can be said to be persistent (*Smith v Thomasson* (1891) 62 LT 68, (1891) 54 JP 596). Watching and besetting have their normal meanings. Using violence or injuring property needs no further analysis, and other offences feature such behaviour.

"Intimidation" in this context has been judicially explained. In *Connor v Kent* [1891] 2 QB 545, (1891) 65 LT 573, (1891) 55 JP 485, Lord Coleridge CJ said:

> "Intimidate is not, as has often been said, a term of art – it is a word of common speech and everyday use; and it must receive, therefore, a reasonable and sensible interpretation according to the circumstances of the cases as they arise from time to time."

Violence or threats of violence to the person fall within intimidation and, despite initial doubts, so do threats or violence towards property. In *R v Jones* (1974) 59 Cr App R 120, it was said:

> "'intimidate' in this section includes putting persons in fear by the exhibition of force or violence or the threat of force or violence; and there is no limitation restricting the meaning to cases of violence or threats of violence to the person."

A picket in the form of a mass demonstration is likely to intimidate others and to fall within s 7 (now s 241 of the 1992 Act), especially in the light of the observations of Scott J in *Thomas v NUM* (above):

> ". . . counsel for the . . . defendants submitted that mass picketing (by which I understand to be meant picketing so as by sheer weight of numbers to block the entrance to premises or to prevent the entry thereto of vehicles or people) was not *per se* tortious or criminal. In my judgement, mass picketing is clearly both common law nuisance and an offence under s 7 of the 1875 Act . . ."

Even where the activity falls short of the picketing described above, picketing may still be intimidatory if accompanied by sufficiently serious threats of violence.

The mischief aimed at is threats of violence which deter people from going to work. In non-industrial cases the threats may be less obvious and more likely to be economic in nature and so do not often fall within the meaning of intimidate. For example, a picket of a company to persuade it not to invest in a particular country or not to experiment on animals might be backed up by threats of disinvestment or a campaign against the purchase or supply of that company's goods. Such action would not be intimidation. But as to whether the activity would fall within "watching and besetting", see *DPP v Fidler* (above), and *Hubbard v Pitt* [1976] QB 142, [1975] 3 WLR 201, [1975] All ER 1 (QBD), a civil case involving picketing of an estate agent's premises. The limited immunity granted by s 220 of the 1992 Act, and its predecessors, does not extend to consumer picketing, although Lord Denning in the Court of Appeal in *Hubbard v Pitt* attempted to assimilate the immunity into the common law of private nuisance.

The information should identify the acts which it is alleged the victim was compelled to do or was deterred from doing (*R v Mckenzie* [1892] 2 QB 519, and *ex p Wilkins* (1895) 64 LJMC 221, (1895) 72 LT 567). For the purposes of s 7(1)(a), the information should specify whether it is alleged that there was intimidation (*R v Edmondes* (1895) 59 JP 776). This would indicate that the section creates several offences, although there are authorities which suggest that it creates only one offence, capable of being committed in a variety of ways.

3 Disorderly Behaviour in Relation to Meetings

As well as the offences dealt with in Chapter 4 and the preventive powers at common law dealt with in Chapter 2, there is legislation on offences at public meetings. These provisions seem rarely to be invoked, and the common law power to control those breaching or threatening to breach the peace allows ample scope to police officers and stewards.

3.1 Public Meetings

Section 1(1) of the Public Meetings Act 1908 makes it an offence to act or incite others to act in a disorderly manner for the purpose of preventing the transaction of business of a lawful public meeting. This offence is triable summarily only and punishable by up to six months' imprisonment or a fine up to level 5 of the standard scale.

Where a constable reasonably suspects a person of committing an offence under s 1(1), he may, if requested to do so by the chairman of the meeting, require that person to declare his name and address. Failure to do so, or declaring a false name and address, is an offence (s 1(3)). This offence is triable summarily only and punishable by a fine on level 1 only.

The meeting must be shown to be lawful, and for these purposes a meeting on the highway is not necessarily unlawful unless some other factor is present, eg obstruction (*Burden v Rigler* [1911] 1 KB 337, (1911) 103 LT 758, (1911) 75 JP 36). Section 1 does not apply to election meetings to which s 97 of the Representation of the People Act 1983 applies (s 1(4)). Putting questions to a speaker, shouting "hear, hear" or simple disapproval are insufficient to merit action under the Acts (see *Wooding v Oxley* (1839) 9 C & P 1 NP 170). There must be conduct aimed at preventing the transaction of the business.

The provisions on arrest for failure to give name and address to a police officer acting on behalf of the chairman were repealed by s 7 of the Police and Criminal Evidence Act 1984, s 25 of which now contains the effective power of arrest in these situations and for the offences under s 1(1) and (2).

3.2 Meetings of Local Authorities

As far as meetings of local authorities are concerned, the Public Bodies

(Admissions to Meetings) Act 1960 (see now also the Local Government Access to Information Act 1985, s 1, which added s 100A to the Local Government Act 1972) are relevant, as is the Public Meetings Act 1908, discussed above. Generally, the public is allowed access to meetings of local authorities, but for the preservation of order the common law powers to suppress or prevent disorderly conduct or other misbehaviour at a meeting have been preserved. These powers include a power to expel or exclude from a meeting those who are causing or threatening disruptive behaviour. It is also possible to exercise the power in advance of the meeting, provided the discretion to do so is exercised properly (see *R v Brent Health Authority ex p Francis* [1985] QB 869, [1985] 3 WLR 1317, [1985] 1 All ER 74 (QBD)).

3.3 Illegal Election Practices

Section 97(1) of the Representation of the People Act 1983 makes it an illegal election practice to act or incite another to act in a disorderly manner with the purpose of preventing the transaction of business at certain election meetings specified in s 97(2). A person guilty of an illegal election practice is liable to a fine up to level 5 of the standard scale (Representation of the People Act, s 169).

Where a constable reasonably suspects a person of committing an offence under s 97(1), he may, if requested to do so by the chairman of the meeting, require that person to declare his name and address. Failure to do so, or declaring a false name and address, is an offence (s 97(3)). This offence is triable summarily only and punishable by a fine on level 1 of the standard scale only. The arrest provisions, which were similar to those under the Public Meetings Act 1908, were repealed by Sch 7 to the Police and Criminal Evidence Act 1984, and s 25 of that Act provides the power of arrest for offences contrary to s 97.

4   Educational Premises

The Education Act 1996 s 547 makes it an offence for a person who is not lawfully on school premises (including playgrounds, playing fields or other outdoor recreation areas) maintained by a local education authority to cause or permit nuisance or disturbance to the annoyance of those lawfully using the premises. This offence is punishable by a fine up to level 2. Police officers have a power of removal, as does anyone else with the authority of the local education authority or governing body (s 547(3), (4) and (5)). Presumably a suitably authorised security guard would have this power. Proceedings may be brought by either the police or the local education authority (s 547(6), (8)).

Whether a person is lawfully on premises falls to be judged according to normal principles, although there may be factual or even legal difficulties from time to time. In *London Borough of Wandsworth v A, The Times* 28 January 2000 (QBD), it was held that an implied licence in favour of a parent may arise in respect of school premises (but not on the facts of that case).

The Local Government (Miscellaneous) Provisions Act 1982, s 40, created a similar offence in connection with further or higher education premises maintained by a local education authority.

5   Protection of Worship

A range of provisions concerns protecting worship from interference. These were reviewed by the Law Commission in its report on *Offences against Public Worship* (No 145), which favoured retention of some and repeal of others. Church wardens have powers at common law and under statute to maintain order and decency in the church; including powers to expel those who create a disturbance.

Section 2 of the Ecclesiastical Courts Jurisdiction Act 1860 was reviewed by the Law Commission which favoured its retention. The Act penalises behaviour of two sorts. The first offence concerns "riotous, violent or indecent behaviour" at any time in churchyards, burial grounds, churches, chapels and any other certified place of religious worship, whether during divine service or at other time.

"Indecent" is given a wide meaning which includes, but extends beyond, sexual connotations and that which tends to deprave or corrupt, although the offence is often charged in respect of activities of a sexual nature committed in churchyards (see *Blake v DPP*, *The Times* 19 January 1993 (DC)). "Indecent" means anything which creates a disturbance in a sacred place (*Abrahams v Cavey* [1968] 1 QB 479, [1967] 3 WLR 1229, [1967] 3 All ER 179 (DC)). Interrupting a church service to complain about the church's views on Sunday trading was held to fall within the Act and merit a £30 fine (see *The Times*, 22 May 1986) and Mr Peter Tatchell was famously convicted in 1999 and fined the symbolic amount of £18.60. The nature of the place where the behaviour occurred is the context in which the behaviour falls to be construed; the question is not whether the behaviour would be condemned had it occurred elsewhere (*Worth v Terrington* (1845)13 M&W 795).

In *Girt v Fillingham* [1901] P 176, a clergyman was properly convicted when he went with a crowd to a church and cried out during prayers, "Idolatry! Protestants leave this House of Baal":

> "It was pointed out that on the authority of Sir John Nichol in *Palmer v Roffey* (1824) 2 Add 141 that the sacredness of the place was the object of the protecting law, and that controversial matters could not be dealt with in church without a violation of the statute."

It might be otherwise where the words are spoken as an aside and not in a loud voice (see *Jones v Catterall* (1902) 18 TLR 367). See also *R v Farrant* [1973] Crim LR 240 (using magic incantations at night in a churchyard); *Abrahams v Cavey* (above) (interrupting a Methodist service to protest about the Vietnam War was indecent behaviour).

The second sort of behaviour penalised by s 2 of the 1860 Act is that which obstructs a clergyman or preacher. The Act makes it an offence to "molest, let, disturb, vex or trouble, or by any other unlawful means disquiet or misuse" any preacher or clergyman celebrating any sacrament or rite, etc in a church or burial ground. Offenders are liable, on summary conviction, to a fine on level 1 or two months' imprisonment without fine. Other minor Acts relating to disturbances in cemeteries and burial grounds were recommended for repeal by the Law Commission, but remain extant.

Section 36 of the Offences Against the Person Act 1861 makes it an offence to obstruct by threats or force a clergyman or other minister from celebrating divine service. This is triable either way under the Magistrates' Courts Act 1980 and is punishable by up to two months' imprisonment.

6 Byelaws

Byelaws often apply to the conduct of processions and assemblies or otherwise affect protest, demonstrations or more general matters relating to public places. The licensing powers of local authorities in relation to activities on or near the highway, and the associated offences, are also relevant.

Typically, byelaws relate to a wide range of activity including the display of posters, the use of particular language, the use of loud-hailers, the distribution of handbills, the collection of money, and the playing of musical instruments. Byelaws commonly restrict the holding of meetings in certain places or require consent to meetings and assemblies. Byelaws often make it an offence to use riotous, violent, disorderly, indecent or offensive behaviour, or conduct which causes annoyance. The use of indecent, offensive or obscene words may also be an offence. There are wide variations in the formulae employed, and there are extensive decisions on specific formulae. The meaning attributed to some of the words employed has tended to be specific to the context of byelaws; for example the word "indecent" does not necessarily bear the meaning attributed to it elsewhere in the law, and "riotous" is not necessarily synonymous with "riot" for the purposes of the Public Order Act 1986.

The principles of judicial review apply to challenges to the validity of byelaws, whether directly by way of application for judicial review or indirectly by way of a defence to a criminal charge under byelaws (*R v Reading Crown Court ex p Hutchinson* [1988] QB 384, [1987] 3 WLR 1062, [1988] 1 All ER 333 (DC) and *Boddington v British Transport Police* [1999] 2 AC 143, [1998] 2 WLR 639, [1998] 2 All ER 203 (HL)). The principles of unreasonableness have been applied to byelaws with particular care to avoid undue interference with locally made decisions (see *Kruse v Johnson* [1898] 2 QB 91, [1895–9] All ER Rep 105, (1895) 78 LT 647).

The punishment for a breach of byelaws is a fine not exceeding level 2 on the standard scale, but there is also the possibility of a binding over order. In extreme cases, a local authority may seek an injunction to prohibit persistent breaches of byelaws and to stop repetition (see *City of London Corporation v Bovis Construction Ltd* [1992] 3 All ER 697, 84 LGR 660 (CA) and *Runnymede Borough Council v Ball* [1986] 1 WLR 353, [1986] 1 All ER 629, [1986] JPL 288 (CA)).

7 Offences under the Town Police Clauses Act 1847

The offences under the Town Police Clauses Act 1847, s 28 are legion and concern activities which obstruct, annoy or place in danger residents of a street or passengers in the street (which must be indicated: *Cotterill v Lampriere* [1890] 24 QB 634, (1890) 59 LJMC 133, (1890) 62 LT 695). The offences range from those concerning housekeeping (beating or shaking a carpet) to childrens' games (flying a kite); and from immorality (indecent exposure) to public safety (leaving a cellar unprotected). Section 28 also prohibits wilful obstruction of the highway.

8 The Vagrancy Act 1824

The Vagrancy Act 1824, s 4 penalises a wide range of conduct including indecent exposure, which is also an offence at common law. Section 4 applies to a person found within certain premises for an unlawful purpose and being deemed a "rogue and vagabond". The scope of the Act was considered in *Talbot v Oxford City Magistrates' Court* [2000] 2 Cr App R 60, *The Times* 15 February 2000 (QBD), in particular whether or not Oxford University fell within the range of premises wherein an offence under s 4 might be committed: "dwellinghouse, warehouse, coachhouse, stable, or outhouse, or in any inclosed yard, garden or area . . .". It was held that an enclosed area did not include a room within a building. In *Knott v Blackburn* [1944] 1 All ER 116 (KBD), the expression was found to apply to the basement of a house.

The power of arrest in s 6 of the Vagrancy Act was held to have survived the Police and Criminal Evidence Act 1984 in *Gapper v Chief Constable of Avon and Somerset* [1999] 2 WLR 928, [1998] 4 All ER 248 (CA).

9 Uniforms

Of paramount importance at the time the 1936 Public Order Act was passed, were the provisions of the Act relating to uniforms worn in connection with political objectives, and quasi-military organisations. They have since been invoked only sporadically, although they remain important as a deterrent. Section 1 of the Public Order Act 1936 states:

"Subject as hereinafter provided, any person who in any public place, or at any public meeting wears uniform signifying his association with any political organisation or with the promotion of any political object shall be guilty of an offence:

Provided that, if the chief officer of police is satisfied that the wearing of any such uniform as aforesaid on any ceremonial, anniversary, or other special occasion will not be likely to involve risk of public disor-

der, permit the wearing of such uniform on that occasion either absolutely or subject to such conditions as may be specified in the order."
The offence is triable summarily only and is subject to a maximum penalty
of three months' imprisonment or a fine not exceeding level 4 on the standard scale, or both (s 7(2)). A constable may arrest without warrant any person reasonably suspected by him to be committing an offence contrary to s 1
(s 7(3)). Although a person may be charged with an offence contrary to s 1
without the consent of the Attorney-General, such consent is required before
further steps in proceedings may be taken (s 1(2)).

9.1 Definitions

"Meeting", "public meeting" and "public place" are defined by s 9(1) of the
1936 Act, as amended by s 33 of the Criminal Justice Act 1972. Section 9
was unaffected by the 1986 Public Order Act:

"'Meeting' means a meeting held for the purpose of the discussion of
matters of public interest or for the purpose of the expression of views
on such matters;

'Public meeting' includes any meeting in a public place and any
meeting which the public or any section thereof are permitted to attend,
whether on payment or otherwise.

'Public place' includes any highway and any other premises or
place to which at the material time the public have or are permitted to
have access, whether on payment or otherwise."

The meaning of "public place" was considered in a number of cases under s
5 of the Public Order Act 1936:

- *Marsh v Arscott* (1982) 75 Cr App R 211, [1982] Crim LR 827 (QBD):
  a car park attached to a shop is not a public place at 11.30 pm;
- *R v Edwards and Roberts* (1978) 122 SJ 177, (1978) 67 Cr App R 228,
  [1978] Crim LR 564 (CA): the front garden or driveway of a house was
  not a public place since entry was under licence;
- *Cawley v Frost* [1976] 1 WLR 1207, [1976] 3 All ER 743, [1976] Crim
  LR 747 (DC): a football ground is capable of being a public place even
  though there are places within to which the public does not have access;
  the premises should be considered in their entirety.

Cases on the meaning of "public place" for the purposes of other legislation
are mentioned on page 217, although interpretation may vary from Act to
Act, and the context of each statute affects the meaning to be ascribed.

"Uniform"

Early cases on the Act are *R v Wood* (1937) SI Sol Jo 108 and *R v Charnley*
(1937) 81 SJ 108. "Uniform" is undefined in the Act, but it was analysed in
O'Moran v DPP [1975] QB 864, [1975] 2 WLR 413, [1975] 1 All ER 473
(DC), where it was said to imply one or more items of wearing apparel such
as a beret, dark glasses, pullover, trousers, jacket. Whether one item alone is

sufficient is a question of fact, but there is no reason to doubt that it may be.

Whether or not the wearing apparel can be described as uniform does not necessarily require proof that it had been worn as uniform in the past; the matter is to be judged by reference to the adoption of the items to indicate that a group of people are together or in association. The deliberate adoption of identical apparel showing association is sufficient to show that the apparel is uniform.

9.2 Association with a Political Organisation or Object

To establish an offence under s 1 of the Public Order Act 1936 it must be proved that the wearing of the uniform shows the wearer's association with a political organisation or object. Uniform worn in a range of contexts – eg in a charity parade or a play – clearly falls outside the scope of the Act. "Association with" tends to suggest a willingness to adhere to the tenets of the organisation, even if falling short of membership. In any event "association with" is an ordinary phrase and ought to receive no special construction (*Brutus v Cozens* [1973] AC 854, [1972] 3 WLR 521, [1972] 2 All ER 1297 (HL)).

The meaning of "political" has not been reviewed in this context but it would seem to be capable of a very broad meaning. Whether a body could properly be said to be a "political" organisation would be answered by reference to its central tenets and aims and objectives. In the context of the law relating to extradition, "political" has been extensively examined and the meaning there may be adopted. The meaning of "political" in the context of the law relating to charities, extradition and the Broadcasting Act 1990, s 92(2)(a), was reviewed in *R v Radio Authority ex p Bull* [1995] 3 WLR 572, [1995] 4 All ER 481, (1995) 145 NLJ 1297 (QBD). Since it is an ordinary word of the English language, again it ought to receive its ordinary meaning (see *Brutus v Cozens,* above).

A body which could not be said to be a political organisation may, on occasion, participate in seeking to achieve a political object, and a uniform worn in that context might fall within s 1. Whether the wearing of a uniform on the occasion of a demonstration to press for some change in the law (eg a protest march by uniformed firemen) would fall foul of the Act is unclear. And there is a serious issue whether clothing of a highly specialised sort could be said to be uniform; for example, the clothing of a priest might be described as uniform, and wearing it at a protest outside an embassy might be said to be an association with a political object. It is to be hoped that the discretion of the Crown Prosecution Service prevents the inappropriate application of the Act.

Other Items

Where what is alleged to have been worn is not wearing apparel, but an object such as a badge, tie or arm band, then s 1 of the 1936 Act may not apply, but wearing the object may be likely to occasion a breach of the peace (see *Humphries v Connor*, (1864) 17 ICLR 1, page 39) in the context in which it is worn, or it may amount to a visible representation within the meaning of s 4, 4A, or 5 of the Public Order Act 1986 (see Chapter 4).

As for masks and other objects worn with a view to concealing identity see page 225.

Terrorism

Section 13 of the Terrorism Act 2000 makes it an offence for a person in a public place to wear an item of clothing or wear, carry, or display an article in such a way or in such circumstances as to arouse reasonable apprehension that he is a member or supporter of a proscribed organisation. This summary offence is punishable by imprisonment for up to six months, a fine up to level 5, or both. Proscription is dealt with in s 3(1) and Sch 2. In the light of the extended meaning of terrorism (s 1) there is greater scope for this provision to be invoked.

9.3   Other Provisions on Uniforms

There are various offences connected with the wearing of uniforms, including bringing contempt on a uniform (Uniforms Act 1894, ss 2 and 3; British Mercantile Marine Uniform Act 1919, s 1; Official Secrets Act 1920, s 1; Police Act 1964, s 52; British Transport Commission Act 1962, s 43).

There are also offences under the Unlawful Drilling Act 1819 which relate to training or drilling in the use of arms or military exercises (punishable by up to seven years' imprisonment); and attending a meeting where such training or drilling occurs for the purpose of being trained or drilled (punishable by up to two years' imprisonment). Meetings for such purposes are prohibited "as dangerous to the peace and security of his Majesty's liege subjects and of his government". Justices of the peace and constables have the power to disperse such unlawful meetings and to arrest and detain any person present (s 2).

10   Quasi-military Organisations

Section 2 of the 1936 Public Order Act states:

"(1)If the members or adherents of any association of persons, whether incorporated or not, are:

(a) organised or trained or equipped for the purpose of enabling them to be employed in usurping the functions of the police or of the armed forces of the Crown; or

(b) organised and trained or organised and equipped either for the purpose of enabling them to be employed for the use or display of physical force in promoting any political object, or in such manner as to arouse reasonable apprehension that they are organised and either trained or equipped for that purpose;

then any person who takes part in the control or management of the association or in so organising or training as aforesaid any members or adherents thereof, shall be guilty of an offence under this section.

Provided that in any proceedings against a person charged with the offence of taking part in the control or management of such an association as aforesaid it shall be a defence to that charge to prove that he neither consented to nor connived at the organisation, training, or equipment of members or adherents of the association in contravention of the provisions of this section."

As the preamble to the 1936 Act remarks, the offences concern the development of private armies to usurp the functions of the state. Thus, private security firms patrolling housing estates, for example, do not fall within s 2(1)(a) or (b).

The expression "political object" in s 2(1)(b) can be contrasted with the different emphasis in s 2(1)(a) from which that phrase is absent. There is also a difference between being "organised and trained" and being "organised and equipped" (see *R v Jordan and Tyndall* [1963] Crim LR 124 (CCA)). There are two limbs to s 2(1)(b). The first is, in essence, being concerned in the management of an organisation whose members are organised etc for use or display to attain a political object. The second is being concerned in the management of an organisation whose members are organised etc in such a manner as to arouse reasonable apprehension in the mind of a sensible man, aware of all the facts, that they are organised etc for such a purpose (see *R v Jordan and Tyndall*).

The provision and proper identification of stewards at public meetings on private premises are specifically excluded from the scope of the Act (s 2(6)).

The consent of the Attorney-General is required for the institution of proceedings (s 2(2)). A search warrant may be granted by a judge of the High Court to enter and search premises and anyone found on them; there is also a power of seizure (s 2(5)).

The offence is triable either way and is subject, on summary conviction, to a maximum of six months' imprisonment or a fine not exceeding the statutory maximum, or both; and on conviction on indictment, a maximum of two years' imprisonment or a fine, or both (s 7(1)).

11   Bomb Hoaxes

Before the enactment of the Criminal Law Act 1977, bomb hoaxes were dealt with as offences of making false claims as to the presence of a bomb or similar device under, for example, the Criminal Damage Act 1971, s 2(1), or the Post Office Act 1969, s 78; or as the common law offence of public nuisance (*R v Madden* [1975] 1 WLR 1379, [1975] 3 All ER 155, 61 Cr App R 254 (CA); *R v Norbury* [1978] Crim LR 435). But these provisions were seen as defective and not appropriate to the mischief. Accordingly, specific

legislation was enacted. Section 51 of the Criminal Law Act 1977 states:
"(1) A person who—

    (a)   places any article in any place whatever; or

    (b)   dispatches any article by post, rail, or any other means whatever,

with the intention (in either case) of inducing in some other person a belief that it is likely to explode or ignite and thereby cause personal injury or damage to property is guilty of an offence.

    In this subsection 'article' includes substance.

(2) A person who communicates any information which he knows or believes to be false to another person with the intention of inducing in him or any other person a false belief that a bomb or other thing liable to explode or ignite is present in any place or location whatever is guilty of an offence.

(3) For a person to be guilty of an offence under subsection (1) or (2) above it is not necessary for him to have any particular person in mind as the person in whom he intends to induce the belief mentioned in that subsection.

(4) A person guilty of an offence under this section shall be liable–

    (a) on summary conviction, to imprisonment for a term not exceeding six months or to a fine not exceeding the statutory maximum, or both;

    (b) on conviction on indictment, to imprisonment for a term not exceeding seven years."

Penalties imposed tend to be high, bearing in mind the impact such hoaxes have both on the general public and the emergency services, and the need for deterrence.

12   Tampering with Goods

At a very late stage in the passage of the Public Order Act 1986, the government introduced an amendment, which subsequently became s 38, to reflect its concern about the apparent growth of tampering with products, often food products, carried out with a view to extorting money from manufacturers or to publicise a cause. Both before and after the 1986 Act, offences contrary to any of the following Acts may be committed by those who tamper with goods: blackmail contrary to the Theft Act 1968, s 21; administering a noxious substance contrary to the Offences Against the Person Act 1861, ss 23 and 24; criminal damage under the Criminal Damage Act 1971, s 1(1) and (2). Where death or serious injury occurs, charges of other offences may be appropriate.

    All these offences present difficulties. In criminal damage, for instance, the property damaged is often that of the defendant himself and there may be difficulty in establishing the necessary *mens rea*. In any event, these provisions were not designed to deal with the creation of apprehension among consumers or the general public by actual or claimed tampering.

Section 38 of the Public Order Act 1986 created specific offences to deal with those who seek to promote a cause or objective by tampering with products supplied to the public, or by claiming to have done so. Such tampering or claim must be accompanied by one of the intentions specified in s 38(1). The provisions in s 38 might sit more happily in an enactment other than one on public order, but the view of the government at the time was that since the offence concerns public alarm or anxiety, it was appropriate to a Public Order Act.

There have been several examples of campaigns against particular manufacturers or stores in the UK, but extreme examples may be drawn from the United States and Japan, where deaths and serious injuries have occurred. Police forces have arrangements to co-ordinate measures in the event of occurrences of this nature. The nature of the crime has led to the growth of insurance, and the development of tamper-proof or tamper-resistant packaging. One of the problems is the risk that publicising investigations by the police or affected companies may itself deter the public from purchasing particular products, and thereby achieve the very aim pursued by the perpetrators, or cause considerable commercial damage to the company in question.

12.1 The Offences

Section 38 of the Act states:

"(1) It is an offence for a person, with the intention—
  (a) of causing public alarm or anxiety, or
  (b) of causing injury to members of the public consuming or using the goods, or
  (c) of causing economic loss to any person by reason of the goods being shunned by members of the public, or
  (d) of causing economic loss to any person by reason of steps taken to avoid any such alarm or anxiety, injury or loss,
  to contaminate or interfere with goods, or make it appear that goods have been contaminated or interfered with, or to place goods which have been contaminated or interfered with, or which appear to have been contaminated or interfered with, in a place where goods of that description are consumed, used, sold or otherwise supplied.
(2) It is also an offence for a person, with any such intention as is mentioned in paragraph (a), (c) or (d) of subsection (1), to threaten that he or another will do, or to claim that he or another has done, any of the acts mentioned in that subsection.
(3) It is an offence for a person to be in possession of any of the following articles with a view to the commission of an offence under subsection (1)–
  (a) materials to be used for contaminating or interfering with goods or making it appear that goods have been contaminated or interfered

with, or
(b) goods which have been contaminated or interfered with or which appear to have been contaminated or interfered with.
(4) A person guilty of an offence under this section is liable–
    (a) on conviction on indictment to imprisonment for a term not exceeding ten years or a fine or both, or
    (b) on summary conviction to imprisonment for a term not exceeding six months or a fine not exceeding the statutory maximum or both.
(5) In this section 'goods' includes substances whether natural or manufactured and whether or not incorporated in or mixed with other goods.
(6) The reference in subsection (2) to a person claiming that certain acts have been committed does not include a person who in good faith reports or warns that such acts have been, or appear to have been, committed."

12.2 Definitions

"Contaminate" and "Interfere"

The words "contaminate" and "interfere" are undefined and ought to be given a common sense and broad interpretation. They are wider than "damage" and cover instances ranging from:
(a) the addition of a harmless but discolouring substance;
(b) the addition of an adhesive label to a package or item indicating that it may have been tampered with;
(c) the injection of a harmful substance into food;
(d) the removal or damage of part of a product so as to create a danger, eg in an electrical item.

"Goods"

The meaning of "goods" is partially explained in s 38(5); the definition there has been used in earlier legislation (see the Consumer Safety Act 1978) and is wide enough to encompass ingredients or parts for incorporation into another product. Goods during all stages of manufacture, processing, cleaning, production, storage, and sale are within the scope of s 38.

The term "goods" may be interpreted to include part of a building; thus, a claim that a lift has been interfered with may fall within the terms of the offence. A claim that a circus big top has been damaged or that apparatus in a fair has been interfered with seem to fall within the "causing public anxiety and economic loss". Whether the definition of "goods" is fulfilled in such instances is unclear, but there are other offences relevant to such conduct.

Relevant Places

The phrase "place goods . . . where goods . . . are . . . otherwise supplied" relates to the "placing offence" and seems to create a *genus* of place where goods are supplied. The supply need not be to the general public or to members of the public, but the necessary *mens rea* must be demonstrated. Where a person places contaminated goods on a production line, eg on a conveyor belt leading to a packing system, he should be charged under the contamination or possession arm of the offence, since the place is not one where goods are "consumed, used, sold or otherwise supplied". The "placing" offence seems to be aimed at the substitution of goods on supermarket shelves, or in cafes or warehouses, etc.

As the terms "the public" and "members of the public" indicate, the mischief at which the Act is aimed appears to be the creation of public alarm or anxiety, injury to members of the public or economic loss. Where there is a campaign aimed at a company with the intention to cause alarm, anxiety or injury to that company's employees, it may be difficult to argue that these are in fact "the public" or "members of the public" for this purpose, although a relevant consideration might be the size of the workforce.

12.3 The Defence of Good Faith
It is difficult to envisage the prosecution of a newspaper, or TV or radio company, which reports an acknowledged claim of interference or contamination, but the defence of good faith would apply. Proceedings under s 38 are more likely where a newspaper or TV or radio company runs a campaign to report alleged occurrences concerning a company which denies the suggestions. Even in the unlikely event that the relevant intention could be established, it might still be possible to demonstrate good faith, eg the editor's belief that it is in the public interest to report the alleged events.

Index